# Little Winners

# Little Winners

### Inside the World of
### the Child Sports Star

## Emily
## Greenspan

**Little, Brown and Company**
**Boston  Toronto**

The author gratefully acknowledges the following for permission to reprint previously copyrighted material:

"Schooling for the Olympics," by Holcomb B. Noble © 1981 by The New York Times Company. Reprinted by permission.

"The Exploitation of Dorothy Hamill" by Philip Taubman is reprinted by courtesy of *Esquire.* Copyright © 1978 by Esquire Associates.

*Chrissie: My Own Story* by Chris Evert Lloyd with Neil Amdur Copyright © 1982 by Evert Enterprises, Inc. Reprinted by permission of Simon & Schuster, A Division of Gulf & Western Corporation.

*Winning Is Everything and Other American Myths* by Thomas Tutko and William Bruns © 1976. Reprinted by permission of Macmillan Publishing Co., Inc.

*Life on the Run* by Bill Bradley Copyright © 1976. Reprinted by permission of Times Books, a division of Quadrangle/The New York Times Book Co., Inc.

"Swimmer Seeks Own Success" by Barry Temkin © 1981. Reprinted by permission of the Chicago *Tribune.*

FIRST EDITION

Library of Congress Cataloging in Publication Data
Greenspan, Emily.
  Little winners.

  Includes bibliographical references and index.
  1. Athletes—United States—Biography. 2. Sports for children—Psychological aspects. I. Title.
GV697.A1G695   1983      796'.092'2 [B]      83–9437
ISBN 0–316–32667–4

VB

Designed by Patricia Girvin Dunbar

*Published simultaneously in Canada
by Little, Brown & Company (Canada) Limited*

PRINTED IN THE UNITED STATES OF AMERICA

In memory of my father,
who instilled in me a love of sports.

# Contents

Introduction   3

1. The Rise and Fall of Lisa-Marie Allen   7
2. Child's Play   24
3. Getting Started   35
4. Buckling Down   49
5. The Home Front   62
6. The Coach   93
7. The Education of the Superstar   121
8. Sportspolitik   145
9. Growing Up: Physiology and
   the Role of Sports Medicine   166
10. The Sift   188
11. Turning Pro   214
12. The Pro Life   243
13. Life after Sports   270

   Acknowledgments   291
   Notes   293
   Index   301

# Little Winners

# Introduction

*Six forty-five A.M. The Playland Ice Casino in Rye, New York, is unheated at this hour. Beer cans lie crumpled under the empty bleachers after last night's hockey game. A blue haze of stale cigarette smoke hangs over the ice. There is silence, except for the occasional scrape of steel blades, as twenty of us kids with "potential" trace and retrace our figure eights.*

*My toes ache from the cold. Only fifteen more minutes until free skating, when music will fill the arena and I can jump and spin with abandon. I pass the interminable minutes by contemplating the quickest route to the candy machine or, better yet, an escape to the locker room to thaw my frozen fingers over the radiator. But if I leave the ice my mother will spot me, in which case at dinner I'll hear her familiar refrain, "Why can't you be more like Dottie?"*

Dottie was an eight-year-old friend and rival whose concentration waxed when mine waned. What neither my mother nor I knew was that Dottie's determination would one day make her Dorothy Hamill, Olympic champion, while my lapses in concentration left me behind with the rest of us mortals.

Now, twenty years later, I remember the tugs-of-war between

me and my potential. In my attempt to live up to my athletic promise, I felt considerable pressure from myself, my parents, and my coach. I felt anxious about falling short of the Olympic podium. But considering the time and money my parents had invested, I felt guilty about expressing my anxieties. So, at age ten, I was faced with pressures that my classmates did not experience until many years later in choosing a college or a career. On the other hand, being one of the kids with "potential," I had the opportunity to develop a love of music and movement, some degree of discipline, close friendships, early experience with winning and losing, and a feeling — when I walked into school late and my classmates turned in admiration — that I was special.

My complicated feelings as a child athlete are now being shared by an increasing number of children, some of them even younger than I was then. While I was growing up, sports became a national obsession. During the sports booms of the sixties and seventies, millions of Americans became physically active, sometimes for the first time in their lives, and in some cases spending as much time, energy, and money on recreation as on their careers.

The media were quick to latch onto the trend, and television has been perhaps most influential in making sports big business. Hours of programming are devoted to everything from surfing to skiing, body building to bellyflop diving, and the commercial breaks are filled with the financial and social trappings of the sports superstar — Vitas Gerulaitis taking his immigrant father for a drive in one of his five cars; Joe Namath snaring beautiful blondes with his Brut after-shave; and Walt Frazier hooking his checkbook to the drive-in bank teller through the sunroof of his pink Rolls-Royce.

Sports have extended even beyond big business into politics. Winners are no longer simply victors of a game, but superheroes credited with abilities that extend far beyond the playing field.

## Introduction

At the 1980 Winter Olympics, for example, Eric Heiden and the U.S. Olympic Hockey Team generated more excitement than the presidential candidates mustered in the previous year-long campaign. Similarly, the boycott of the Moscow Summer Olympics suggested that the absence of our athletes could state national policy more forcefully than the words of our politicians. Red Smith wrote in the *New York Times*, "In these confusing, turbulent times when we are torn between wisdom of patience and the perils of inaction, our athletes' skill is our only weapon. . . . Far from being wasted, their long labors have endowed them with a prestige, hence a power, that nobody else has. . . . Of that power they must be proud; for that power, we must be grateful."

The mystique seems to intensify with the youth of the athlete. The accomplishments of child athletes are special, almost sacred. For if our hearts warm at the sight of a twenty-one-year-old breaking a record, the achievement seems even more remarkable if the athlete is under fifteen. In fact, we consider child athletes "pure" — immune from the cutthroat competition and violence of professional sports.

Traditionally, a sports career signaled a way out of the ghetto. Today, with greater opportunities within the professional realm and more role models for both men and women, more middle-class children and their parents are latching onto the dream. As sports leave the playground and enter arenas where the interests of children, their parents, coaches, agents, corporate sponsors, fans, and the media converge, the pressures on a young athlete multiply.

It is time to take a long, hard look at the changing conditions and attitudes that affect the child athlete. Has competition— which literally means "to seek together" — now become primarily a drudgery for children, a showcase for parents, and a financial outlet for big business? Does entering competition at earlier ages increase the risk of psychological burn-out and physical injury? How do young children and their families juggle daily training, year-round competitions, schoolwork, worldwide travel, and the demands of college recruiters, agents, sponsors, and the media? How has the cult of the child athlete affected those who do not excel? And what are the chances of little winners later becoming big losers?

This book will seek to answer these questions by examining the lives of children under twenty who compete — or are training to compete — at the highest levels of their sports. It will deal primarily with children in individual sports, where the pressures mount before and during adolescence. (A team player's career peaks later, usually during or after college.) Here, then, is a glimpse inside the lives and minds of those involved in competitive sports today.

# 1
# The Rise and Fall of Lisa-Marie Allen

**F**ebruary 1981. The National Figure Skating Championships in San Diego, California. This was the moment that Lisa-Marie Allen had waited for. Her chief rival, Linda Fratianne, had turned pro after winning a silver medal at the 1980 Olympics. After being runner-up to Fratianne for three years, it was Lisa's turn to win. She promised to restore to the sport an elegance that had been missing during Fratianne's reign. For while Linda was short and dark, wore shimmering pink and orange sequined costumes, and skated boldly, Lisa was a statuesque and strikingly attractive platinum blonde. Her costumes bore no fancy trimmings. She pulled her long hair back in a neat bun. And like Peggy Fleming, she floated over the ice with an almost ethereal fluidity.

As she began her $4^1/_2$-minute freestyle program, Lisa's cheeks flushed with confidence. But halfway through the routine, she fell on a difficult triple jump. The rest of her program was lackluster. Her graceful lines couldn't hide her wobbly landings, her fading rapport with the audience, and her loss of competitive instinct.

At age nine she had entered her first regional competition and had spent the next decade climbing the skating ladder, battling for one of the top three positions at regional, sectional, national, world, and Olympic competitions. She had made it to fifth at the 1980 Olympics. The next Olympics was three years away. Lisa-Marie was twenty years old. She wanted to get on with her life. She had been through so much in her chase of Fratianne that her only goal now was to win the elusive national championship. But she knew her performance would not earn

David Leonardi

**Lisa-Marie Allen**

her high marks from the judges. In all probability, the title had slipped away. At the program's finale she automatically struck her pose. But as the music ended, so did the script for her life. Her amateur career was over. Her head dropped, her eyes filled with tears, and she quickly left the ice.

She had done everything right. Trained hard. Followed the prescribed path to success. There *had* been alternatives. At fourteen she had forsaken a promising riding career that had begun at age four. In fact, the year she won the Novice Pacific Coast title in skating, she also won the Pacific Coast riding championship. By the time she was ten a riding instructor with an eye on the future suggested that to add a touch of distinction, she hyphenate her first and middle names to Lisa-Marie.

She began sweeping riding shows, mainly, she says, because her mare Abril (Spanish for the month the mare was born) was such a calm and intelligent horse that she could compensate for Lisa's mistakes. Her competitors grew disgruntled as Lisa rode away with all the trophies. But after a show in northern California, Abril inexplicably grew fatter and fatter. Her daily rations were cut down, she was placed on a special diet, but still she grew bigger. A veterinarian provided the diagnosis: the mare was pregnant. At the show, late at night, someone had sneaked a stallion into the stall. Lisa's trainer cursed the unknown saboteur.

At the same time, her increasing involvement in two sports was sapping Lisa's strength and her mother's. Dorothy Allen had been devoting four hours a day to chauffeuring Lisa from skating rink to riding ring to school — a schedule complicated by her job as a payroll clerk at a construction company. For Lisa, the schedule was even more exhausting: skating from 5:30 A.M. to 8:30, school from 9 to 2, skating from 2:30 to 3:30, training horses from 4 to 6, skating from 7 to 8:30 at night. Little time remained for homework, friends, meals, or sleep. After three years of this routine, Lisa and her mother realized that Lisa had to make a choice. She could compete in horse shows all her life, but if she were going to compete in skating she would have to reach the top before she was twenty. Lisa also remembered the unfortunate incident with Abril. Skating seemed like a fairer sport because the results rested on one's own labors. If she worked hard, she knew she could win. She decided to devote all her time to skating.

Lisa left public school after sixth grade and began taking correspondence courses with a private tutor. She would finish high school at the Valley Professional School, a classroom for a handful of skaters, dancers, and other athletes located next to the skating rink in Garden Grove, California.

Lisa's progress, though not meteoric, was rapid and steady. Six years after first putting on skates she won the national junior title and entered her first international competition in Obersdorf, West Germany. "I was scared to death," she recalls. "I was only fourteen and competing in a strange country. As I stepped onto the ice to do my first compulsory figure I thought, 'I don't know what I'm doing. Why am I here?' The rest of the team was older. They were always off drinking beer at night and having a good time, while I sat in the hotel with my mother. But you've got to start somewhere, and I sensed that I was on my way."

After winning the junior title, Lisa was automatically promoted to senior competition. Suddenly things changed. While rising through the ranks, one can skate aggressively and attempt difficult jumps even though they may not be completed successfully. But in the seniors there is no higher level to attain. Skaters who have leapfrogged through the junior divisions often come to a virtual standstill when they encounter seasoned senior-level competitors. Also, at the senior level every important competition is nationally televised.

Life in the skating world is something like life in a commune. High-ranking competitors become enmeshed in a network of parents, coaches, judges, and influential officials of the United

States Figure Skating Association. The progress of each skater, informally tracked for years, now becomes the object of closest scrutiny. Few details of a competitor's life are unknown — what she eats, what kinds of clothes she wears, how she presents herself, who she associates with, when she goes to sleep, how much money her parents earn. Such constant appraisal ferrets out the unsuitable claimants and determines who will best represent the figure skating association and the country.

The senior level also imposes new financial and time demands. Although the United States Figure Skating Association (USFSA) picks up the tab for international competitions, the top-level skater must also skate in hundreds of exhibitions that require new skating outfits, new show routines, and more travel expenses. For the Allens, the financial sacrifices were enormous. Lisa's father and mother had separated when Lisa was six. There was no child support for Lisa and her four older brothers. Dorothy Allen's secretarial job could not possibly cover the rising costs of ice time, lessons, costumes, new skating boots and blades, and travel. To finance Lisa's career, Mrs. Allen started to speculate in real estate. She'd buy a home, sell it, and then buy a smaller one. The family would stay in the second home until the money from the first ran out. She also started taking in boarders for additional income.

Mrs. Allen's greatest fear was that her daughter would quit. "Because the boys didn't have a father, I tried to be like a buddy to them, introducing them to lots of sports," says Dorothy Allen. "But it didn't work. The only thing they did with any consistency was play baseball. They all played very well. But none of them wanted to do anything with it. It was just a passing phase.

"And then Lisa came along, a girl after all those boys. And someone with such absolute direction. Perhaps I'm one of those mothers who live through their children, but I couldn't face it if Lisa started and didn't continue. It was like a personal obsession with me that she wouldn't quit."

The two made a pact. If they were in the sport, they were in it for the long run. The goal was the national championship and perhaps an Olympic medal.

In 1977 Lisa placed second to Linda Fratianne in the Nationals. In 1978 she was second again. In 1979 second again. Yet Fratianne was far from invulnerable. Although technically brilliant, she lacked the charisma of her predecessor, Dorothy Hamill. As one sportswriter put it, "she and her audience might as well have been in separate buildings." And when Lisa-Marie Allen was on, she could bring the house down.

The cat-and-mouse chase between the ice princess and her lady-in-waiting was pounced upon by the press. "People said that Linda and I didn't get along," says Lisa. "Well, her coach virtually ran her life. He even told her when to smile. I told the reporters that I wouldn't want a coach to run my life." The two skaters had had a fairly typical competitive relationship marked by politeness and pleasant chatter, devoid of strong affinity or animosity. The highly publicized "bad blood" between the two temporarily caused hard feelings, but they discussed the problem and relations were soon restored. Each still respected the other's talents and accepted her personal differences.

When Lisa reached her sixteenth birthday her mother, eager to be relieved of her chauffeuring duties, bought her a car. The first day, as Lisa drove away from practice, a group of her skating cronies clustered in the doorway and watched her disappear into the California sunset. "There goes Lisa's skating career," someone predicted. Her mother also now permitted her to date, and this was viewed as another source of career corruption. When she finished high school Lisa took it upon herself to restructure her schedule. She practiced in the morning and late afternoon. The midday hours she spent at the beach. Her coach was incensed. The sun would rob her energy; she would become a beach bum. Yet even with the car and the boys and the beach, Lisa never missed a day of practice.

Barbara von Hoffman

Lisa's freewheeling attitude nevertheless had serious consequences. Because the inner circle of skating is so small and so self-protective, those who show less than total dedication to the sport, who question the emotional healthiness of a one-track existence, quickly lose support within the inner sanctum. Such was the case with Lisa-Marie Allen.

By the 1980 Nationals Lisa's skating style had fully evolved. She had attained such grace and poise that her simplest spin became classical sculpture in motion. She was ready to make another run at Linda Fratianne, who was by this time not only the reigning national champion but world champion as well.

At the Nationals in Atlanta, only one month before the Olympics, Fratianne fizzled. During the two-minute short program she fell twice. The next day she skated the final four-minute freestyle routine as if she were still in a daze. Although Lisa-Marie won both the short program and the freestyle competition, she was placed second overall. The rankings were nothing short of a scandal. In an article entitled "Judging is Clouded for Miss Fratianne," Neil Amdur of the *New York Times* wrote, "The seven judges were not talking publicly because they are prohibited by international rules. But private conversations with some coaches and officials suggested that the disparity in scoring during the women's competition had reflected, once again, a 'don't rock the boat' philosophy in this country that appears to be geared more towards Olympic medals than towards fulfilling meet requirements or fostering improvements in the sport." In the simplest terms, it seemed that the skating establishment had decided that Linda Fratianne had what it took to go all the way and Lisa-Marie did not. Their scoring reflected this belief rather than what they had seen on the ice at Atlanta.

But the Allen camp was undaunted. After the loss came new encouragement from the press, fans, and friends. "The thing that's difficult as a parent, and must be torture for the athlete, is to be told time and time again, 'All you have to do is do it this time and they'll give it to you,' " says Dorothy Allen. "After the Nationals in Atlanta, everyone came up to us and said, 'Don't worry. She should have won here, but the Olympics are an open competition and things will be different.' But people were just plain conning us, because at the Olympics, when Lisa saw her marks after the first compulsory figure, she knew it wasn't open."

At the 1980 Olympic competition at Lake Placid, Lisa found herself in eighth place after the first compulsory figure. Her mother, superstitious about seeing the first figure, had remained back in the hotel room. "Please don't worry when you see where I'm placed," Lisa said to her mother over the phone. "That's not what I did." Mrs. Allen walked up to the Olympic Arena in time to see Lisa skate the second figure. In the arena's hush, Lisa traced the complex pattern on the ice. When she finished the figure, the hint of a smile crept over her face. She knew she had done well. But again the judges' marks were unconscionably low — low enough to keep her in eighth place. When one of the judges was questioned, he shook his head and said, "Yes, I know. Her figure was better than Anett's [Anett Poetzsch, the eventual winner] but that's the game." Mrs. Allen dumbfounded, walked out of the Olympic Arena. The U.S. judge had probably scored Lisa low in order to leave room for Linda to place higher. It seemed that the international judges, who were familiar with the established pecking order from the previous year's world championships (which Linda had won) were also scoring accordingly, perhaps bending slightly to accommodate their own nationalistic preferences. As Dorothy Allen disappeared into the crowds she thought grimly, "They said it would be different here. Why did I believe them?"

With a strong free-skating performance, Lisa pulled up to fifth in the final standings. Linda Fratianne, who had been groomed and packaged by the United States Figure Skating Association after Dorothy Hamill won the Olympics in 1976, finished second. Carlo Fassi, who would later coach Lisa-Marie, remarked, "If the USFSA had focused less exclusively on Linda and given more attention and encouragement to Lisa, the result probably would have been better for American skating."

After the Olympics, it had become apparent that the sport itself was changing. Elaine Zayak, a fourteen-year-old sprite from Paramus, New Jersey, had electrified the audience at the Atlanta Nationals with six triple jumps, moving her up in the standings from eleventh to fourth. It was clear that in the future triple jumps would be the rule rather than the exception. But the movement toward athleticism was unkind to Lisa-Marie Allen. First of all, her forte was style. Each of her movements was carried to its natural completion, rather than hurried in preparation for another triple jump. While Elaine Zayak had spent her youth bouncing on a trampoline, practicing snappy midair rotations that would later serve as the basis for her triple jumps, Lisa-Marie Allen had been in ballet class, mastering extension and flexibility. Lisa could reliably perform four triple jumps, but practicing them ravaged her body, for unlike shorter skaters like Dorothy Hamill, Linda Fratianne, and Elaine Zayak, if Lisa erred in midair she couldn't fall compactly. Her arms and legs splayed out awkwardly, her neck twisted. Several times she suffered whiplash, and only the skilled hands of a chiropractor could straighten her out.

As jarring as a jump's landing could be, the takeoff could cause even greater damage. Although some triple jumps are executed by lifting off from the outside of the skate, others, like the triple toe loop, use the toepick in the front of the blade for propulsion, in much the same way that a pole vaulter plants his pole. But the force needed to lift a five-foot-nine-inch, 130-pound woman is considerable. On the world tour following the Olympics, Lisa, while practicing the triple toe loop, jammed her ankle, tearing several ligaments. She spent the next five weeks in a cast.

The injury caused the relationship with her coach, which had been tenuous, to rupture. Barbara Rolles was perhaps the finest skating teacher in southern California, a marvelous motivator of young, unformed talent. Lisa had started taking lessons from Barbara at age nine and during the next ten years their relationship deepened. The charmed circle included three other young girls who would also compete in the elite Senior Ladies division in national and international competition — Barbie Smith, Wendy Burge, and Jeanne Chapman. As the four girls matured, Barbara Rolles seemed ready to join Carlo Fassi, John Nicks, and Ron Ludington as a Svengali of skating, a coach to whom aspiring skaters from all over the world flock.

Yet, as Barbara approached the peak of her power, Wendy, Barbie, and Jeanne left her. Whereas Barbara had once gone out of her way to spend extra time with them, now she would not give them the number of lessons they had agreed upon. Whereas before Barbara had giggled with them like a fellow schoolgirl, taken them shopping, and shown a sincere interest in them as individuals, now she was cold and silent. Barbara was in the throes of a divorce, which might have partly explained her behavior, but the way she harped away at everything from their sunbathing habits to their social lives indicated to the girls that Barbara was having a difficult time adjusting to them as independent young women. The skaters were confused and upset by the change in their teacher. One by one they decided that their relationship with Barbara could no longer work without trust and respect.

Lisa was the last to leave. When Rolles got an offer to teach at the prestigious Broadmoor Arena in Colorado Springs, the Allens had relocated from California to Colorado. Unlike the others, Lisa had never taken lessons from another skating coach. She felt an immense loyalty to Barbara. But their relationship deteriorated until it became a hopeless tangle of mutual frustration. For like Lisa, who had the misfortune to reach her peak after Linda Fratianne had appropriated the spotlight, as an amateur Barbara Rolles had had the misfortune to skate in the shadow of national and Olympic champion Carol Heiss. When Lisa was injured, all the fears that had been festering on both sides exploded.

"She wouldn't speak to me," says Lisa. "Here we had worked together for ten years. We were so close — like mother and daughter. And all of a sudden she didn't like me anymore. I said, 'Okay. You aren't the same person I knew ten years ago. I'm not the same person either. We aren't good for each other anymore. So I'm saying good-bye.' Then Barbara blew up. She told me, 'You're only going to embarrass anyone who coaches you.' "

Lisa rested her ankle over the summer and began training in the fall with Carlo Fassi. She had already been approached by the Ice Capades after the Olympics. They were eager for her to sign a pro contract whenever she was ready. Not yet, she told them. Just one last try. Among all the other things she wanted, she wanted to show Barbara Rolles. Lisa left for the Nationals in San Diego in high spirits. "I had prepared myself totally. My body was in great shape, and I was geared up to do what I had to do," she says. "Then, four days before the competition, during the run-through of my long program, I landed a double flip–double loop combination and felt my ankle pop. It hurt a little, but I only had about thirty seconds to go. So I finished my program, went home, and put ice on it. The next day I couldn't walk. This was three days before the competition. I went over to the rink and tried to skate. I almost fell over on a simple outside eight. That's when I knew it wasn't in the cards for me to win."

She could have withdrawn. She had seen her lifelong friends Tai Babilonia and Randy Gardner withdraw from the Olympics because of an injury and become heroes by not competing. But they already had a national and a world title and she didn't. Keeping her chin up, she began her final program. She fell while attempting the only triple jump in her routine and skated the remainder in physical and mental anguish. As she skated off the ice, ABC-TV commentator Dick Button wistfully acknowledged that this was, in all probability, Lisa-Marie Allen's swan song.

Carlo Fassi suggests that Lisa was an unfortunate victim of circumstance. "When I began to coach Lisa, everyone was upset about the way the Olympics in Lake Placid had gone — the fact that Linda didn't win. The judges and the people in the association wanted to forget about Lake Placid and get in all new skaters. I think Lisa was a casualty of that mood. Although I believe her major problem was still the injury, I feel that even without the injury, the mood of the association was to establish a clean slate."

And what of Lisa's reaction? "It hurt," she says. "I cried for a good two weeks afterwards. But when I got it out of my system, I realized that it just wasn't meant to be. In any type of athletics, something unfortunate can happen at any time. Unfortunately," she sighs, "everything happened to me at the wrong time."

Four months after the Nationals, Lisa-Marie Allen is sitting by the pool at the Broadmoor, a sprawling salmon-colored resort nestled in the foothills of the Rockies. Behind the pool, across a placid mountain lake, lies the World Arena, where she had trained and where other young hopefuls are now attending summer skating school. Lisa is tanned and relaxed, her relief at the end of her competitive career almost tangible. She has bought a condominium up the road, where her mother will live while Lisa tours with the Ice Capades. At first she was ambivalent about signing a two-year contract. "I wasn't really sure if it was what I wanted to do," she says. "I've done so much traveling. I really wanted a home, maybe to get married and have a family. But at age twenty, you can't just decide that. So I decided that I'm going to go. Now I'm very excited about it."

Yet in the back of her mother's mind, at least, there are still traces of anger and remorse. She knows her daughter's $1,200-a-week salary is paltry compared with the reported million-dollar contracts of Dorothy Hamill, Linda Fratianne, Tai Babilonia and Randy Gardner. "The last four years were so totally agonizing, I wished I was an alcoholic," laughs Dorothy Allen. "At the level of skating Lisa attained, you're suddenly made aware of the games that are played. I guess it's fine being a parent if you're in a particular set of shoes where you know you have a backing — not just financial support, but also the emotional support of a club and the figure skating association. If I'd been the parent of Linda or Elaine, somebody who was the chosen one, I'd have gone through anxiety, but not the absolute frustration.

"Looking back," Mrs. Allen continues, "I feel a twinge of guilt because I didn't approach skating with the right attitude. My whole theory behind raising children was that your job was to bring that child to adulthood to function as a worthwhile human being. But in helping Lisa develop into a well-rounded, emotionally responsible adult, I didn't help promote total devotion to skating. She didn't live and breathe the sport. Therefore, she didn't think that the president of the association was God Almighty or the judges were to be revered. I think if she had that attitude, she might have been more successful."

Often judges and skating association members want total devotion from skaters because their own lives revolve around the sport. After the debacle in San Diego one judge said to Mrs. Allen, "Gee, that's too bad about Lisa. But you only get out of skating what you put into it." Dorothy Allen's reaction: "This woman seldom sees her husband. Her four children virtually raised themselves. That's not my idea of marriage or living. This atmosphere in skating — it isn't healthy. Families separate because of it. Wives leave their husbands and move with their little darlings to another city to train under the 'best' coach. And some of the kids — their only knowledge is of an ice rink. One seventeen-year-old who trains here said that when she dies she

21

wants to be buried under the Broadmoor Arena. And I partic-
ipated in this too," she says softly, ruefully.

But then her eyes light up. "Well, except for the emotional
frustration, Lisa's had experiences she couldn't have gotten any
other way. There's no way she could have gone to China or
have been presented to the Queen. It also gave her a good taste
of what life is about. That it isn't always fair and things don't
always go your way."

Lisa's dreams have not come true, and yet she hasn't crum-
bled. Her ability to face and surmount her difficulties has given
her unusual maturity. Stability may also have been instilled in
childhood by the resilient Mrs. Allen and the opportunities she
provided in allowing Lisa to explore many avenues.

Despite the thirty-year difference in their ages, four months
after the Nationals in San Diego, mother and daughter both found
themselves starting anew. After twelve years of working toward
a common goal, their lives are going to take different direc-
tions. Lisa says, "My mother never pushed me in skating. She
only guided me when I had a question. I never liked having her
in the rink when I was training, so she never came. But I knew
she would always be there if I had a problem. Now she doesn't
have to be supportive any more. When I leave it will probably
be a blow for her, because we've been so close. But she's a
trouper. She'll pull through. And it will be difficult for me, too."

Dorothy Allen echoes her daughter's sentiments: "I'm excited
about starting anew, yet I also dread it. For the past few years
I've wanted to do something different with my life, but I don't
know what to do. I'm terrified of jumping off the high dive and
finding the pool empty.

"But I'm also relieved that it's all over. I had a very active
social life until Lisa was twelve and skating took over. It was
difficult to be entertaining on a date when you've been up since
4:15. I've really been anxious just to be myself. That's what I'm
looking forward to."

22

\*   \*   \*

Lisa had contemplated college, and after losing in the 1981 Nationals she had toured the University of Colorado at Boulder as her most likely destination. But after visiting the campus, she decided not to go. The students, hanging around the student union drinking and smoking, seemed to lack direction. Her life had been so focused and she had seen and experienced so much that she feared she would not fit in. She realized that for a while longer she could only feel comfortable in the world she knew so well — the skating world. She says that she is happy simply to travel to different cities, to perform nightly without having to train daily, and to go to bars and discos with Barbie Smith and Olympic bronze medalist Charlie Tickner, skating friends from her California and Colorado days who are also Ice Capade stars. Within a few years she hopes to return to her mountainside condominium in Colorado Springs, marry, and settle down.

Dorothy Allen is recovering too, working as a payroll officer at Colorado College during the day, taking courses toward a college degree at night, tending Lisa's dog and cat, and conversing with the golfers who pass by Lisa's deck overlooking the Broadmoor golf course. She looks forward to the day when Lisa comes back and reclaims the condo, when she will return to her home and friends in California to resume life as she knew it before skating determined its course.

Lisa-Marie Allen's skating career is a paradigm of the issues that shape the child athlete's life — the early start, the parental involvement, the importance of the coach, the danger of injury, the politics of the athletic establishment, and the merciless pressure to mount a successful career within a few short years, always aware that unless you're a winner, you're a loser. Little winners, like child movie stars, experience childhoods full of excitement, tension, and crisis. The impact of such early attention and adult demands is liable to affect the athlete for life.

# 2
# Child's Play

Play is a pagan part of the human beast, our natural expressiveness. It flows from inner and perennial energies, and needs no justification. . . . One does not play for the sake of work; one plays for the sake of excellence. The point of the excellence is that there is no point.

— Michael Novak, *The Joy of Sports*

**T**he age at which children enter competition is steadily dropping. The boy who drifted into sports between the ages of eight and twelve and reached his peak in his early twenties has been replaced by the precocious preschooler of either sex who enters competition between the ages of three and seven, wins world championships in his or her teens, and often becomes a multimillionaire shortly thereafter. At age two Tracy Austin was presented with a sawed-off tennis racket and given her first lesson. Three years later she was a cover girl for *World Tennis* magazine. At fourteen she reached the quarterfinals of the U.S. Open. By the time she turned pro — shortly before her sixteenth birthday — she had captured twenty-five national junior titles. And by age eighteen, she had pocketed the U.S. Open title and deposited a million dollars in her trust fund.

In sports like tennis, the child athlete is no longer a remarkable specimen. When sixteen-year-old Chrissie Evert battled to the finals of the U.S. Open in 1971, it seemed amazing that someone so young could be so good. But then came Pam Shriver, Tracy Austin, Andrea Jaeger, Hana Mandlikova, and Kathy Rinaldi. Right now on some tennis court there is no doubt another girl wonder in braces and pigtails slugging her way toward the pros. This parade of child superstars may have taken the sports goddess image down a peg by making sports accomplishments seem more accessible, but the sight of these *wunderkinder* also makes parents aware of the possibilities for their own children, possibilities frequently shaped by parental athletic experiences.

In the past two decades Americans have gone fitness crazy.

ɔarents run, swim, ride, or skate their way into shape, they
...ɹ1 to share their enjoyment with their children. Recent con-
verts and late bloomers want their children to have the opportunities they either missed or muffed. Parents today are not only
alert to signs of athletic precocity in their children but are examining their own body types, aptitudes, and interests in order
to plan an athletic program they can do with their children—
sometimes while the child is still in the womb. According to a
recent national poll, 89 percent of parents with sons and 82
percent of those with daughters feel it is important for their
children to be active in sports.

As a result, the junior athletic ranks are swelling at an unprecedented rate. At the 1981 Maclay Championship, the most
prestigious event in junior riding, 182 equestrians made the final,
forcing a 4:30 A.M. start. More than 22,000 girls from the greater
New York City area competed in a $2^1/_2$-month-long track and
field event — the 1982 Colgate Women's Games. And when
veteran golfer Tommy Bolt decided in 1981 to give the PGA
tour one last shot, he registered at a tournament, dumped his
street clothes into a locker, and stepped onto the practice putting
green, where he was confronted by a horde of new young professionals. Raising his golf club skyward he implored, "Lord, who
are all those *children?*"

For almost every parental ambition there is a well-organized
outlet. Parents who want to get a jump on the competition can
enroll their children in age-group swimming programs at three
years, ice hockey at four, and football, baseball, or soccer at six.
Children who are barely tall enough to reach the cookie jar are
swinging golf clubs, tennis rackets, and polo mallets; riding bikes
and bucking broncos; competing against themselves, the clock,
and each other. The winners are not only glorified; they also
receive commercial endorsements, cash prizes, travel expenses,
sterling silver trophies, and crystal goblets.

The expansion of the competitive pool, along with advances

in training techniques, equipment, and nutrition, have expanded the parameters of sport. Gone are the days when the naturally gifted athlete could coast through regional competitions to a national championship. Now the athlete has to train hard year-round to meet the escalating standard. World records in track and field and swimming are broken almost as soon as they are established. The record-breaking time that won Mark Spitz a gold medal in the 100-meter freestyle at the 1972 Olympics wouldn't even qualify him for the event today.

In figure skating, gymnastics, and diving, athletes are regularly doing things that no one dared attempt ten years ago. At the 1981 National Figure Skating Championships, fifteen-year old Elaine Zayak dazzled the judges and the audience by completing six triple jumps in a $4^1/_2$-minute program, a feat unmatched by any man or woman. Since then, triple jumps have been the standard. Lilliputian eleven-year-olds are flinging themselves skyward (with great trepidation and at physical risk) in an attempt to emulate the Zayak model. To see that their children master triple jumps in skating, double back flips in gymnastics, or the equivalent skills in football, basketball, and hockey, gung-ho parents are shaping an Eleventh Commandment: Thou shalt shepherd thy child to the nearest gym, swimming pool, golf course, riding ring, tennis club, or skating rink—and the sooner the better.

Ivan Bell, a thirty-one-year-old former wrestler, is the director of the Toddler Movement Education Program at the 92nd Street YM-YWHA in New York City. His program is one of hundreds of "diaper gyms" and infant swim classes being organized at local "Y"s and private clubs across the country. Since Bell took over the program two years ago enrollment has grown from 100 to 1,200. The location of this particular "Y" attracts parents who are upper-middle-class professionals, ambitious both for themselves and for their children. "Every day I see parents longing

Kevin W. Reece                    Kevin W. Reece

Michael Hnatov                    Michael Hnatov

"Wee Wizards" at the 92nd Street YM-YWHA
in New York City.

for an athlete in whom they can invest emotionally and financially," says Bell. "The parents of a child who shows some prowess at three has dreams of an adult champion."

The strollers are parked outside the basement gym at the 92nd Street "Y". Snowsuits are unzipped, earmuffs removed. Bell calls out to his two-year-old Wee Wizards, "Hiya Jason." "Good to see you Kimberly." "How was your weekend, Alexandra?" The responses run toward grunts and baby talk, but the youngsters haven't come to the gym to master the art of conversation. With a parent or babysitter in tow, they hitch up their Oshkosh overalls and scamper around the room, stopping to bounce on the trampoline, walk across the balance beam, swing from the uneven parallel bars, swat a tether ball, climb on a jungle gym, or tumble down a slide constructed from gym mats.

A phonograph plays "Frosty the Snowman." Shrieks of laughter are punctuated by occasional yelps of resistance. One girl on the trampoline soars into the air, drops down to her seat, and bounces up to her feet again thirty-five times while her mother loudly applauds. Periods of unstructured play, group games, and sing-alongs are broken by requests for bottles, teddy bears, and toileting. Spurred on by Ivan, who has inexhaustible energy and enthusiasm, and his assistant Kay, everyone seems to be having a wonderful time.

Preschoolers were once regarded almost as inanimate objects — you waited until they were older and more verbal to develop their athletic skills. Today increasing numbers of parents are aware that the first few months and years of life offer unique opportunities for learning. Two-year-olds are extremely flexible. They are eager to emulate almost any adult model and show little spontaneous fear or self-consciousness.

Several of the children are already veterans of sports programs. Amy, a spunky two-year-old, was "drownproofed" in swim class at six months. When she was one, she mastered the slide in the "Y" Park Bench program. At seventeen months she had her introduction to the basics of gymnastics as a Tumbling Tot. Now, in the 2-to-2$^1/_2$ age group, she is refining her skills as a Wee Wizard while also attending a nursery school specializing in music.

In the break of the hour-long class, as Amy opens her lunch box (complete with peanut butter and jelly, apple juice, and pacifier), the parents discuss plans for next semester. "At this age there's a limit to what the kids can do with the equipment," says one mother. "There's so much repetition in the classes; the instructors don't lead them on to more difficult things. Even I'm bored."

Amy's mother nods in agreement. "I'd like a program geared a little more to her age, something that's more challenging. Maybe I'll put her in a dance class or another swim class. As long as it's in the afternoon and doesn't interfere with her nap."

Some of the other mothers have already experienced the down side of sports. At the end of the break instructor Kay announces, "Let's go bowling!" Two miniature pins and a rubber ball are handed to each youngster. With varying degrees of success the children set up the pins and knock them down. Except Todd, a thirty-pound blond bruiser, who rushes around the room brandishing his bowling pins.

"Todd," his mother screams. "Stop that!"

"It's those darn golf clubs his father gave him," she moans. "Now he's going around swinging at everything. They're baby clubs, so they aren't real long, but they *are* metal. He could break a window or put someone's eye out. I finally took the clubs away, which greatly upset my husband. He said that I was telling him what to do. Sports, he said, are his area.

"My husband is a good athlete. He could have been a pro football player — he got an athletic scholarship — and he's a good golfer. He says golf should be Todd's game because football's too dangerous. I'll give Todd back his clubs, but one and

a half was just too young. He's got to be old enough to know
how to use them."

In another corner of the room a sturdy-looking boy with a
thick thatch of brown hair is skillfully kicking a soccer ball back
and forth with Ivan. Ben started coming to the gym when he
was one. Lately, his father has been taking him to the park to
play baseball, Frisbee, and soccer. One can't help but notice his
well-developed coordination. Although his mother is heartened
that through sports Ben and his father are developing a special
rapport, she is wary.

"In the two years we've been coming to the gym, I've noticed
how frequently the kids' interests change," she says. "One day
they'll love the trampoline, the next day they won't get near it.
My attitude is that you've got to allow kids to try new things
and change along with them. After all, it's their happiness. I
think it's nice that Ben likes sports and it's exciting that he's
well coordinated, but so what? He could become a doctor who
just likes to throw Frisbees.

"I'll give him the opportunity to enjoy sports, but I won't push
him into anything. I believe that whatever he wants will happen.
This year Ben asked to come back to the program. I feel confident that when he wants something badly, he'll continue to ask
for it."

After the final strains of the Mickey Mouse Club anthem fade
and Ivan has kissed the last Wee Wizard good-bye, we have a
chance to talk. Most of the parents, he says, initially enroll their
children in the program to give them the opportunity to socialize
with other children. In the beginning, the parents tend to be
extremely protective, indeed overprotective. The balance beam,
like all the equipment in the gym, is regulation size. Although
it stands almost four feet off the ground, as the children walk
across it holding Ivan's hand, they show little fear. They may
even misstep and begin to fall. He grabs them, plops them back
on the beam, and they continue as if nothing has happened. But

if a child happens to glance at his mother, he sees that her face is ashen. She is grimacing, almost crying. Even though she knows Bell is a good spotter, she almost instinctively reaches out to grab her child.

It is the grimace of dread, the catch in the voice, the desperate clutching, that telegraphs fear to the child. If the parent continues to transmit silent messages of fear or physically restricts free play, she may unconsciously limit her child's growth. For movement is the connection between the child's natural expressiveness and his overwhelming desire to understand and synthesize the world. It is through movement that the child realizes that he is not part of his mother and begins to establish himself as an independent human being.

Children are not competitive between the ages of two and three. They don't spontaneously compare their abilities and skills with others until later, usually between the ages of four and six. Yet each semester Bell watches the parents' initial desire for the child's socialization shift to a concern with performance. While the children are intent on emulating Bell, the parents' eyes wander around the room, focusing on the abilities of other children. If a mother sees another child in the class who is two months older or younger doing a forward roll, she'll say to her child, "C'mon, you can do it," even if the child is not physiologically prepared for the stunt.

One mother, whose $2^1/_2$-year-old girl was practicing seat drops on the trampoline, was thrilled by her daughter's rapid progress. "Okay, Lisa," she gushed, after the girl had done four consecutive seat drops. "Let's have the next one be perfect." The mother then turned to Bell and gasped, "My God! What am I doing? She's only $2^1/_2$ and already I'm demanding perfection."

No one is a great athlete at two or three years of age. The child who shows exceptional early ability is likely to have developed faster physically. In a few months or years, as others catch up and grow bigger, stronger, and more agile, the gap may narrow. Nevertheless, Ivan is frequently asked to assess a child's ability and to make predictions. He feels hard pressed to respond. "If the child is really good, I'll say that he or she does show advanced skill at this level. But I have to caution the parents that what we're dealing with is potential. I don't think it's a bad idea to encourage children who show exceptional ability to enter a program where they can really work on their skills. But parents should think of training as creating and nurturing talent, rather than polishing what is already a gem."

Bell believes that in the younger age groups children should be reinforced for participating, for trying things rather than for doing them well. The goal of programs like the Wee Wizards is to instill the attitude that movement is fun. And the programs are structured so that the child's imagination, as well as athletic abilities, are stimulated.

"It is important that children have flexibility, creativity, and spontaneity. And the way to get that is via play," says sports psychologist Dr. Thomas Tutko, coauthor of *Winning is Everything and Other American Myths*. "Well, what we as parents are usually doing is rigidifying play. There is no room for creativity, alteration, or adjustments. You play the game the way God told you to play the game. And that actually undermines what kids need."

Tutko recalls how joyous play can be for children when they are allowed to direct it themselves. One day when his son was about seven, the neighborhood kids gathered in the Tutko living room to watch the Super Bowl. The kids were so excited by it that they decided to stage their own Super Bowl the following Sunday. They put down crepe paper for yardlines and erected broomsticks for goalposts. The field was crooked to conform to the shape of the backyard.

"Everyone arrived early that afternoon with some piece of equipment," Tutko recalls. "One had a helmet, one a big jersey, another a pair of football pants. It was really a comical sight.

My son begged me to come out and watch. Then he asked, 'Do you think the girls would be cheerleaders?' So I went inside and found my daughter, who was upstairs with her girlfriends. Sure enough, they became pompom girls.

"Then it started to rain. The crepe paper began to disintegrate and the kids got soaked. The sight of them — everyone lined up, still playing and cheering as it poured down — that is going to stand out as one of the moments when I really understood kids."

Tutko believes that when parents inject their fantasies and organizational techniques into the world of child's play, they commit a form of emotional child abuse. And indeed, within the Wee Wizard class, one could sense that this was the stage at which many parental fantasies start to operate. Excellence was demanded and rewarded. The athletic blueprint was being drawn.

# 3
# Getting Started

I wasn't that crazy about starting tennis. It meant giving up swimming at Kara Bennett's house on weekends, and hitting tennis balls didn't seem as much fun as cannonballing into the water. But I didn't question my dad's decision at the time, and the more balls that cleared the net, the prouder I became; tennis emerged as a form of self-expression, an outlet that I lacked within the structure of the classroom.

— Chris Evert Lloyd, *Chrissie: My Own Story*

**F**ew children pick up a golf club or tennis racket and return to practice day after day by themselves. Most often one or both parents initiate and help develop a child's career. For example, Jack Nicklaus's introduction to golf occurred when his father injured his ankle and was instructed to walk two hours daily. Charlie Nicklaus decided that playing golf was preferable to pacing the streets and twelve-year-old Jack followed his father onto the course. One day Charlie belted a 260-yard drive and quipped to his son, "Beat that and I'll buy you a Cadillac." After driving the ball 290 yards, Jack didn't get the Cadillac, but he did develop a taste for the game.

Similarly, Jimmy Connors might not have been a tennis champion if it weren't for his mother, Gloria, a tennis instructor who dreamed of becoming a touring pro until she married. She took Jimmy out on the court when he was two, played with him every day, and stoked his competitive drive by yelling at her son, "Get those tiger juices going!"

From the beginning, most parents are aware of the powerful impact they have on their children. In particular, they worry about whether they have crossed the thin line between encouraging a child and pushing him too hard. Some parents won't nudge their children into sports at all, for fear of being labeled pushy parents. But children often need a gentle shove: how many of us, adult or child, have loved anything we do from the start? Many champions who at first were lukewarm about their sports are now grateful that their parents made them get out and try. And many people whose parents steered them away

A beginner's ballet/gymnastic class in Atlanta.

from sports and competition are now resentful that they didn't have the opportunity to develop themselves athletically during childhood.

Nevertheless, some parents push children into competition before they have an opportunity to grasp the essentials. Sports psychologist Thomas Tutko explains:

Adults are so anxious to test the skills of young athletes, and are so worried that children will grow bored unless they 'play for keeps' that they try to build the roof of the house before they have the foundation. They put [the child] in a situation where he must learn to perform skills under pressure before he is comfortable with the sport. He may still be overcoming his fears of getting hit by a baseball, making a head-on tackle, or falling on the ice at full speed, when suddenly he also has to win. His coach wants to win. His parents want to see him win. The child who just wants to learn how to pick up a ground ball and throw it correctly to first base is confounded by the fact that he has to throw out the runner and kill a rally. Not only that, he stands to be accused of not listening or not trying if he goofs up. If he continues to fail, he may be relegated to the bench.

Children who begin too early and who suffer setbacks because of their slow physical maturation inevitably suffer loss of self-esteem. They may not be able to put winning and losing in perspective (it's hard even for adults) and they exaggerate the scope of their losses.

Parents of potential young sports superstars may also end up inhibiting their child's potential for more complex reasons. One well-known competitive marathoner started running casually with his four-year-old son. By the time the child was six, it looked as if he could be a world-class runner, so the father started serious training with his son. He organized the national age-group running program simply to give his son competition. By the time the boy was ten he had set world records for his age group in several distances. He was featured in *Sports Illustrated* and the *Washington Post* and interviewed on television. But something wasn't right. The father insisted on workouts twice a day and the son wanted no part of it. He wanted to play football and basketball instead. He stopped training and a year later, at age twelve, he ran his last race.

Parents of children who begin competing before eight years and are still competing ten years later share certain characteristics. In the very beginning, these parents were able to convey enthusiasm without conveying expectation. They rewarded their children more for trying than for winning. And they adopted a stepladder approach to training — that is, they helped their children set readily attainable goals. Once these goals were achieved, they then helped them set higher standards.

Perhaps one of the most successful athletes today is Chris Evert Lloyd, who not only has developed consummate skill at tennis, but also has evolved into an articulate and concerned spokeswoman for the sport. In some ways, having been the pioneering teenage tennis queen was as trying as it was glamorous. She lived, suddenly, in the spotlight, surrounded by a swirl of fans, reporters, and financiers eager to personalize, analyze, and cash in on her success. Perhaps what enabled her to handle the situation so well was her low-key attitude. She did not stop to question what it meant to be a pacesetter. When reporters grilled her about her two-fisted backhand, she preferred to talk about her nail polish.

How she was able to make her way through the newly created underbrush of the media, agents, and corporate sponsors becomes clear when you listen to her father, Jimmy Evert: "I didn't think anything would happen with my kids. Even though both Chris and Jeanne won national titles, I still didn't think in terms of superstar. We just played it day to day. Today I think a lot of the kids look to the future too much. They want to become champions so badly. And their parents want that too."

Chris's introduction to the game was low-key because that was the way Jimmy Evert was introduced to the sport. "I was a poor kid, living in Chicago. But my family lived about a block from one of the biggest tennis clubs in the Midwest. My friends and I used to peer through the fence when Don Budge and other players of the 1930s came to Chicago. Soon I began playing with my friends, because it was the thing to do. I was lucky in that the tennis pro chose me as a ballboy. So when I wasn't working, I'd get to hit with him. Eventually, I made it to the top three in the country, won the national doubles title, and earned a tennis scholarship to Notre Dame."

After graduating, Evert followed his parents to Florida. His first job was with the Fort Lauderdale Parks and Recreation Department, teaching tennis at Holiday Park — a job he still holds today. When Jimmy Evert got married and had children, visions of his early years in tennis flooded back. It had made his childhood exciting, and he thought his kids would also enjoy the sport. So when each of them turned six, he put a full-size (but lightweight) racket in their hands and took them to Holiday Park.

"All five of my kids played tournaments at an early age and everyone enjoyed it," he says. "Chrissie, for instance, didn't have a big weapon, but she was always a thrill to watch. She was smaller than most kids her age, and couldn't hit the ball as hard. But that helped her establish a mental edge. She learned to think well on the court and devise strategies to outmaneuver her opponents. She also developed an amazing ability to concentrate. So when she gained strength at sixteen or seventeen, she began hitting the ball harder and her game really jelled. But it wasn't until she reached the semifinals of the U.S. Open at sixteen that I realized how far she might go."

Jimmy Evert believes that Chris's low-key early start has been an advantage, and an unpressured early introduction to a game like tennis does have its benefits. Muscular coordination developed before maturity becomes programmed into a child. An adult trying to learn the same skills may stumble along for years and never achieve the same mastery as the child who literally grew up with the sport and has a message locked into the muscles. The message may grow fainter with time, but it is never truly forgotten.

While Herbert Amyx seems, at first impression, to be a more high-pressure father than Jim Evert, his handling of his daughter Jennifer, a talented marathon runner, does not differ markedly in its fundamentals. Jennifer ran her first marathon at age five and has since run in ten other marathons and one thirty-six-mile ultramarathon. She logs more than a hundred miles a week and can complete a marathon in an eminently respectable three hours and two minutes.

Herbert Amyx has the classic runner's build — long, lean, and hollow-chested. He also has a runner's mind, crammed with minutiae about training schedules, oxygen uptake, lactose intolerance, heat exhaustion, and blisters. A medical researcher for the National Institute of Health, he speaks of running as a science, spewing information about statistics, studies, and theories. Part of this no doubt stems from the barrage of criticism he receives for allowing his children David and Jennifer to run marathons. It makes him angry. It also makes him scared.

"I've seen a lot of mistakes among parents whose kids are precocious in athletics," he says with a slow shake of his head. "So many people don't have an understanding of the event. There's a girl who competed in ten-kilometer [6.2-mile] races whose coach ran with her the entire course, ducking out of sight at the timing stands and water stations. At one race he was pacing her with the express purpose of beating Jennifer. He kept turning around and yelling, 'C'mon, she's right behind you.' At the finish line they disqualified the girl."

The muscles in Amyx's face tighten as he shifts gears from parent to preacher. "I thought that was a mistake. It wasn't her fault that she had an atrocious coach who didn't understand that distance running is about personal goals and improvement, not

Janeart Ltd.

Jennifer Amyx, age eleven, finishing her 11th marathon.

eleven-year-old girls going out to beat each other. And the girl's parents only made things worse. Their only knowledge of running came from what they heard from the coach. At Susie's first ten-kilometer race she ran a miraculous thirty-seven minutes. About a hundred yards from the finish line she launched into a desperate sprint, using her last ounce of strength. Afterwards, she was more dead than alive. Her parents saw her hunched over and said, 'Well, not a good race today, huh?' I felt so sorry for her. She was a great talent, perhaps a world-class talent. I just wish someone could have told her that running could be an enjoyable pursuit. Instead, she got fed up and quit."

Herb Amyx knows he is walking a physiological as well as psychological tightrope with his children. Rumors continue to fly that marathon running permanently stunts children's growth or turns healthy children into middle-aged invalids. The growth question appears settled, for eleven-year-old Jennifer is already a lanky five two. But because children have only just begun running marathons within the past ten years, no formal long-term studies exist in this country. Some people claim that the continual pounding on a child's ankles, knees, and hips may lead to a pain-riddled adulthood. Ninety percent of coaches, the Amateur Athletic Union (AAU), and the Road Runner's Club suggest that children only run short and middle distances. In fact, the Road Runner's Club has banned children under eighteen from competing in the Boston and New York marathons.*

This infuriates Amyx, who believes that for children who train properly, running long distances is not only safe, but safer and less painful than running short, fast sprints. Children's play, he points out, is naturally continuous, with bursts of activity interspersed with rest periods. If directed, a child's daily running

---

*In an informal study, Dr. Arthur Grayson of Torrance, California, has observed eleven children marathoners who began running a decade ago between the ages of five and twelve. Today these high school and college students are suffering no physical ill effects from their early training. Some are still running marathons; others are competing in water polo, swimming, and crew.

would surely total several miles. In the absence of any scientific evidence of physical injury caused by marathon running, Amyx suspects the real reason behind the Road Runner's ban is abusive parents and coaches.

"Training for the event is everything," he says. "Because we run thirty miles every Saturday morning, Jennifer isn't scared of the distance. To her, twenty-six miles is an ordinary run. But other kids go into the race never having gone the distance. Their parents and coaches expect them to finish the race and run faster than they've ever run before. When the kid starts to lose steam, which is almost inevitable, the parents get upset and scream for him to hang in there. The race directors see a miserable-looking kid and a near-hysterical parent and yank them both off the course. It's terrible to see that happen, because it's so senseless. It wouldn't happen at all if they trained properly."

His voice grows louder and more belligerent. "But does that mean you deprive all kids of the chance to run a marathon? Can you imagine if they decided to ban youth hockey because some father beat up his kid? Parents yell and vent their anger at their kids in many sports, but that doesn't mean you ban the sport."

It was Herb Amyx who initially sparked Jennifer's interest in running. "When my father turned thirty," Jennifer says in a soft Maryland twang, "he kinda thought he was getting old. So he started to jog to the park and back, which was about a half mile. My older brother David wanted to go too, so he took him. I wanted to go too, but Dad said I was too small, 'cause I was only about four and a half. But I kept begging and finally he let me tag along. Actually, I just wanted to get to the park and go on the swings.

"After that, we decided to see how far we could go. So we ran to the fishing pond that was a little farther away than the park. I'll never forget the day I made it around the pond for the first time. It felt really great."

But from one mile to twenty-six in less than a year?

"We just decided to keep seeing how far we could go," Jennifer explains. "We did it real gradually, increasing a mile or so every few weeks. Then when I went off to kindergarten, I'd run after school too. Mom picked me up at school and waited while I ran around the playground for forty minutes. Later that year we decided to try our first marathon. It took us over five hours, and by the time we finished all the trucks and people had gone home. We came in next to last. But we made it."

Child's play. But what could keep a child doing anything for five hours? And didn't the kids at school think she was strange?

"Yeah," she sighs. "Not just the kids at school. Everyone thinks it's kinda strange. Even my relatives think we're weird. They can't understand about running. Because they don't like it they think it's boring or something."

And she is never bored?

"No, not really," Jennifer replies. "If you vary the course all the time, run with other people, and love the outdoors. In fact, I like running long distances best. So Saturday morning's my favorite. We get up at five-thirty and run thirty miles with some of our friends. Not everyone runs the whole way, but we all go as far as we can. Mom follows us in the car and hands us water and Cokes every three miles, or if Mom can't make it, another friend will leave us stuff in the bushes. Afterwards we all go back to our house for breakfast. It's lots of fun."

But doesn't she ever just want to stay in bed? Or turn back? Or quit altogether?

"Well, sometimes in winter when it's cold and dark I don't want to get out of bed," she acknowledges. "But I tell myself if I go out I'll be that much better than anyone else. Plus, once I'm out there, I enjoy it. If I quit, I think I'd really miss it. Right now, I'd like to run my whole life. But if I get tired of it, I'll stop."

I am beginning to accept that she likes to run. She is smart and well adjusted. She plays the cello and piano, considers religion and family life more important than running, and brings home report cards filled with A's. Her smile is so endearing it could melt an iceberg. But is she a marvelous little actress, playing out a script written by her father?

"Who is in charge of your running?" I ask.

"I am," she replies firmly. "Dad keeps a record of my mileage, 'cause I'm not that well organized. And he'll set up our training schedules, deciding how much we should be running at different times of the year and based on that, deciding which races we'll enter. But he doesn't push us. He wants us to improve our time from one year to the next, but David and I set our own goals."

Ottawa, the capital of Canada, upholds the British tradition of the Changing of the Guard in front of the Parliament buildings every day at 10 A.M. The site is also where the 1981 Avon International Women's Marathon will begin and end the next day, and where the bus that has taken Herb and Jennifer Amyx and the other runners on a tour of the course now deposits them, precisely on the dot of ten. Herb Amyx wants to confer with Jennifer about the course — how to run the metal grids, where to run in the center of the road and where to run along the sides. Jennifer's face screws into a knot of agony. Since they arrived in Ottawa the day before, the main thing on her mind has been seeing the Changing of the Guard. Now the Governor General's Foot Guard, with their bright red uniforms and bushy black headdresses, are marching in formation to Parliament Hill.

"Dad, please," she begs, partly asking but mostly telling her father that she has no intention of talking shop. In a gait combining the controlled stride of a marathoner and the excited lope of an overanxious child, she flies across the lawn and disappears into the crowd.

Her father's mind, however, is not so easily distracted. The heat is his main concern. They had been training in cool fifty-degree morning temperatures in Maryland, and now they have traveled five hundred miles north only to have the temperature climb into the eighties. If the heat keeps up and Jennifer begins too fast, slipping into the six-minute-a-mile pace that to her feels like a slow jog, she'll have nothing left in reserve for the second half of the race.

Jennifer is not only the youngest competitor in many marathons, she also often emerges as the women's victor. She has set several world records for her age group, and has her sights on the 1984 Olympic trials and beyond that, a berth on the 1988 Olympic team. Recognizing her talent, Avon invited her to this race — the official U.S. Women's championship and the unofficial world championship — and paid her hotel and travel costs.

But sometimes Jennifer can't regulate her pace and burns out. She is used to running with her father and brother. In the last marathon she ran alone she started out too fast and had to quit after eighteen miles.

The entire Amyx family bears a heavy burden. Their pride of accomplishment is tempered by their reputation as pariahs, not only in the nonsporting world but also within the running establishment. Although they may like to think of running as a pleasurable pastime, it clearly represents more than simply placing one foot in front of the other for twenty-six miles. It has become a crusade. As its leader, Herbert Amyx exudes anger, resentment, pride, and parental concern. He knows his kids enjoy and excel at running. He knows that if he becomes too domineering they'll eventually resent him and quit. He knows they may quit anyway, as other interests arise during adolescence. He knows that nine people out of ten think he and his family are crazy. He tries not to listen.

The day of the marathon is even hotter than expected. Although the race is scheduled to begin at eight-thirty, few of the runners would finish much before noon. At five-thirty, the sun is already a bright orange disc on the horizon. "You know, many top marathoners won't even start a race if it's this warm. Bill Rodgers, Grete Waitz — they've been known to just get in their cars and go home," says Herb Amyx, muttering skyward.

Jennifer sits quietly, looking pale and nervous, as she stares into her bowl of instant rice and potatoes, a special prerace concoction to appease her queasy stomach. Avon had invited her to the race and paid her expenses. Brooks had provided her running shoes. She also had an endorsement with Moving Comfort, who gave her running clothing. And her father, mother, and three brothers had driven all the way from Maryland to cheer her on. She feels that she owes them all something. She has to finish this race — and finish in a way that will make herself, her family, and her sponsors proud.

During the race the heat soars to ninety. Of the 625 starters, only 389 finish the race. Those who stay in find the last few miles especially brutal. The sun splinters off the Ottawa River and there is no shade to afford relief. When the finishers begin to filter in, many collapse into the arms of friends, family, and race officials.

Although Jennifer starts out too fast, running $6^1/_2$-minute miles for the first few miles — she settles down and finishes in three hours and two minutes, earning forty-sixth place. More impressive, at least to her parents, is the excellent physical condition in which she finishes. Her tangled pigtails are the only testament to her having run a marathon. As she rests with her family, reporters begin to cluster around, wanting to know how, on a day when almost all the top runners had either dropped out or were off their best times, she had managed to improve her time by a substantial five minutes. A huge smile lights up her face. "It's simple," she beams. "I just like to run."

# 4
# Buckling Down

Until one is committed, there is hesitancy, the chance to draw back, always ineffectiveness. At the moment one definitely commits oneself, then Providence moves too. A whole stream of events issues from that decision, raising in one's favor all manner of unforeseen incidents and meetings and material assistance which no man could have dreamed would come his way.

— W. H. Murray

*I* *walk into the Playland Ice Ca-*
*sino for my first group figure skating lesson. I am eight. In the*
*center of the ice a blonde girl, only a year or two older than I,*
*is doing a one-foot spin. Working up a head of steam by skating*
*backwards, she then turns forward, centers herself over her right*
*leg, whips her arms around her body and then like a bird soaring*
*into flight, she begins to spin. Folding her arms across her chest,*
*she spins faster and faster. The outlines of her body blur. She*
*whirls for a minute or two, wrapped in her self-made cocoon.*
*Then the edges of her body reappear, her arms unfurl, and she*
*skates away.*

*I am mesmerized. What would it feel like to spin so fast?*
*Somewhere within me something clicks. I resolve that one day*
*it will be me in the center of the ice spinning, loosing all my*
*energy, and watching the world disappear in an intoxicating blur.*

The first stage of a sports career, when the child's natural
talents flower, is a time of high excitement. Progress is rapid
and enjoyment is not yet dampened by the rigors of training.
Mark Spitz has exceptionally strong legs that actually curve
backward. By age ten his legs had propelled him to seventeen
national age-group records. He says, "My interest in swimming
didn't have much to do with training. It was all pure natural
ability. Because of my early accomplishments, swimming interested me a lot more than Little League baseball, where I might
have been a bench warmer."

Sometimes outstanding achievement begins not with physical
ability but with disability. Elaine Zayak, the 1983 Ladies' World

Figure Skating Champion, had three toes severed from her left foot in a lawnmower accident at age three. Her mother enrolled Elaine in a local Tots on Ice program shortly thereafter to improve her balance. Fellow skater Scott Hamilton, the 1983 Men's World Champion, suffered from a rare childhood digestive disease that temporarily threatened his life and permanently stunted his growth. He too began skating to regain his strength. When Jackie Hampton was thirteen years old, her schoolmates taunted her about her scoliosis (curvature of the spine). She hated her twice-weekly trips to the chiropractor. To her his office and his hands on her back became symbols of her disability. She was shy and introverted, and when she walked it appeared that she wanted nothing more than to disappear forever into her hunched shoulders. At the same time, Jackie longed to stand out from the crowd. But in her poverty-stricken neighborhood there were only two ways to shine: the boys became basketball stars and the girls became cheerleaders.

One day a young man named Tom Gettling gave a karate exhibition at the local day care and recreation center. Jackie was fascinated by the tall blond seventeen-year-old who twirled the *menshakas* (two sticks connected by a metal chain) over his head, around his back, and through his legs. He demonstrated set-pattern routines called *katas*, combining arm punches and leg kicks into a balletic dance. Then an assistant held four boards together high in the air, and with one leap Tom shattered them with his flying foot.

Jackie recalls, "I couldn't believe anyone could *do* all those things. I was determined to follow him across the country, if necessary, to learn karate." Jackie didn't have to travel far. Tom lived nearby and based on the success of the exhibition was hired by the recreation center to teach karate. Jackie soon became his star pupil.

Four years later, Jackie is a black-belt karate champion. She practices seven hours a day, memorizing and perfecting the thousand *katas* that Tom, her *sifu* (master), calls out in Japanese, Chinese, or Korean. "*Empikata!*" he says. Jackie gets down on her hands and knees, straightens her *ghee* (robe), and begins to bend and stretch, extending her legs, thrusting her arms, and coordinating her movements in a startling display of grace and power.

Her trips to the chiropractor have ceased. Jackie now stands straight and proud. No longer a loner, she works with younger children, passing her knowledge along to them. Moreover, knowing that Jackie has the power to break a concrete block with her hand, her classmates no longer jeer.

Sometimes dreams are passed down through the generations. Fourteen-year-old Robby Unser's father, Bobby, is a three-time winner of the Indianapolis 500. So is his uncle Al. Great-uncle "King of the Mountain" Louis was a forty-six-time entrant in the annual Pikes Peak Fourth of July climb until race officials forced his retirement at age seventy-two. Great-uncle Joe was killed while practicing for Indy and Uncle Jerry was killed in the big race itself. Possibly young Robby was born with motor oil in his veins. He's been racing go-karts since age seven, sleeps in a bed shaped like a racing car, and his bedroom is cluttered with his father's and uncle's trophies as well as a healthy collection of his own.

The sources for a young athlete's dreams are legion. Television, with its superstars neatly packaged for maximum effect, exerts a powerful influence. The sentimental "Nadia's Song," which accompanied the endless replays of every perfect 10 that Nadia Comaneci received at the 1976 Olympics, propelled a swarm of little girls into gymnastics classes. Fantasies are also stoked by the "Up Close and Personal" style of television interviews. The camera zooms in on the superstars, transporting them from their living rooms to ours, personalizing their athletic accomplishments and making them seem accessible.

The dream that is born at the very beginning of a sports career is an important component of athletic success. It may fade to the vanishing point, but its traces remain as time goes on, the stakes rise, and the athlete's play becomes work. The dream helps competitors detach themselves from the vagaries of individual wins and losses and focus instead on an internalized image of themselves. Expectations become their own, not those of parents or coaches.

Richard Migliore is a wisp of a boy, five feet five, 104 pounds, seventeen years old, with sandy hair and pale brown eyes. He is dressed like the other jockeys who loll on the terrace outside the jockeys' room at Hialeah Park, in a white T-shirt and thin white nylon riding pants. But most of the other jockeys are dark and swarthy, and look as if they've seen more of life than they cared to. Migliore is wide-eyed and baby-faced, embryonic.

His background, too, sets him apart. While many of the other jockeys were raised around the track, Migliore's father is a New York banker, a manager in charge of auditing for the Queens region of Citibank. His mother teaches English at Brentwood Junior High School in Bay Shore, Long Island. Neither they nor Richard's three siblings had ever been to the track. He fell in love with the sport by watching Saturday morning races from Aqueduct and Belmont on television, handicapping his favorites, and cheering from the living room. When Richard was eleven, the family moved from Brooklyn to Bay Shore; when Richard was twelve his father broke down and he and Richard put up twenty dollars apiece to buy a Shetland pony named Cochise.

Although his parents hoped that he would show the pony, Richard quickly tired of controlled paces and jumping. "It just wasn't exciting enough," he says. "It didn't have the competitive edge that I like so much." At thirteen he visited a farm on Long Island where a man named Bill George put him on a horse for the first time. Watching the tiny boy ride, George knew he was a natural. Good seat, good hands. He helped Richard as much

Bob Coglianese

Richard Migliore

as he could and then sent him to a nearby quarterhorse track where Richard rode for the next seven months, making the first step from a farm to a minor-league racetrack.

One day, during his stint at the quarterhorse track, Richard had a stroke of luck. He was at a gas station, filling his bicycle tires with air, when he noticed a racetrack sticker on a car bumper. He introduced himself to the owner, who was a ticket puncher at Belmont. As they talked, sharing their love of the track, the ticket puncher said he knew a trainer at Belmont and promised to introduce Migliore to him. And so he took the fifteen-year-old to meet Steve DiMauro.

"I knew I was too young," says Richard, "that you had to be sixteen to work at the track. So I told Mr. DiMauro that I was sixteen, and he put me on a horse that morning. He said, 'You've got a job. Come back tomorrow morning.' " Migliore rustled up some working papers and forged the school guidance counselor's name. The next morning, back at the track, he received his official badge.

His dream of racing thoroughbreds was fast becoming a reality, but it was a reality that placed almost impossible demands on him. Brentwood High School in Bay Shore was then on split sessions, and the fifteen-year-old sophomore was scheduled for afternoon classes. So he'd get up at 4:30 A.M., his father would drop him off at Belmont at 5:30, and he'd work the horses for four hours. Then he'd run to catch a bus outside the track's gates at 10:30, transfer to another bus to Bay Shore, take a taxi home, and at 1:00 P.M. catch another bus to school. He attended school from 1:30 to 6:30 and, returning home at quarter to seven, fall asleep. "I did that for four months," he says, tilting forward on his narrow waist. "I was so exhausted you couldn't even talk to me, I was so out of it." The school worked out a curriculum that could be administered by individual tutors. With this intensive, personalized system of education, he could accomplish ten hours of schoolwork in three.

The next step was to become an apprentice jockey, or "bug boy." The "bug" is actually the star that appears next to the apprentice jockey's name in the racing program. The system is complex. In order for an apprentice jockey to get the necessary riding experience, he is given an extra weight allowance. He is allowed to weigh in at ten pounds less than the experienced jockeys, thus making it easier for the horse to move faster, until he has ridden five winners. After the fifth win, the weight allowance drops to seven pounds. After the thirty-fifth win — or a year after the fifth win, whichever comes first — he "loses his bug" and becomes a full-fledged jock. Migliore lost his bug in the fall of 1981, at age seventeen.

By the end of 1981 his horses made more than $5,300,000 in prize money and he personally netted over half a million dollars. He also received the Eclipse Award. "It's the ultimate honor, like getting an Academy Award," he says excitedly. "It makes you stand out from the crowd." Enormous praise and adulation descended on him, and although owners and trainers are only obligated to pay the jockey 10 percent of the purse, fancy gifts began to drift his way. He had a contract with Steve DiMauro, which meant that he was obligated to ride one of his horses whenever one was entered, but when DiMauro's mounts weren't running, other owners and trainers sought Richard's services through his agent, Joe Shea. To sweeten the deal, one owner, who also owns a chain of camera stores, gave Migliore and Shea expensive cameras. Another, a furrier, gave Richard a substantial discount on a fur jacket he wanted to give his mother for Christmas.

In 1981 Richard Migliore became a valuable commodity. The year also marked the point where play became work, the point where the rigors of sport begin to offset that first fine careless rapture. Every morning he had to arrive at the track at six to exercise the horses he would ride that day. Then at noon he had to report to the jockey room to ensure that during the afternoon races he could have no interaction with the public.

"It's hard to be in the jockeys' room all afternoon," he says. "We're pent up like animals in the zoo. They take us out for the show and bring us back in. I guess it's like any nine-to-five job where you've got to be in your office. But here it is *law*," he says, waving his hands for emphasis. "You get fines, or face suspension if you leave this area. I didn't mind it last year because at Aqueduct, Belmont, and Saratoga they had nine races a day and I rode in all nine. When you're riding nine a day you don't have time to think, 'Well, I'm sitting here, but I'd love to get out in the sun or go to the beach.' You're just back and forth. Riding, changing clothes, and riding again.

"Today I'll ride five," he continues. "So I'll be pretty busy. But there will be times when I've got nothing better to do than maybe watch a little TV or shoot a little pool in the jockeys' room or come out here on the terrace and watch the people go by. I wish I could ride the first five races and leave. But it doesn't work out that way."

"But," he says, the dejected tone suddenly leaving his voice, "the riding part is what makes it all count. If it wasn't for that, it wouldn't be worth waiting for anything. Winning races is something you can't even explain. There is no better feeling than having a horse under you, striding out, giving it his all. It's such a fantastic high."

There have also, however, been less exhilarating moments, such as the 1981 summer races at Saratoga. Never before had a bug boy been the leading rider. And finishing a meet on top means more than money. It means prestige, self-esteem. With only two days left in the series, Angel Cordero and Eddie Maple, two of the country's leading jockeys, had twenty-one points apiece. Migliore had twenty. He was up all night, calculating that if he won six of his nine races (Cordero and Maple were running far fewer) they'd never catch him. The first race, he figured, would be his worst shot. "Not that she didn't have a chance," he points out, "because anything can happen. Any horse can win on any given day. If she feels good that day, great. But if she doesn't, you're out of luck. But the first horse was the one I gave the least chance to win."

As it happened, Migliore won the first race. The second race was less successful. He finished second. But by the start of the third race his confidence had returned. He was riding his favorite horse, a horse he had won with twelve times during the meet. "I was coming up on the outside and I was going to win," he says with a knowing smile, "but as I was coming up the horse bolted and turned me sideways. The other horses ran into me like the Green Bay Packers. I got hit in the head, and there was a horse trailing the field that stepped on my hand. I was out of action for two weeks."

Migliore confirms there is wisdom in the old saw about getting right back up on the horse after being thrown. His first day back he ran two races and won them both. "There are some things you just can't avoid," he states matter-of-factly. "If a horse breaks a leg when he's running forty miles an hour it's like a blowout in a car. If he doesn't have the balance, he'll fall. It's kind of like walking toward a staircase at the end of a pitch-black room. You know it's coming, but then you hit it, and it's over.

"If I was afraid to ride," he continues, "I'd quit. Because I'm having fun doing it. If I was afraid to ride, I couldn't have any fun. I'm going to be eighteen years old in a month or two, and if it wasn't any fun it wouldn't be worth it, no matter how much money I was making. I've had three serious falls this year, but after all three, I won the first race back. It picks up your head and makes you feel good."

When Richard talks about riding, he sits on the edge of his seat, his eyes gleaming with boyish enthusiasm. Yet his words are informed by experience and a touch of cynicism uncommon for a boy his age. Although he lives with his parents in Bay Shore most of the year, he spends at least six days a week, fifty-two weeks a year, at the track. (Which track and which race is decided by Joe Shea.) Sometimes he races at two tracks in a single day — for example, riding at Belmont in the afternoon and then helicoptering to the Meadowlands in New Jersey in time for the evening races. His is a frenetic, exhausting, and often lonely existence. At the core of his life are the horses he rides.

"The jockey's got to get along with the horse, not just as number six, but to really understand the animal. He's also got to have a good sense of pace — to tell how fast he's going and to sense when to make his run and when to hold back a little longer. You can't have any idols, because what would happen if you hooked up with him head to head in the stretch? If he's my idol, right there, he's got the psychological edge. And you've got to be sharp all the time.

"The biggest thing is staying cool. Nothing can sway you. You've got to stay on the straight and narrow, both on and off the horse. There are people screaming at you in the paddock, and they can get pretty nasty. They can never understand what my typical day is like and what I go through. To them it's 'that goddam jockey, he blew it for me.' But they don't see if I rode the horse good or bad. They just see that they lost their money. And with the owners, too, you can't get to thinking about what they expect for you. Because if you start thinking about them too much, you can't think about the horse.

"Ultimately, I don't know how much is physical, how much is mental. How much it's the jockey and how much it's the horse. Some horses need more from a jockey, while others all you have to do is sit there. A horse couldn't do it without a good jockey and a jockey couldn't do it without the horse. I'd like to think of it as a partnership. I go out there and try hard every race. That's all I can do."

59

*Little Winners*

Richard is scheduled to run in the second race. The horses, on the far side of the track, are beginning to enter the starting gate. Richard is riding number nine — April Lovebug. The odds against him are a mighty twenty-five to one.

"And they're off!" explodes the voice over the loudspeaker. The horses congeal in a distant blur. But on the outside, a yellow-jacketed arm flies into the air. Yes, it's him, the one in the yellow jacket with black stripes, raising his arm faster and faster, whipping the horse on the left hindquarters and then on the right. As they round the first turn, the horses establish their positions. Richard is now third or fourth, it is impossible to tell which. The furious swatting has ceased. He is now cruising, maintaining his pace. Then, rounding the back stretch, he whips the horse two more times. April Lovebug takes off. She roars down the home stretch and wins by a nose.

The crowd goes wild at a twenty-five-to-one shot winning the race. The scoreboard lights up, registering the payoffs. In the winner's circle the owners and other jockeys pump his hand. He has won a seven-thousand-dollar purse for his spectacular ride, but his mind isn't on money. His face, almost dwarfed by the yellow cap, is covered with an ear-to-ear grin.

Richard Migliore's three-month stint at Hialeah Park was like a busman's holiday. Instead of running nine races a day, he'd race only five. At the end of the day he could return to his rented apartment five blocks from the beach and plunge into the surf, freeing himself from the owners and trainers who have thousands of dollars riding on him every time he mounts their gleaming thoroughbreds, and the gamblers who poke their noses into the paddock asking for hot tips. While fighting the waves he could forget the three serious falls he suffered the previous year and how, as winter descended on New York, he was beginning to wake up stiff and achy, like an old man. After a year of riding himself as hard as the horses, entering more than two thousand

60

races and winning more than three hundred, thinking of nothing but racing from sunup to sundown, he could soak in the warm bathtub of the ocean and finally relax.

While athletic training may begin in a leisurely fashion, Migliore's story indicates how the pace can soon accelerate. One lesson a week turns into three or four. The *wunderkind* is enrolled in special schools, camps, and clubs. Long hours of practice, year-round competition, and extensive travel constrict outside interests and friendships. Proponents of children's sports claim that early athletic training primes youngsters for a lifetime of fitness. But according to sport psychologist Dr. Bruce C. Ogilvie, the pressures may even exceed those of adulthood. "There are very few activities where one is asked for excellence on command," says Dr. Ogilvie. "How can anyone expressing any ability constantly live on the finest edge of their talent? Yet that's one of the expectations we place on the competitive athlete."

Parents can push, coaches can inspire, and fellow athletes can nourish, but the training is done by the child alone. Young athletes must be willing to work hard, sometimes suffer, be lonely, and feel isolated by the love of what they do. Later on, near adolescence, they may reassess their goals and leave the sport. But as athletes begin to drill to the music of "practice makes perfect," their lives start to lock into place. They begin to think of themselves as jockeys, skaters, swimmers, or gymnasts. At an age when their friends may be frolicking in the schoolyard, they have made a commitment.

# 5
# The Home Front

No child can skate without a parent. You couldn't even hire someone to do the things a parent has to do. It is the parent who enables the child to get to the rink, to have instruction, and to simply survive in the sport.
— A skating mother

I probably should tell you I support my son's tennis because he gets so much out of it. That it improves him mentally and physically and, as my tennis-mother pals and I like to tell ourselves, it teaches children so much about life. Though all that is certainly true, the real reason I support my son's tennis is because it adds drama to my life — along with thrill, danger, and hope. The hope is that he'll be good enough to earn a lot of money someday.
— A tennis mother

**T**en-year-old Susan Sloan's skin is burning under the Florida sun but her mother, Pat, doesn't seem to notice. Susan is a tennis "prospect." Last November the ten-year-old whipped a field of older competitors to win the National twelve-and-under title. Her parents have become totally dedicated to Susan's tennis. Pat works at the tennis club in Lexington, Kentucky, where Susan practices, and travels with her daughter to tournaments year-round. Her father, Jim, works long hours in his drycleaning business to support his daughter's expensive habit.

Right now mother and daughter are spending three weeks at Nick Bollettieri's Tennis Academy in Bradenton, Florida. They have come to the academy at the suggestion of Susan's hometown pro, who wants her to sharpen her strokes. So as Susan pounds her forehand to Bollettieri across the net, Pat, a platinum blonde with oversize white sunglasses shading round blue eyes, talks about her favorite subject, her daughter: "From the first time Susan saw her older sister hit a tennis ball she started bugging us to play. I thought she was too little, but she wasn't. She's always had great coordination. She was already jumping rope when other kids were learning to walk."

Susan's abilities were soon evident to all who saw her play. At the club she was the local prodigy. Widespread admiration of their daughter's talent set the Sloans on a course of action. "When someone tells you your child is going to be great at something — and she's been told that since she was seven — then it puts an awful lot of responsibility on the parents," says Pat Sloan. "You have to decide if you're going to go all the way

63

and make a total commitment to it. If she had that type of talent, we felt we owed it to her to do everything we could. And that's exactly what we're doing."

Commitment to sport must begin with the child. Yet as he or she starts to achieve, the parental role expands. Mothers are called upon to chauffeur the child to daily practice sessions, competitions, exhibitions. Fathers must annually produce thousands of dollars for equipment, coaching, and travel. Siblings, too, must make sacrifices. Often their share of their mother's attention dwindles. And they see that a sizeable proportion of the family budget is allotted to their sister or brother, not to them.

A child's sports career is like a flooding stream, sweeping the entire family into the current. By necessity, the family must draw together to coordinate schedules and juggle finances. Psychic boundaries between family members blur as joys and sorrows are communally shared. Yet keeping the family together, identities separate, and the athlete's career going requires a flexibility and continuing commitment that only a few families can successfully muster.

Five years ago Cathy Annacone was in a situation identical to Pat Sloan's. She, too, sat on a bench at Nick Bollettieri's Tennis Academy monitoring the progress of her fourteen-year-old son Paul. A small, compact woman with dark eyes and a thick mane of black hair, Cathy Annacone has the energy and resilience peculiar to those women who have survived predominantly male households. Growing up with three brothers, her athletic talents were overlooked, so as an adult, Cathy set her mind to mastering tennis. A few years later Cathy's husband, Dominic, took up the game when he was sidelined with a broken ankle. Itchy for activity, he learned how to play while still in a walking cast. When their sons Steve and Paul

Paul (top) and Steve Annacone, 1980

were old enough to swing rackets, Cathy, especially, was eager to introduce them to the game. Tennis became the family religion.

When Cathy and Dom temporarily moved from Shoreham, Long Island, to Puerto Rico to teach school at Ramie Air Force Base, the Annacones could play tennis every day. Their youngest son, Paul, emerged as the star of the family. "Though Steve's shots were good, Paul's were just as good — and he was four years younger," Cathy recalls. "Because Paul was precocious and little, everybody paid attention to him. He never really had a childhood. It seemed as if he zoomed straight from infancy to preadolescence."

While in Puerto Rico, Paul's talents were noticed by Charles Joslin, owner of a tennis club in Massachusetts. Joslin invited the eight-year-old to spend the summer touring with his club's junior team on the prestigious New England junior tennis circuit. Although reluctant to let Paul go, Cathy and Dom realized that it would be an excellent opportunity for Paul to improve his game. They finally succumbed to their son's pleas, and Paul's tennis career was set in motion. That winter, when the Annacones moved back to Shoreham, Paul played the eastern boys' circuit. By sixth grade Paul had already decided that tennis would be his life. At fourteen he would announce to his mother, who was then employed as a high school guidance counselor, "I'm not going to do it the way you and Dad did. I'm not going to be an academic or a scholar. I want to be outside playing tennis, not sitting behind a desk."

Both parents were dismayed, though not surprised. They had watched Paul's grades fall as his tennis improved. His father was especially concerned that Paul not shut any doors in his young life. But both parents were equally determined to let their son make his own choices. "I tried to support both his schooling and his tennis," says Cathy. "I'd help him with his schoolwork, and make sure that he wasn't letting it slide. But I really felt that his love was tennis. And I wanted to support that as best I could."

But supporting Paul's tennis involved more than simply lending a strong shoulder. By the time Paul was ten, Cathy and Dom were taking turns chauffeuring him an hour each way to the Port Washington Tennis Academy after school. Cathy often sat on the floor doing macrame as Paul practiced for two hours. As she watched Paul her thoughts often wandered to Steven. Steve was now fourteen, an inscrutable age. When Paul had declared that tennis was going to be his life, Steve had stated that tennis wasn't going to be his. He seemed happy, making new friends in high school, absorbed with his schoolwork and a variety of intramural sports. Although he seemed happily independent and eager to share in his brother's growing success, what was going on in Steve's mind?

Perhaps she should have pushed Steve in tennis. When Charles Joslin had spotted Paul and escorted him around New England for three summers, she had not pushed Steve to go too, not only because she felt that Steve was less enthusiastic about the sport than Paul was, but also because she feared that sending both boys with Joslin would be too much of an imposition, especially when Joslin had specifically requested Paul. But would Steve later resent Paul if Paul turned out to be good? She pushed these thoughts from her mind. After all, Paul was only ten. It was too early to start thinking about a career.

By the time Paul was thirteen, virtually all family life revolved around his schedule. Tournaments at Port Washington and other clubs in New York and New Jersey were scheduled for almost every weekend. One parent would drive Paul to his Friday evening match; the other would do the 9:00 A.M. match on Saturday. If he won the early match, Paul would have to wait several hours to play again late in the afternoon. If he made the finals, both parents and sometimes Steve would return on Sunday. "It was exhausting," says Cathy, "driving and worrying the whole weekend, trying to keep Paul's mind occupied between his Saturday matches, and then going back to work on Monday." Holidays like Thanksgiving and Christmas were times not for family reunions, but for special tournaments. The turkey was roasted, but around Paul's match schedule.

Dom had earned a Ph.D. and was named superintendent of schools in East Hampton, Long Island. While he was busy with his new administrative career, Cathy was dissatisfied with her job as a guidance counselor. As a result, although the whole family made sacrifices for Paul's tennis, it was Cathy who became most emotionally involved in Paul's career. She became increasingly ambitious for her son. Even watching him play became too stressful. At tournaments she would go down to the locker room and jump rope, telling Paul, "All the energy I'm using down here, I'm sending up to you."

Although tennis was clearly Paul's choice, she started to feel responsible for his losses. "Parents are most willing to give, give, give," she says, "and it's great when you're riding the highs. But when you see the pain when your child loses, it just tears your heart out. I hated to see him suffer so. And I felt that it somehow was my fault because I had gotten him interested in the sport. I knew that it was an irrational feeling and that, in fact, I am not responsible. But there's some thread in me that just won't let go."

"I became very fragile," she adds. "I didn't want to feel responsible for him when he didn't do well. And I didn't want my feeling good about myself to be contingent on Paul's success. I knew I had to get us both out of the situation."

At the same time, the family was living in East Hampton, fully two hours from Port Washington. Commuting was impossible, and the closest tennis facilities didn't offer enough competition. So when Paul was fourteen, Cathy went to Florida and scouted tennis academies. She chose Nick Bollettieri's and asked

Dom to fly Paul down. Cathy stayed for a week to get Paul settled and then returned to East Hampton.

The family splintered. Steve was happily settled at the University of South Carolina, studying business administration. Cathy was living in New York City five days a week while taking courses toward her Ph.D. Dom was home alone in East Hampton, accumulating household bills and the monthly thousand-dollar tab from Nick Bollettieri.

There had always been a certain tension in Dom and Cathy's marriage resulting from differences in their personalities. Dom enjoys the role of the Italian-American patriarch. Disciplined and reserved, he sometimes masks his deep love for his family by affecting a gruff manner. Cathy's temperament thrives on change and diversity. Before she went back to graduate school she had enjoyed juggling her career, marriage, Paul's tennis, and the management of the household. She bubbles, while Dom speaks slowly, measuring each word. As their career paths diverged, the differences in their personalities became more pronounced. Dom was upset and lonely during Cathy's five-day-a-week absence. Moreover, when she had been employed, Cathy had shared the financial burden of Paul's tennis, a responsibility that now rested solely with Dom. The couple teetered on the edge of divorce, but their interest in Paul's tennis held them together. "We felt that it was important for Paul that we stay together as a family," says Cathy. "We were scared that by separating we'd destroy what we all worked so hard to build."

During Paul's three years at the academy, however, the Annacones seldom saw their son. He spent nine months a year at Bollettieri's; during vacations he was away at major tournaments like the Orange Bowl in Miami Beach. He spent the summer months on the junior circuit, sometimes making whistlestops in East Hampton to practice with Steve, who spent summers as a tennis pro at a local club.

When Paul was seventeen and entering his last year at the academy, Steve graduated from college and got a job teaching tennis not far from Bollettieri's. The two brothers found themselves growing closer, their four-year age difference less significant that it had once been. Although he had gone to college and indulged other interests, Steve realized that his first love was coaching tennis, especially his brother's rapidly improving game. At the same time, by the first half of his senior year, Paul felt that he had learned as much as he could at the academy. He had risen to number one in his age group in the East. Moreover, he felt stifled by the restrictive social life at the academy. He also missed his family and wanted to graduate from high school with his East Hampton friends. Paul and Steve devised a plan. Steve would quit his teaching job in Florida and both would return home, where Steve would coach and manage Paul until Paul left for college eight months later.

Cathy was still in New York taking graduate courses; Dom was excited at the prospect of having his sons home again. But at first they had problems. Under Cathy's tenure, the household had become flexible to the point of benign anarchy. Cathy accepted it when one of her brood came home late for dinner, and if someone didn't like the menu, she'd cook separate meals to accommodate individual tastes. Dom, however, tried to schedule everything and everyone. He set meals for specific hours and was insulted when Paul snubbed his special linguini with white clam sauce. And since neither Paul nor Steve had a paying job, for the first time in years Dom was bombarded by requests for pocket money.

"It was a mess," laughs Paul. "Dad was still having difficulty trying to accept my mom's absence. And he had trouble adjusting to Steve and me — to the fact that we were no longer boys but young men. I mean, he had hardly seen me except for a week or two here and there from the time I was fourteen to seventeen. Those are pretty important years. And Steve had grown a lot in college, too. Dad could no longer treat us as he had. It took a while for him to get used to our idiosyncrasies and us to his. But at the end of the eight months, we were all closer than we had ever been."

In the fall Paul left for the University of Tennessee, a school he had chosen from the more than fifty that had offered full scholarships. He picked Tennessee because Mike DePalmer, a long time associate of Nick Bollettieri's and a prominent coach at the academy, had just been named tennis coach there. The relationship with DePalmer soon became a focal point in Paul's life. DePalmer was friend, mentor, father-figure, and alter ego, the man who gave Paul a kick in the pants when his motivation started to lag. His support system expanded further when he began seeing a sports psychologist to sharpen his competitive drive and when Bill Shelton, who had followed Paul's career for several years (and who is now an agent at Donald Dell's management firm, ProServ), helped Paul select pro tournaments that he might be eligible to enter as an amateur in the fall. For these various sources of assistance, the Annacones have been grateful. "Neither Dom nor I are really familiar with the inner workings of the tennis world," Cathy concedes. "I know the sport is filled with politics in terms of getting into tournaments and being ranked. I'm glad that people like Bill Shelton and Mike De-Palmer, who are familiar with the politics, will be helping us out."

As Paul's supporting cast has expanded, his focus has narrowed almost exclusively to tennis. During his first year at college he played in a major intercollegiate tournament every weekend from December to May. He made academic sacrifices by taking courses in military science and music appreciation, spent evenings doing push-ups while his roommate studied, restricted his drinking to an occasional beer, and imposed an early curfew on his social life to prevent anything or anyone from interfering with his training. He had hoped to turn in a strong performance at the last and most important tournament of the season, the NCAA championship — the springboard to the pros — but he was eliminated in an early round.

After his freshman year Paul spent the summer on the rough-and-tumble Grand Prix "satellite" circuit in Canada. There he met a number of twenty-five- to thirty-five-year-old pros who were desperately trying to support themselves — and sometimes a family — on paltry prize money. He knew that after the regal treatment he had received as a junior and at college he could not stand to be ranked below two hundred, having to qualify for every major tournament and play the inferior satellite tour in the meantime. For the first time he realized that all his eggs were in one basket. "Ma, I'm scared. I'm nineteen. I'm running out of time," Paul whispered to Cathy over the phone.

But during the summer and his first exposure to pro tennis, Paul's game jelled. He finished third on the satellite tour, beat several of the best young pros in the country, and qualified for the U.S. Open. Although Paul played poorly in the Open and was beaten in the first round, he saw his peers Eric Korita (against whom Paul had played evenly at Nick Bollettieri's) and Scott Davis (a former NCAA champ whom Paul had beaten in the satellites) advance several rounds. He now feels sure that his day is coming.

"No matter how much I tried to pump myself up before, deep down I was never really convinced that I could hold my own. Now I realize I can and should beat the best college players in the country. And they know it's going to be tough to beat me. This year I think I can win the NCAAs and then turn pro. Losing at the U.S. Open was a real disappointment — it was the worst match I played all summer — but I know I'll be around for several more."

"It would be really great if Paul could make it in tennis," says Cathy. "But if he doesn't make it by his mid-twenties he's smart enough to realize it and he'll move on — perhaps playing professional doubles, working as a representative for a sporting goods firm, or setting up a tennis club with his brother and teaching. I know in my heart that he will have options. And when he is thinking clearly, which is most of the time, he knows he does too. But when he loses he forgets he has any options. That's when he really needs our support.

"We're lucky in that Paul's a very social and communicative kid," Cathy continues. "He will talk to me about everything from his fears of letting us down after all the money we've put into his tennis to the advisability of having sex before a match. When he really feels I'm overstepping my bounds he'll say, 'Look, you've really got to trust me.' And it's true. I've put in all the energy I can for him. Now the decisions are his."

Cathy is now using her counseling skills to help brother Steve. "Now that Steve is twenty-five and has shown a renewed interest in competing, I've asked him, 'How come you're doing all this stuff now that I was trying to get you to do at fifteen?' And he said, 'It's all in my head, Ma. I was confused then. Unlike Paul, I didn't have any goals for myself. But now I'm becoming more focused. And I just have to learn not to expect too much because I don't have the training Paul does. Most of the time it's still a lot of fun to play. But losing is still the pits.' "

After a short stint in the corporate world in New York City, Steve once again decided that he preferred coaching tennis. He has relocated to Knoxville, Tennessee, where he teaches at a country club. When his schedule permits, he attends Paul's matches and offers moral support. Says Cathy, "Whereas Paul is very world-wise, sophisticated, and articulate, Steve is more analytical. He can see a problem, consider its facets, and then work it out. They're a fine compliment to each other. And I'm thrilled that they get along so well and can pump each other up about whatever the other is doing. But I also want Steve to be growing, rather than riding Paul's coattails. And I don't want Paul to feel that he is his brother's keeper."

Dom Annacone estimates that Paul's tennis has cost well over $50,000. Cathy admits that combining the roles of wife, mother, sports mother, and career woman has produced tension and a rather erratic household. Steve says that he sometimes felt superfluous in a family where Paul's tennis became the number one priority. Yet when asked whether knowing what they know now, they would do it again, no one hesitated. Says Dom: "My parents were Italian immigrants and instilled in me the belief that it's each generation's responsibility to try and boost the next generation to a higher level. To me, that's what evolution is all about. So although the financial responsibilities for Paul's tennis were enormous, I never resented making those sacrifices. In fact, I feel it has been one of the best accomplishments of my life."

Cathy adds, "There is a lot of denial that goes into being the parent of a precocious child, because you are constantly trying to separate your own identity and ambitions from the child's. And because you don't know how things are going to turn out, you don't want to blow your horn too loud or too soon. But now, as I sit at tournaments and others tell me that Paul is a fine, handsome young man I feel very proud. When Paul loses, I still feel devastated. I just have to keep reminding myself that the bad is part of the good."

Says Steve, "There were times when I felt that if I received half the attention Paul did, I could have made it myself in tennis. But I didn't have his direction. And I realized that for Paul to make it in tennis he would need the support of the entire family and so I accepted the situation. When Paul started to do well on the national junior circuit and became very goal oriented, it made a deep impression on me. I've learned that even if you set goals too high and then have to adjust them, it's a necessary part of getting to where you want to be. So after a childhood of having no goals, I now have several. Paul will probably be turning pro in a year or two, and my short-term goal is to coach and travel with him. I'd then like to use that experience to start

a junior development program or academy similar to Nick Bollettieri's."

Paul concludes, "Basically my brother and I are like best
friends. Even though it's me out on the court physically and
mentally, it's good to know that he's with me 100 percent. When
I win he gets all excited with me, and when I lose he helps me
sort it out. And my dad and mom are just great. To help me
gain and improve my tennis skills they've driven me to practice
and competitions, dishing out $300 or $500 or whatever it takes,
knowing it means they're not going to have a vacation or they
can't buy things for themselves. I just hope someday I'll be the
one who can say 'Merry Christmas' and give them a $10,000
check or something. It would be nice to make it big enough
someday to help them with whatever they want or need."

Cathy Annacone discovered how difficult it was to separate
her own ambitions and needs from those of her son. Sport psychologist Dr. Bruce Ogilvie says that the very nature of our
American sports system, which places the sole responsibility for
supporting the career in the lap of the parents, promotes parental
intrusion:

It is an unfortunate necessity that parents get involved in individual
sports like golf, tennis, and skating. They foot the bills financially and
make a lot of sacrifices in their own personal lives so their child can
get into regional, state, national, and international competitions. As the
child progresses, the involvement gets more intense and the parents
grow increasingly neurotic. This neurosis takes many forms. The most
prevalent is the parent who for whatever reason is dissatisfied with his
or her own life and climbs right into the child's bloodstream until it's
no longer the child's activity. The parent is so needy and the child's
performance is so important to the parent that soon the child gets lost.
The experience is no longer theirs. Everything is sucked out by the
ever-present parent. And then the youngsters become alienated from
the activity. Even though they dearly love what they do, they aren't
allowed to experience it in a personal way. So what starts out as a
natural vicarious satisfaction on the part of the parent becomes an

obsession. They lose conscious awareness of what they are doing. They deny and rationalize. And they're very hard to push back. Even if you try to tell a parent to pull back, to get out of the child's life, it's very, very difficult to accomplish.

In parent groups I tell them that as parents they mustn't use guilt to manipulate the child. They'll quickly assure me, "Oh, I would never do that." And what shoots out of the parent's mouth a minute later but, "After all I've done for you, you lost that match to a nobody." Parents can develop savage, brutal mouths without realizing it.

Dr. Ogilvie's mission is to ally himself squarely with the child athlete. "My strategy with the athlete is to neutralize parental intrusions," he explains, "to help them engineer their lives so that if the parents make distracting verbal noises, the child will no longer hear. I tell the children that greatness and excellence is a very selfish pursuit. It has to be all theirs. But even if I keep telling them that, it would surprise you to know the number of kids — the Olympic kids — that still need to hear it."

Bruce Ogilvie speaks from personal experience. When his daughter Terrie was fourteen, she announced over dinner one night that her coach at the Santa Clara Swim Club had informed her that she had qualified for the Nationals in Cincinnati. Her father's immediate response was, "Great! I've never been to Cincinnati or a Nationals." His daughter's rejoinder was, "And you're not going this time." Dr. Ogilvie says, "I knew at once that this was not in any sense a rejection of Daddy, but her need to control the types of pressures that would allow her to compete effectively. My presence was one more pressure she didn't need."

Dr. Ogilvie's prescription for parental overzealousness: "The parent should become a guest in the life of the child. This would permit the child to remain in control and invite the parent to share whatever they might be experiencing based upon their personal need."

Emotional threads are most likely to fray when the sport claims a major share of the family's budget or time and when parents have put their own interests — or lives — on hold for the sake of the child's career. Some years ago Mark Spitz remarked in a television interview: "I think with any great success story there's a tragedy. And I think my tragedy is that my parents spent so much time devoting their attentions to my well-being, that I think they failed to devote enough attention to their own growth. After I became an adult, moved out, and my athletic career was over, my parents were really left with themselves. And now they're looking at each other eye-to-eye saying, 'Well, now what do we do?' "

Parents who themselves have achieved a high level of professional success in sports are perhaps the least likely to intrude in a negative fashion. In fact, their experience usually offers the child distinct advantages. Take the 1982 All-American College Golf Team: three of the selections were sons of professional baseball or football stars. Jay Delsing's father, Jim, played with the New York Yankees when they won the 1929 World Series; Billy Ray Brown's father, Charlie, was an all-pro tackle for the Oakland Raiders; Chris Perry's father, Jim, was a major league pitcher for seventeen years and his forty-three-year-old uncle, Gaylord, is still pitching.

Stan Wood, chairman of the All-American Selection Committee, says, "Coming from these families has been a positive factor for all three boys. They all idolized their fathers and early in their lives they hung around locker rooms and decided that they, too, wanted to make a career in sports. And coming from athletic families, they have a good deal of inherent athletic ability, as well as very competitive natures."

Chris Perry started playing golf when he was eight by taking chip shots in the backyard with his father's nine iron. At the same time he was becoming a star baseball pitcher like his father. Knowing that Chris wanted to make sports his life, his father took him aside when he reached eighth grade and told him it was time to make a choice because it was time to start developing skills for one sport exclusively. Chris sensed that it might be difficult to live up to his father's and uncle's reputations, and watching his father play a team sport strengthened his commitment to individual accomplishment. "I remember a couple of times when my dad had a no-hitter going into the ninth and someone hit a routine fly ball and the center fielder dropped it. I knew I would have trouble dealing with that." Chris chose golf, a decision his father supported. Three years later he was Minnesota state champion and had earned a golf scholarship to Ohio State University.

But perhaps the most valuable lessons Chris has learned from his father and uncle have been unspoken. "My dad and Uncle Gay played on fairly good teams, but they always worked harder than anyone else in training camp to get themselves in shape. I saw them setting goals for themselves all the time. Seeing how hard they worked has inspired me in my golf game. This year I got to play in the U.S. Open. I saw how good those guys really are. They hit unbelievable shots and control themselves so well over the days of competition. So now I know what level I have to reach. And I'm willing to work hard to get there by the time I finish college."

It is true that when a parent's pro career ends in frustration because of injury or dismissal, or the child's ability does not equal the parent's, being the son or daughter of a sports star can be a curse rather than a blessing. But in most cases having a parent who is an experienced competitor gives the child an early intuitive knowledge of sports, and as the child's competitive career unfolds, the parent-child roles usually remain firmly fixed. In families in which both parents and children are neophytes, the leader often becomes the child.

As parent-child roles become set, the parent-parent relationship often shifts. Sometimes a sports career provides parents with the opportunity to ignore their marital strains by focusing on the child. Most children are not fooled. They usually feel more pressure because they think they have to perform well to hold the marriage together. More often the sports career itself creates marital discord. Sometimes this starts when one parent moves to another city to live with the child while he or she trains with a famous coach. Or, as the number of financial and emotional sacrifices mount, parents may become increasingly competitive about who is doing more for the child.

Linda Fratianne, twenty-one-year-old former world figure skating champion, earns approximately one million dollars annually with a professional skating show, drives a white Mercedes-Benz, and owns a condominium in Beverly Hills and a house in West Hollywood. But she is hurt and angry. The fallout from her parents' troubled marriage, a marriage ruptured by her skating career, has descended on her shoulders.

Things began happily, with Linda as an exceptionally motivated young skater and Virginia Fratianne as an exceptionally devoted skating mother. Before dawn Virginia nudged Linda awake, fed her breakfast, supervised her between six and eight hours of practice, fixed her dinner, and trundled her off to bed. The lives of mother and daughter became more tightly entwined over the years. By the time Linda was sixteen, the two were seldom apart. Linda refused to get a driver's license, for example, because she didn't want her mother to feel unwanted.

However, it appears that Robert Fratianne, a superior court judge in Los Angeles County, *did* come to feel unwanted. According to an interview Linda gave to Linda Kay of the *Chicago Tribune*, her father began to spend time with the mother of one of Linda's skating rivals. Linda told Linda Kay: "I'd go out to lunch with my father and he used to tell me how his girlfriend's girls were doing, and he'd say, 'One of them is so beautiful. I've never seen anyone as beautiful as her, and we're putting her in modeling school, she's just so nice.' And I felt like saying, 'Dad, I'm your daughter, too.' "

According to the article, Virginia and Robert Fratianne split for good during what Linda had hoped would be her finest hour, the 1980 Winter Olympics at Lake Placid. Her status as reigning world champion and pre-Olympic favorite, were not enough to protect her, however. Linda finished a disappointing second. The divorce became legal in February 1981; thirteen days later, on Valentine's Day, Robert remarried.

In an attempt to work out their feelings, Linda and her mother saw the same psychologist. He made Linda realize how her mental state had become dependent on her mother's emotions. To recover, she had to set her mind on her own career, but it wasn't easy. Especially when Robert Fratianne argued in court that he couldn't afford to pay Virginia alimony and child support for their five children because Linda's training expenses depleted his savings.

The strife within the family has left Linda bitter and confused. "For a while, I didn't even want to be around men," she told Linda Kay. "I don't need [my father] in my life anymore. [But] I would just like him to come up to me and tell me why things have happened the way they have."

Another potential family trouble spot is sibling rivalry, in which the crucial factor rests with the personalities of the siblings and the extent to which each is naturally empathetic. Says Cathy Annacone: "I've often thought about Steve, and how Paul's success has affected him. My own sense is that if Paul were my brother, I probably would not love him as much as Steve did. I'd resent the hell out of him. But Steve is incredibly supportive of Paul and always has been."

Another important factor is the age and sex of the siblings. The four-year difference between Paul and Steve Annacone, although not very significant now, represented a large emotional gap during childhood. By the time Paul was proving himself in tennis at age nine, Steve was in high school, where he had his own circle of friends. And by that time Steve had already decided that tennis wasn't going to be his life. The number of siblings is also important. Because Steve and Paul were the only two children in the family and because both their parents worked, it was natural that they would be drawn together.

But most siblings will, at some point, feel conflicting emotions of pride and envy when a brother or sister's accomplishments receive more attention than do their own. Jealousy can be extremely strong when a major part of the family's income is directed only to the sports star.

For several years Richard Zayak, part owner of Lou's Tavern in Hillsdale, New Jersey, has spent more than $25,000 annually in an effort to meet the training and travel expenses of his daughter Elaine. In 1981 his investment paid off when Elaine won the national figure skating title. In 1982 the sixteen-year-old became world champion. Her nineteen-year-old brother, Ricky, and eighteen-year-old sister, Cindy, feel immensely proud of Elaine. "The most exciting moment of my life was when I first saw Elaine on television when she won the Junior World Championships in Germany," says Cindy. But Ricky and Cindy sometimes also felt resentful. When Ricky was sixteen, he asked his mother for $600 to buy a used car. She refused. The money was needed for Elaine's skating. He stormed away, got a job, and bought the car himself. Cindy Zayak has felt equally annoyed. "Sometimes I'll get angry inside," she says. "Like if I ask for a new pair of shoes and my mother says, 'You have a job, you pay for them.' Then I'll see Elaine get another pair of $425 skates.'"

Yet Cindy and Ricky are not hostile, embittered children who feel that their lives have been spoiled by Elaine's success. They know the financial sacrifices their parents have made to help Elaine on her way, and they are generally sympathetic to the exigencies of the family finances. Mrs. Zayak has tried to defuse sibling rivalry by getting Ricky and Cindy to think of the long run. "I know you are making sacrifices now," she tells them,

David Leonardi

David Leonardi

Elaine Zayak, at fourteen, winning the
National Junior Championship, 1979.

"but eventually it may pay off. If Elaine does well and gets into a show she'll have a lot of money. If you ever get in financial trouble and need a loan, Elaine might be able to help you out."

When two siblings are involved in a sport, the bond that forms when they practice together, learn from each other's experiences, and share competitive pressures usually far outweighs the negative effects. In pro tennis there have been at least fifteen sibling teams in recent years, including Tracy and John Austin, Chris and Jeanne Evert, Gene and Sandy Mayer, Andrea and Suzy Jaeger, Tim and Tom Gullikson, Sammy and Tony Giammalva, and Vijay and Anand Amritraj. In other sports there are other dynamic duos: Phil and Steve Mahre (skiing); Faye and Kaye Young, Dick and Tom Van Aarsdale, Gus and Ray Williams (basketball); Phil and Tony Esposito, Marty and Mark Howe (hockey). In professional riding, there are three Leone brothers — Armand, Peter, and Mark. One family has become a dynasty in squash. Launched in the tiny village of Peshawar, Pakistan, in the 1920s by Hashim Khan, the family now boasts more than fifty squash-playing Khans from the Khyber Pass to Colorado. It is not unusual for five or six Khans to be playing in the same tournament. Sharif, Hashim's son and twelve-time winner of the prestigious North American Open, describes competing against his brothers and cousins as "a friendly rivalry" and then points to his bottom teeth held together by braces — "My cousin Mo," he explains. "When members of the family compete against each other, we play twice as hard as against outsiders." Nothing like the Khan legacy exists in the annals of sport. "Only in the circus," laughs Sharif.

For Sharif Khan, family tradition has been an important motivating force. "Winning the first four or five North American Open squash titles was relatively easy," he says. "I was young, strong, extremely motivated, and playing a thin field. Then the game boomed. Superbly conditioned college players turned pro. It got harder not only to physically fend off these new challengers, but also to motivate myself to defend the title for the ninth or tenth time." The inspiration came from glancing at the silver trophy. Since the North American Open began in 1954, the names of his father Hashim, uncle Roshan, and cousin Mohibullah have been etched again and again on the silver bowl above his own.

But in some cases the tradition set by a parent or older sibling can lead to desperation rather than inspiration. The normal self-doubt that is part of any competitor's makeup can become overwhelming when one's measuring stick is a superstar sibling. For instance, Jeanne Evert was thirteen and a promising junior player when her sister Chris stunned the tennis world by reaching the semifinals of the U.S. Open at age sixteen. Her internal pressure to excel, magnified by Chrissie's example, was aggravated still further by the press, who began spinning tales about Jeanne and predicting how one day she might supplant her sister. Jeanne rose to the number nine ranking in the country, but feeling unable to live up to her sister's precedent, she quit the game. Now married to Brahm Durbin, a Canadian accountant, she told Frank Deford of *Sports Illustrated*, "The strains were probably my fault. But she was always so confident. . . .She was always there when I needed her. But it was just that she was so . . . so assured on the court. And finally it was too much for me."

"There's no question that my success adversely affected my brothers and sisters," Chris admits in her autobiography. "Drew and John were singled out at local and college tournaments. Some hecklers at college matches would shout, 'C'mon Chris' when they played, which was unfair. Local radio and television stations requested interviews, even when my brothers weren't the No. 1 players on their teams. The interviewers, of course, were more interested in whether I was going to win the Open or Wimbledon."

Now the burden of Chris's legacy is falling on her youngest sister, fourteen-year-old Clare, who reached the finals of the national championship in her age group in 1982. "Sure I'd love to have my own tennis identity, but I haven't done enough yet to earn it," Clare said to a newspaper reporter. "Some people have wanted to meet me just because who my sister is, but I've learned that's natural."

Whereas the three-year age difference between Chris and Jeanne resulted in a natural competitiveness, the thirteen-year gap between Chris and Clare has brought an ease to their relationship. When Chris was single and often lonely on the tour, Clare was the bright spot in her life. She loved coming home to baby-sit and practice with her kid sister. And Clare maintains that she is never envious of Chris. Now more than ever, she loves being with her famous older sister. Chris is confident that because of Clare's happy-go-lucky, independent nature, she will be able to handle the pressures that inevitably will arise if Clare continues to do well. To help ease the pressure for Clare, Chris plans to retire from the tour before her sister joins.

A small age difference coupled with predictions from the press also caused misery for speed skater (and later world champion bicyclist) Beth Heiden. Before the 1980 Winter Olympics she was billed as a sure winner. Beth and brother Eric appeared together on the cover of *Time*. Their Madison, Wisconsin, home was invaded by the press and charity groups. When she left for Lake Placid, Beth told her mother that she hoped to win one medal, the bronze in the 3,000 meters. That's exactly what she did win. But the pressures of always being mentioned with Eric, winner of five gold medals, proved too much. In a press conference, the tears that had been welling up for months angrily spilled out: "I like to skate for myself, and this year I feel I have to skate for the press. And to hell with you guys."

Perhaps the greatest potential damage occurs when more than one sibling has excelled in a sport and a younger child can't seem to get a toehold. Twenty-year-old Murray Howe is the third son of hockey's all-time leading scorer, Gordie. Murray's

Six-year-old Clare Evert hugs a bouquet of roses given to
sister Chris after a 1974 Wimbledon victory.

two older brothers, Mark and Marty, followed their father into the National Hockey League. Playing in the NHL was also Murray's dream. He began skating at two and was on a team by five. He skated five days a week, lifted weights, learned karate, and took vitamins to improve his performance. At sixteen, Murray joined a junior team in Toronto where one of his teammates was future NHL star Wayne Gretzky. "The good players were leaving me in the dust," he told Steve Marantz of the *Boston Globe*. "No matter what I did I didn't feel like I was improving." Even at sixteen, recruiters were sizing up Murray, comparing him with Gordie, Mark, and Marty. He felt he had to live up to his name and began to put a lot of pressure on himself.

As Murray pushed himself harder and harder, he began to lose more often. After two more years of junior hockey, he finally stepped back and reevaluated his life. "I was very unhappy with everything," he said. "I felt at the bottom of the pile in hockey. But in school I was always getting the highest scores on tests. A very definite change occurred in my goals." While he had once thought of school as "not leading to anything," he enrolled at the University of Michigan as a premedical student. He gave hockey one last shot but failed to make the varsity team. It was the final crushing blow. He realized that hockey would never be his life and he began rechanneling his energies into medicine. Now that he is a student at the University of Michigan Medical School and his future is assured, he can look back and laugh. No one will ever know how much of Murray's inferior performance was due to the pressure of having to equal his relatives, but at least the story has a happy ending.

Another sticky sibling situation arises when young boys are compared with talented older sisters, another situation that can be exacerbated by the press. Mrs. Sue Cassiday shivered when she read in the *Chicago Tribune*: "For Grant Cassiday, it could be a most uncomfortable situation. On the one hand, there is his older sister Stacy, one of the best age group swimmers in the country, a budding star who, just past her fourteenth birthday, has already earned the right to swim for the 1984 Olympic Trials. On the other hand, there is Grant. At age ten, he is a fine swimmer in his own right, one who recently helped Lake Forrest win the State Junior Olympic title. But partly because girls develop more quickly than boys, he is not matching Stacy's ten-year-old performances."

"I was so mad at that article," fumes Mrs. Cassiday. "Grant is not like his sister, in personality or physique. He looks up to Stacy, but hasn't felt overly pressured to match her accomplishments. We have all done our best to keep the comparisons to a healthy level. And then this comes along . . ."

Children who have a superstar for a sibling can't run under a rug and hide. Every day they watch as adulation is heaped onto their brother's or sister's shoulders. They can take one of two paths. They can either abandon the sport or they can confront the problem head-on by choosing to compete in the same arena. As siblings mature and establish their own lives, they are better able to put the relationship into perspective. Sometimes children who have felt shortchanged and initially lashed out at the offending sibling in childhood relocate the blame. The relationship between siblings may grow stronger as the bond between the shortchanged child and the parents deteriorates.

John Austin, the twenty-five-year-old brother of Tracy Austin, is also a tennis professional, one with perhaps not as impressive a record as Tracy's, but with enough talent to play on the highly competitive Grand Prix circuit. Said John in an interview for *World Tennis*: "There's no competition between Tracy and me. But there was competition for my parents' attention. I always felt as if *my* tennis was secondary, that if push came to shove, I would be left behind." John finally exploded after the 1980 Wimbledon championships. First, his mother watched Tracy practice instead of watching John's first-round match. Then his

John and Tracy Austin win the
1980 Wimbledon Mixed Doubles title.

father didn't arrive in England until Tuesday, after John's Monday match. Further, before he and Tracy were about to play their mixed doubles final match (which they won) the NBC announcer proclaimed that Tracy was going for her first Wimbledon title, but neglected any mention of John. John was understandably "pissed off." He finally sat down with his parents and voiced his resentments. Now, says John, the family is closer.

Although the families of talented athletes may make their financial and economic sacrifices on the assumption that sport will "build character," sports in themselves will neither mold nor destroy moral fiber. A sense of morality usually develops in children between the ages of eight and twelve, when the child loses an egocentric orientation and begins to develop the ability to put him- or herself in someone else's place. This role-taking ability allows youngsters not only to note the actions of others but to begin to understand that behind every action lies intent. From this new capacity to reach beyond superficiality into deeper levels of meaning, the superego or conscience begins to form. A sense of fair play starts to develop.

But the ages between eight and twelve are also the years in which outstanding athletic ability begins to be noticed. As the child becomes recognized by his parents, peers, coaches, and community, more attention may be paid to his physical development than to his emotional growth. Says sports psychologist Dr. Thomas Tutko, "People are so worried about his temperament that they fail to correct him; they compensate for him and excuse him from mundane activities for fear that he will be unhappy and not perform up to par. By pampering him, paving his way, taking care of his needs, and providing special privileges, people help perpetuate any immaturity that may be there."

The pressures mount rapidly on the young superstar, often before he is emotionally ready to handle them. "If he performs well, people begin to expect that he will perform well all the time," says Dr. Tutko. "When he doesn't, they are disappointed. If the athlete sees the disappointment and is immature, he may begin to blame many other things for the failure, such as officials, field conditions, poor coaching, teammates, and so on. Part of maturity is admitting one's mistakes and adjusting to them. If people help the superstar excuse himself for making errors, they are really helping him to evade reality."

The family is the first, and perhaps most critical, social environment in the young athlete's life. It is here that a child not only tunes into parental interests, but also picks up adult attitudes toward aggression and fair play. If a parent screams at the referee, calling him a bum, the child learns that verbal abuse is acceptable. If parents give the impression that it is okay to cheat in order to win, if you're not detected, then children learn that any means justifies the desired end.

"The child may have great talent, but the parents can make or break him emotionally," says Dr. Tutko. "They are the ones most responsible for counterbalancing the pressures that their child will face from his teammates, his coach, his public, and himself."

According to Dr. Tutko, the role of the parents is not only to help the potential superstar gracefully handle fame and face failure, but to also alert them to the difficult path that lies ahead. "The talented youngster who seems determined to devote his teenage years to acquiring an athletic scholarship or a pro contract needs to be warned that the problems he will face are different from the problems faced by most athletes. First, a number of people will use him and try to live vicariously through him. Second, he will find that everyone wants to be his friend and to be around him as much as possible. This may seem nice at first, but eventually it can wear away his patience and tolerance. . . . Third, everyone wants to possess him. Some use him to make money; others seek a feeling of importance through him. And fourth, one of the prerequisites of handling athletic success is the ability to live with fan rejection. The *f* in *fan* stands for fickle. They love you today—but you had better win tomorrow. The youngster won't always be a winner and so he must learn to tolerate unfair and unreasonable fan reaction. In fact, even when he is winning, his fans can grow restless if he doesn't perform to an expected level of excellence."

The competitive style children learn from their parents, peers, and coaches is likely to permeate other aspects of their lives. If a child is cocky and obnoxious on the tennis court, these behaviors usually carry over into relationships with siblings, schoolmates, and teachers. If competition helps to foster empathy and respect, the child becomes trusting in other areas of life.

What is the most important function a family can perform for the child superstar? "Love and acceptance are what the child wants, but too often what he gets is love with conditions," says Dr. Tutko. "If the parents love the child only because he is a first stringer, a winner, a hero, then the day will come when he will run out of first teams, victories, and heroics, and find he is alone. It is tough enough to find out when you are 20 or 30 or 35 years of age. It is deadly, psychologically, to discover it at age 12 or 13. . . . Love must be shown for the *individual*, not for what that individual is capable of doing in athletics."

# 6

# The Coach

**Winning is the name of the game. The more you win, the less you get fired.**
**— Bep Guidolin, former**
**Boston Bruins hockey coach**

**I** *am nine years old. I have just wolfed down my dinner. My father is taking our two tennis rackets out of the hall closet. It is warm, late spring. We are about to embark on our after-dinner ritual.*

*We live on a quiet, dead-end street. My father ties a string to a tree on either side of the road and pulls it taut to simulate the height of a net. We stand on opposite sides. He delivers a sermon of "racket back" and "eye on the ball." The balls snap off our rackets, back and forth.*

*He grins at me. I beam back. Tennis is his first love. Formerly a member of the Harvard team and now a solid club player, he is bestowing on me, his eldest daughter, his undying love of the game. My forehand sings over the net. He calls it "the best forehand in the business." We continue hitting until it is too dark to see the ball.*

*In a few years I will play on my high school team and win local tournaments. But my game is woefully lopsided. Both of us developed such pride in my forehand that my backhand and serve went bankrupt. To this day they remain half-baked strokes that reek of accumulated bad habits.*

Twenty years ago, a child's first coach was usually a parent, full of enthusiasm but apt to be amateurish and shortsighted as a teacher. Today many athletes are making careers out of coaching — they are not only well trained in the sport itself, but have also honed their teaching skills. And as sports have become central to American life, parents are taking sports lessons more seriously and removing themselves from the picture, substituting more highly qualified — and more objective — professionals.

Sherm Chavoor coached Debbie Meyer, who won three gold medals in the 1968 Olympics after taking up swimming at age seven. Their relationship began when Debbie was fourteen. Her father had been transferred from New Jersey to California, yet still commuted long distances to work and was home only on weekends. As Meyer swam with Chavoor at poolside twice a day for four hours, he stepped into the paternal void. "At first, I looked to Sherm as a professional who I greatly respected and trusted," says Debbie. "If he had told me to jump, I would have asked, 'How high?' "

Their relationship became even closer when Debbie was in high school. She swam seven to ten miles daily and fell into bed exhausted at 9:00 P.M. She classified her peers as swimmers and nonswimmers. Swimmers were mature and disciplined, nonswimmers, who had not yet made career decisions, faced important responsibilities, or traveled extensively, were immature. She didn't associate with the latter. She only went out on dates with groups of swimmers, and only those who met Chavoor's approval. "If I had a crush on someone who Sherm didn't like he'd say, 'What do you see in that guy?' " recalls Debbie. "I quickly got over those crushes." Chavoor may not have consciously been trying to dominate Debbie's life, yet he knew how important it was to keep his young star's attention from wandering. Any minor uncertainty could mean the loss of hundredths of seconds in a race, possibly the difference between winning and losing.

Meyer was secretly grateful for Chavoor's protection. She had little interest in the high school dating scene, and Chavoor, unlike others, understood her competitive nature. He *insisted* that she be tough. Through the years of flaying the water she had indeed become an exceptional athlete — and admired as an

Little Winners

athlete by her swimming friends, her community, the country, and the world. Swimming was the path she had chosen, and swimming was enough to sustain her.

But after winning the Olympics, a sense of her athletic self wasn't enough. "Nine thousand things caved in on me," she says. The first was a broken ankle, the result of a skiing accident. She gained twelve pounds while in the cast and reassured herself that she'd swim the weight off when she recuperated. But when the cast came off she no longer had any swimming goals. She didn't swim, nor did she get any other form of exercise. Instead, she moved to Los Angeles and became a student at UCLA, where she felt like a fish out of water among the "stereotyped beautiful people," as she called her classmates. Her parents were away on an overseas assignment. She was still widely recognized as Debbie Meyer, Olympic champion, but now that she was no longer swimming, the publicity annoyed her. She sought consolation in food. She ballooned from her competitive swimming weight of 135 pounds to 180 in three months. After the Olympics she had been hired by the CBS "Sports Spectacular" show to do swimming commentary. Although her voice was heard analyzing the swimmer's strokes, she wasn't shown on camera because her face was too chubby.

The affront shook her. If the nonsporting world could only accept her as skinny, then skinny she would become. She applied the same diligence to dieting that she had shown during her strenuous swimming workouts. In fact, she was too diligent. When she appeared one day at her parents' house they could only stare in dismay: their obese Olympic champion was now 110 pounds and bordering on anorexia.

Over the next year, Debbie Meyer came to grips with herself. "It occurred to me that I love sports and there was really no reason to stay away from swimming," she told Janice Kaplan, author of *Women and Sports*. "Being like all the other girls is actually very boring. It was time to take responsibility for my

Debbie Meyer with her coach, Sherm Chavoor.

own life and not depend on Sherm. It had taken awhile, but I finally felt like I was grown up." She became a swim coach at Stanford and was then hired to do public relations for Speedo swimsuits in San Francisco. As she gained a sense of herself as a businesswoman, she also regained her self-confidence.

In 1979 Meyer married Douglas Reyes, a swim coach in her home town of Carmichael, California. Now, at thirty, she helps her husband coach 110 youngsters and runs swimming clinics for YMCAs and private swim clubs across the country. She is happy with married life and her new home in Citrus Heights, outside Sacramento. Her weight has stabilized at 127 pounds. Yet Sherm Chavoor still remains a potent force in her life. At Debbie's wedding rehearsal (the service took place at the Arden Hills Swim Club where Debbie had trained), the minister instructed, "Now the father will walk the bride down the aisle." Both Sherm Chavoor and Mr. Meyer stood up. "I'm sorry, Mr. Chavoor," the minister said, smiling sympathetically. "In this case, blood is thicker than water."

Soon after Debbie Meyer and Sherm Chavoor reached their common goals in northern California, another notable athlete-coach relationship was forged in southern California. Tracy Austin first learned tennis by osmosis. Her parents, Jeanne and George, took up tennis in 1956, when an Air Force transfer brought them back to southern California from the East. Jeanne played every day; George on weekends. When their eldest son, Jeff, was ten, Vic Braden, coach at the Kramer Club where the Austins played, coaxed Jeff out of Little League and into tennis. Sister Pam and brothers Doug and John followed suit. All were ranked nationally as juniors; Jeff, Pam, and John also eventually played in the pros.

Jeanne Austin sold tennis dresses in the Kramer Club's pro shop. Instead of leaving the job when Tracy was born in 1963, she drove to work in the family station wagon and left her youngest daughter sleeping and playing in a crib behind the back seat. It was natural, then, that Vic Braden would go out to the parking lot and roll tennis balls to Tracy in her crib; and that when Tracy was two and still in diapers she'd drag a full-size racket onto the court where her family was playing and yell, "Hit it to me, hit it to me!"

In 1970, when Tracy was seven, Vic Braden left the Kramer Club. The Austins chose Robert Landsdorp, a genial Dutchman, to be Tracy's coach. She was only one in a large group of promising youngsters taught by Landsdorp, a group that included Eliot Teltscher, now the sixth-ranked pro in the world. Although Landsdorp realized that Tracy had unusual tenacity and an innate sense of timing, he was careful not to give her preferential treatment. She received one lesson a week at fourteen dollars an hour.

Over the years, Landsdorp gained an immense respect for Tracy's talents. Off the court they slipped into a close father-daughter relationship. Landsdorp enjoyed teasing his young prodigy, bringing peals of laughter and exasperated "Oh, Robert!"'s to her normally composed countenance. And Tracy loved the attention of her handsome coach. Yet there were bounds to the relationship. Landsdorp's sphere of influence was restricted to the tennis court. Tracy was developing equally close ties to her school friends and family, especially her mother.

"A champion is an independent, willful soul," says Peter Bodo, an editor for *Tennis* magazine who has profiled many of the top tennis players. "A mother is the source. A tennis mother — a good one — isn't the boss, except on a rock bottom level that few outsiders ever witness. A tennis mother is a person who keeps her power only by surrendering it." The bond between Tracy and her mother was formed by a series of pushes and pulls — by Tracy dispensing orders to her mother while Jeanne organized Tracy's career and became her daughter's emotional backbone.

When Tracy was fourteen, she visited her brother Jeff at a tournament in Portland, Oregon, where a professional women's tournament was being held at the same time. As a lark Tracy entered, expecting to lose early and go back to school. Instead she won all her qualifying matches. To continue would mean missing school, and Tracy knew her mother would not approve, so Jeff got on the phone and told his mother, "She's bound to lose. She'll be home tomorrow." Tracy stayed, won several more rounds, flew back home to stop in at school, and then flew back to Portland to win the tournament. By winning at Portland she had qualified to play in other pro tournaments while still an amateur.

Both Jeanne Austin and Robert Landsdorp agreed that Tracy was too young to join the professional circuit, but they also agreed that she *was* ready to try her hand at two major tournaments — Wimbledon and the United States Open. At Wimbledon, Tracy won two rounds before losing to Chris Evert. Then the fourteen-year-old went all the way to the quarterfinals of the U.S. Open. A year later Tracy declared her pro status in a Los Angeles press conference. "The decision to turn pro won't change my life," she told the press. "Except instead of just getting roses I'll be getting prize money."

But turning pro did change her life — and her relationship with Robert Landsdorp. For three weeks at a time, Landsdorp left his club to accompany Tracy and her mother on the pro tour. Yet thrilling as it was to watch his young prodigy, Landsdorp was lonely. He had his own little girl and a wife at home. The Austins wanted him on the tour to practice with Tracy; he wanted to spend more time with his family. Meanwhile, the Austins grew increasingly unhappy with Tracy's serve.

The relationship between Landsdorp and the Austins began unraveling during the 1979 U.S. Open, while sixteen-year-old Tracy was on her way to becoming the youngest champion in the tournament's history. At the Open, former Australian champ

Roy Emerson helped Tracy with her serve, and there were reports that he would be joining their entourage. As the press extolled Tracy as "Super Kid," Vic Braden was often cited as the molder of Tracy's talents. Landsdorp was stung. He returned to his teaching position at the West End Tennis Club. He had wanted to return home, but he had not anticipated losing his power. "Yes, I was hurt," he told longtime tennis commentator Bud Collins. "We'd been through a lot together. It was a close relationship we had, but it had become impossible. Tracy had had a lot of success very fast, and she'd become a know-it-all. Not in the sense of a brat, but that I couldn't tell her anything anymore. The atmosphere was abrasive. I had lost the control I needed, and I left."

Emerson was busy with his own tournament schedule and couldn't travel with Tracy. And Tracy missed her old friend, mentor, and practice partner. Although she won two tournaments during Landsdorp's two-month absence, she also suffered two bad losses. Up popped Landsdorp again, rehired, sitting beside Jeanne in the front row of the Boston Avon Tournament, watching Tracy beat Martina Navratilova for the $100,000 first prize. "Tracy needs me, that's clear," he said.

Though Landsdorp was glad to return to his young starlet, at the same time he told reporters: "I don't like Vic Braden getting credit for rolling a ball at her in the crib and Emerson getting credit for her serve, when it hasn't changed. Maybe it's an ego sort of thing. I've done it and I've done it all. It's like a work of art. An artist would feel robbed if someone else put his name on a painting."

Hearing Landsdorp talk created rumblings in the Austin household. Was Landsdorp too power-hungry? How much did he really add to Tracy's performance? Bud Collins wrote in *World Tennis* magazine: "It will be interesting to watch the triangle going through the changes, to see who's around her when Tracy does conquer the planet. You watch the two of them now on the court: Landsdorp hitting balls to the spots the way a foe will do it, imparting the spin she must watch for, feeding her the difficult angles, and letting her know what her response must be to win. Over and over they go through it. Is this Rasputin influencing the Czarina? A loving professor preparing the prodigy for an exam? An instructor looking to cash in? Probably a little of each because it amounts to an extraordinary tie that has helped pull a little girl from her classrooms to the attention of the world, from playdough to headlines and riches in such a short time. The cord will be severed, but there will be twinges. Perhaps each will always secretly question: 'How much was me? How much the other?' "

Shortly after Collin's article appeared, the cord was severed. Landsdorp was negotiating a new contract with Tracy's business managers and insisted that he was entitled to a share of the $1.5 million Tracy received from endorsing products ranging from tennis gear to cameras. Tracy's attorneys balked. Landsdorp walked out on the negotiations and filed a breach-of-contract suit against Tracy Austin Enterprises for $20,000, a suit that was later settled out of court.

Tracy needed a new coach quickly. Wimbledon was approaching and a back injury had curtailed her training. Jeanne Austin hired ex-Davis Cup champion Marty Reissen to practice with Tracy and hone the finer points of her game. Robert Landsdorp returned to his tennis club to teach pros Eliot Teltscher and Brian Teacher, as well as a new crop of budding prodigies, including twelve-year-old Stephanie Rehe, who Landsdorp predicts may become the youngest winner in Wimbledon — or U.S. Open — history. But now when he talks, the work *control* crops up more often. He is starting the Robert Landsdorp Tennis Academy in Vista, California. The advantage of the academy, he says, is that from the very beginning it can monitor the progress of young players on a daily, rather than weekly, basis. Such an arrangement — which is similar to a boarding school —

also puts the coach, rather than the parents, in the mainstream of the athlete's life.

Despite their thorny relationship, Landsdorp says that he harbors no ill feelings — at least toward Tracy. "She was only a child, after all," he explains. "She was not the one making the decisions." And he acknowledges that the relationship was mutually beneficial. Tracy received fine coaching; she helped boost his reputation. Landsdorp still sees Tracy occasionally and gives her pointers about her game. But now, several years and dollars later, both are older and wiser.

These two stories illustrate the extremely close and often turbulent bond that develops between an athlete and coach, a bond with far more emotional content than the usual teacher-student relationship. From Little League volunteers to luminaries within their sports, coaches exert tremendous influence on athletes, for an athlete's abilities — an important source of self-esteem — are reflected in the eyes of the coach. A study of world-class and Olympic swimmers by Linda Gustavson and Dr. Bruce Ogilvie found that six to twelve years after the swimmers had stopped competing, they still rated their former coaches as the most significant adults in their lives.

Yet coaches, like parents, can put too much pressure on children by evaluating their own success in the child's won-lost record. Even the best coaches may feel conflicting personal and professional interests: on the one hand wishing to understand the youngster's emotional needs, on the other, needing to win in order to keep their jobs.

In a three-year study of world-famous pianists, Olympic swimmers, tennis players, and research mathematicians who reached the top of their fields between the ages of seventeen and thirty-five, Dr. Benjamin S. Bloom of the University of Chicago discovered a pattern. Most of these successes do not limit themselves to one lifelong master, but instead select teachers who mirror their ascending levels of achievement. In an athlete's terms, the first coach is often a local instructor notable mainly for enthusiasm, one who dispenses concrete rewards such as candy and gold stars. At the second stage, the family obtains instruction from a more skilled professional. The student with "potential" becomes a favorite and receives special attention.

At about age ten or eleven, the child moves on to a third teacher, a master who knows how to train top professionals and open the right doors. On the basis of his or her proven success, this coach automatically commands respect as well as high fees. Sometimes this expert may live a distance away. Either the mother devotes a healthy chunk of her life to chauffeuring, one parent relocates with the child, the child temporarily resides with the coach, or the entire family moves to the sports mecca.

How does a coach become a master? Luck plays a part, but the development of a master coach is almost as clearly defined as the careers of the athletes he teaches. Gayna Grant, a former national competitor and a veteran of Ice Capades and Holiday on Ice, is a novice coach. When she reported to her job as an instructor at an Ice Capades Chalet in Cupertino, California, she was besieged by fledgling admirers. "Do an axel," they pleaded. The dimpled, vivacious twenty-five-year-old complied. Only slowly did she learn to resist the temptation to use all her energy demonstrating or practicing her own skating. She had been hired to teach, not to show off. But she soon learned that she couldn't teach until she had earned her students' respect.

"It's like any teacher-student relationship. It's how you define it in the beginning," she says. "I've learned that I can be loving, but I've also got to be firm. A lot of times when you start working with kids they want to know just how much they can get away with. They see you as their bait, not as their teacher. You've really got to put a stop to that and make it clear that you don't like to fool around."

Establishing oneself as an assertive professional is hard enough

Gayna Grant with three-year-old Kelly Welch.

with unruly children; it's even harder to do with their parents. "A lot of parents have an inflated image of their child's abilities," Gayna says. "The United States Figure Skating Association has nine tests that correlate with competitive categories — juvenile, novice, junior and senior. Often the parents want their child to take a certain test before he or she is ready. It's incredibly frustrating. The parents get so involved that they act as though they know what's best and they usually don't. They feel like they can apply the same rules to their child's skating as to some business deal. If you tell them that the child isn't ready for the test they'll get offended and indignant and say, 'Look, I've been paying sixty dollars a week for you to get my kid through the test. What's the problem?'

"Then you have to explain to the parents that it can take a long time to pass one of the tests. You've got to make them understand that there may be other factors, like the child hasn't had adequate practice time or needs another lesson per week. You have to convince the parents that you know the expectations of the judges better than they do."

Even parents who overtly vest authority in the young professional may still be reluctant to let the sport slip from their control. "If a child loves to skate yet starts to do poorly academically or starts to act up at home, the parents sometimes use skating as a pawn," explains Grant. "They'll forbid the child to skate until her grades or behavior improves. But the strategy often backfires. If a girl who loves skating is deprived of the sport, she'll feel badly about herself because she's not being productive. Then everything gets worse. Whereas if parents looked at the skating in a positive way, letting their children do something that makes them feel good about themselves with no strings attached, it could help everything else."

Besides overzealous and manipulative parents, the novice coach must also skirt the designs of other coaches. "Everyone wants to work with a winner," says Gayna. "At the same time, every kid wants to think that his or her coach is the best. So when you find somebody that's like a little sponge and soaks it all in, everybody notices. When the kid wins a competition or passes tests in quick succession, the other kids say, 'Wow, that coach has really got the secret!' And the other coaches are even quicker to perk up their ears. We all know that if our kids don't do well in competitions, our stable will be empty. So when a teacher goes away for a competition or vacation, another coach may sidle up to the precocious skater and tell her how much she likes her style and how she doesn't want the little girl to backslide in the absence of the regular coach. She'll give the girl free lessons, and go out for coffee with the mother. The mother then starts to think what a good-hearted, qualified coach this other woman is. Because the second coach has really put the sales number on, if there is any kind of flare-up between the regular coach and the student, the parent will say, 'We've been thinking, and maybe we'll switch to Miss Melton. Not that we think there's anything wrong with you, but we need a change.'

"But I think a lot of the kids change coaches as a last resort when they know their skating is starting to fizzle out," she adds. "They need an extra hit and they're grappling for someone to pull them up. Sometimes the energy of a new coach will do the trick. But most of the time, it doesn't work."

Like the young athletes, coaches are under time pressure. Unless their competitors are successful, they are easily branded "low-level teachers" or "good at some skills, bad at others." Says Gayna: "It's hard to break out of that framework. Many people who were excellent skaters and are excellent teachers burn out because of the pressure of continually advancing their students just to insure their reputations. If they don't make the effort, their clientele starts to fade. They end up pushing forty-year-olds across the ice. They become bored. And then many of them totally shift careers."

When I wondered why anyone would willingly choose such

a job, Gayna's face began to glow. "I've had kids that I've started from basics, children who couldn't even balance on one foot. And then I see them improve. One day they'll say, 'Oh Gayna, would you watch me do this?' And I'll see them skating just the way I do, using the same arm movements and flourishes. They think they're being very creative putting all these things together. It really makes me smile inside. Then I see that I do have an effect. Even if three quarters of the time they may act as if they're not interested, they really are mopping it up."

The secret of the novice pro is to maintain a steady stream of new pupils. "You've always got to keep them coming, because when you start out with the beginners, only a few will stick with the sport. There's a lot of competition with other things going on in their lives. And some of them just don't want to put in the necessary time and devotion.

"Although there's a lot of shuffling around of coaches, if the coach is doing a good job and the child and the parents are satisfied, the relationship can last several years. And the coaches that are up at the top didn't just turn pro and get Olympic champions. They've been at it a long time, slowly building up their reputations."

The attrition rate of first-level coaches is high. Many find it difficult to make the transition from competitor to teacher, either because they are accustomed to active participation and feel restless on the sidelines, or because their analytical and verbal skills don't match their athletic talent. Advancement is painfully slow. But eventually their work becomes easier. Their reputations spread. Fresh young talent comes to them. And then they enter the second stage.

Bill Sands began coaching women's gymnastics when he was a freshman in high school and a competitive gymnast himself. By the time he was a junior, he had nurtured his first state champion. At age twenty-eight, he has already reached the second level of coaching and is rapidly approaching the third. Hand-

Lissa Doty

Bill Sands with his "A" Team.

some and muscular, with an all-American boyishness, his blue eyes flicker intensely below the bill of a baseball cap. Although there is a lot of camaraderie among his gymnasts, the Mid-America Twisters, the air inside the cavernous former warehouse in Northbrook, Illinois, is filled with Sands's authoritative presence. His voice echoes sharply as his elite athletes, who include two Olympic-level competitors, practice their routines on the balance beam, horse, and bars.

In his office, which is connected to the gym, the atmosphere is livelier. Parents, gymnasts, and two assistant coaches clutter the room. One wall overflows with books on gymnastics and child psychology. A green glow in the corner indicates the computer into which each competitive gymnast daily enters information about her sleep patterns, diet, and health before each six-hour training session. The telephone jingles incessantly and Sands paces the room like a caged tiger.

According to Sands, although the skill level in gymnastics is increasing rapidly, the sport is in serious trouble. Many gymnastic facilities, such as the top-rated academy run by former Olympic champion Muriel Grossfeld, are closing down. "The development of the gymnastics coach is like the evolution of civilization," says Sands. "When man invented agriculture, that gave him time not to worry about survival. He didn't have to go out and kill deer every day. And so when he didn't have to think about that, he could expand the range of things he could do. Gymnastic coaches are usually so poverty-stricken that there is a nip-and-tuck, hand-to-mouth battle just to survive. Most coaches make less than $12,000 a year. And they put up with a lot of frustration. A facility like this runs on class enrollment. You're forced to teach classes in order to pay the bills, which means teaching below your talent. So most coaches really haven't begun to reflect on what they're doing, to ask 'Is there a better way of training? What direction are we moving in? Is this the best thing for the child at this time?'"

Sands cites himself as an example. For the first three years he lived above the gym in a locker room and slept on a fold-out couch. Now he has enough money to get by, but only because he isn't married and can spend his money as he pleases. The things he chooses to buy are new mats for the gym or software for his computer. "Most coaches," he says, "either drop out or get divorced."

Having passed the survival stage, Sands is now acclimating his students to the politics of the sport as well as teaching them specific skills. "The children in gymnastics tend to be very intelligent. They'll be the first to ask the question 'What does it all mean?' Take Kelli Garrison, for example. Here's a girl who by age twelve had gone as far as she could in national gymnastics. She'd been competing overseas and had done well. She qualified for the Olympic team. But that year the international gymnastics committee decided to raise the minimum age to fifteen. So there she was, having made the Olympic team at twelve, having to wait three more years just to try out again. Of course her mind was full of questions.

"The elite-level athlete has to understand, right from the beginning, that international gymnastics are unfair," Sands continues. "I was the coach for our national team at the World Championships in Fort Worth and I know that when you go out on the international floor it's not a performance arena, but a political arena. That's something the girls and I have to talk about. Before they go out on the floor, they have to know that if they have an established name, they'll score two tenths of a point higher. They have to know that the order of the lineup is extremely important, because the first girl to perform will get the lowest score regardless of how good she is. And they have to know that if a coach has a girl who is in contention for the all-around title, that girl will be placed last in the lineup, even for her poorer events. When Amy and Lynne [Amy Koopman and Lynne Lederer, Sands's two Olympic gymnasts] go to Olympic and world meets I tell them, 'You're probably going to be going pretty early in the lineup because you're not a real hotshot in this event and there are probably one or two kids who are better than you are in the all-around, and if another coach is there, not me, he might put his own kids up last anyway. So count on it. You're going to go up first. And if you don't like it, you shouldn't be in the sport."

All of Sands's gymnasts seem to appreciate his direct approach. "Most people want to withhold information from kids, as if they are stupid," says Sands. "But I'll tell you, today's kids aren't stupid. By the time they reach elementary school, they've seen five thousand hours of television. They've seen people slaughtered and countries rise and fall. They have a sense of justice that's unerring. The elite competitor needs to know that everything is stacked against her when she starts. Then at least when she gets into these situations, she's known it can happen."

Most of the athletes Sands trains are willing to endure the political machinations that are part of this subjectively judged sport because the sport itself is intrinsically interesting. Gymnastics involves learning eight events combining different skills — tumbling, dance, acrobatics. Things kids love to do. "While track and field or swimming are just hard work," says Sands, "gymnastics is inherently fun. But it's the approach of most gymnastics coaches that is deadening."

He employs a three-stage model in coaching. "In the beginning, the coach is dictatorial. He stands in front of the gymnast and demands things. The student makes no decisions whatsoever. Then there's a middle stage when the coach becomes more of a comrade. He stands beside the gymnast and together they go toward certain goals. The coach can still step in front and take command if he has to, but he can also step behind the athlete to be more of a resource person. The coach then begins to give the girl exposure to situations where she must take responsibility. She learns to make decisions regarding her performance and to accept the consequences. At the third stage, about 90 percent of the decisions are the gymnast's. She's been in the sport long enough to know how to train. She's generally older by this time and should know what it takes to get her routines ready and how much to warm up before an event. The coach is there if she should suddenly struggle or fall into a new and confusing situation. And he can still help with strategy.

"But the problem is that many coaches never get to steps two and three," he says. "They are afraid to relinquish their control."

Even with his top-level gymnasts, however, Sands occasionally intervenes. During the previous week's competition in Albuquerque, New Mexico, Sands did step in. As fifteen-year-old Lynne Lederer warmed up on the parallel bars, he sensed something was wrong. Lynne was getting more and more angry with herself. According to the coach, "it looked like it was going to mushroom into a real disaster." He went over, kicked the mats on the floor, and told Lynn that her behavior was unacceptable. She instantly understood. It was a part of their tacit agreement. He was extracting his 10 percent.

"I've told the kids that anyone who walks into the gym will give me 90 percent of their potential, just because they're here. I won't allow anyone to train who gives me less than that," says Sands. "Some kids are so talented that they don't need to give you that last 10 percent. They'll still win. Other kids are talented at most events, but occasionally you'll have to extract that last 10 percent to make sure they succeed. With other, less talented children, you've got to get that last 10 percent every time. And so during the warmups, I had to get that 10 percent because things just weren't going right. Lynne didn't like it, but she snapped out of her funk. And she did well enough to make the all-around finals."

He believes that the key to understanding the athlete is observation. "There are certain body language cues that each child gives — when they want you to watch, when they need help, when they feel anxious, nervous, tired, or frustrated. Kids put up these flags all the time. If you're a good observer, you can tell right away if the girl didn't sleep well or isn't feeling good, or had a rotten day at school. But most of the coaches in our country are trying to come up with a magic technique, rather than being good observers."

To corroborate his observations, Sands turns to his prized $8,000 computer. "When I started, I knew virtually nothing about computers," he says. "It took me about two and a half years before I even knew what type of things I wanted to check for, let alone analyze the results. Look," he says, as paper starts spewing out of the machine. Twenty-six records are kept on each gymnast from heart rate to foods consumed in the last twenty-four hours. Sands pays particular attention to the injury records, which tell him when, how, and to which part of the body the injury occurred, as well as showing him the treatment used and his suggestions for any physical limitations on future training.

"Most people coach by adrenalin, not by science," he says. "Our answer to everything is to work harder. But a lot of times that's dumb. Kids should be working less hard. Sometimes it's the girls themselves that push too hard. Other times, I'm the guilty party. But the computer allows me to mediate my own judgments. I can look to the computer to ask, 'Does it look like she's overtraining?' The records on heart rate, sleep patterns, and diet will usually give me the answer."

The computer may also help prevent injuries by supplying collective data. In Sands's first computer study of injuries he found that 85 percent of all his gymnasts' problems occurred from the knees down. His conclusion: too much tumbling on the hard floor. He changed the training regimen, limiting the amount of tumbling on floor mats and increasing time in the foam-rubber-padded pit.

Sands has also found that sometimes his gymnasts will convey important information to the computer that they won't say to his face. "They lie about their weight frequently. And if they're hurt, they won't tell me because that's being a baby, I suppose. But they will tell these things to a computer. They consider the information that comes from the computer as truth, regardless of whether it's truth or not, just because it was processed by some expensive machine."

Unraveling the sheet on Amy Koopman, he shows me that she averages almost nine hours of sleep, has an average weight of eighty-five pounds, had an old knee injury, and has a penchant for Pepsi and tacos. One benefit of the collected data is that when she goes overseas, her data goes with her, giving other coaches important information if her performance should start to lag or any trouble arises. In addition, Sands believes his data gathering is producing better gymnasts. "A lot of the kids in our gym are not as talented as some of the kids they'll go up against, but they'll best them. The information I've gathered has helped me train them better. Twenty percent of the national team comes from this gym."

Sands contends that better methods and more coaches are sorely needed in gymnastics because internationally the American program is in poor shape. "I went to scout the European championships in Madrid for women and for men in Rome and the honeymoon's over," he says. "We can't teach gymnastics the way we have. Right now I would say that the United States is sitting eighth in women's gymnastics and in men's it's a little higher. But it's going to get worse because the reward systems are totally different. If you're a Soviet gymnast, you know that if you get to be a great athlete you can travel, which is something the regular population doesn't get to do. That's a very significant reward right there. Whereas here everyone asks the kids, 'What about all the sacrifices that you make for training?' The whole public attitude is slightly suspicious. The kids find out fast that if you're good, it's uncomfortable. And so they don't stay in competition as long."

If Sands is an example of the new wave in coaching, Carlo Fassi typifies the old master. A short, stocky man who speaks in a thick Italian accent, Fassi has been a skating professional for twenty-eight years. His success rate has been phenomenal. Many Olympic champions within recent memory have been Fassi trained, including Peggy Fleming, John Curry, Dorothy Hamill, and Robin Cousins. All came to Fassi relatively late in their development. Peggy Fleming was national champion and third in the world; Dorothy Hamill was a junior champion; John Curry was on the world team but in a dangerous slump; and Robin Cousins, brilliant in free skating but inconsistent in the school figures, was sixth in the world. They all relocated lock, stock, and skate blades to the Broadmoor Ice Arena in Colorado Springs where Fassi was reported to work his magic.

"Some of my colleagues say that I got these skaters when they had already made it," says Fassi. "That wasn't the case for Robin, because his figures were so poor, but for the others it was partially true. Yet I'm sure Robin, John, and maybe even Dorothy never would have been an Olympic champion without me. I can fairly say that I was the secret ingredient that made them the champion."

And what is Fassi's secret ingredient? "I'm very competitive, a good fighter, and I think I transmit that to the kids. Maybe it's because I help give them the sense that they are the best. I *expect* they'll become champions and they do it. Not for me, but for them. I help them develop an immense feeling of pride in themselves. The best example is Peggy Fleming. She is very sweet and nice, but she has an inside of iron. When she went out on the ice at the Olympics she never doubted that she was the best."

116

Carlo Fassi with 1976 Olympic champion John Curry.

Despite his success, Fassi denies that he has achieved a magic formula. In fact, he claims that the reverse is true. The key to his coaching lies in his ability to adapt his knowlege to each skater. "We are not all born with the same body, the same flexibility, or the same motivation. So 'the best technique' for one skater may be totally wrong for another. Coaches that demand that all their skaters conform to a preconceived pattern may prevent the good skater from becoming great."

Fassi believes that the essential ingredient in coaching success is the personality mesh between coach and athlete. One relationship that didn't work was with Scott Hamilton, the 1983 Men's World Champion. Under Fassi's tutelage, Hamilton progressed from the junior ranks to the world team. Yet, according to Fassi, when it came to the crucial moment, the time when Hamilton would either beat the world or fade into oblivion, "the union wasn't there. We just didn't click. It's never the coach that makes the champion," Fassi adds. "It's the combination of the two. It's the same in baseball. For one coach the team might not do anything and if he goes to another team of equal caliber — bam — he wins the World Series. And nobody knows why."

As the Tracy Austin-Robert Landsdorp relationship illustrated, one of the hardest things a superstar's coach must endure is the appropriation of the spotlight. Says Fassi, "The best coaches are not those who were top-level athletes. You think about the sport more when you've had to struggle to do things well." Perhaps this is why those who were mediocre as athletes develop top-level egos as coaches, egos that may block athlete development. "The skater must feel that the coach is there for the skater's improvement, not the coach's glorification. The skater does the skating and wins the competitions. It is with them that the credit, and at times the blame, should lie. If a skater does well it may reflect on the coach, but the skater is the one who gives the performance that is judged, not the coach," says Fassi.

Yet he too sometimes has difficulty in maintaining an emotional distance, especially in defeat. "I try to keep it as a business and do the best job I can when I teach," he says. "I think I can shut out my work pretty quickly when I get home. At least I think I can. But sometimes, if one of my top skaters doesn't skate well, it's always on my mind. But I think that's part of a lot of jobs. If a lawyer doesn't win a big case, he's got to think about it a little afterwards."

An albatross for many a skating coach is the proverbial skating mother. And when she pays a teacher like Fassi at the rate of a dollar a minute, she feels entitled to voice her opinions. "Skating mothers are often a problem," he concedes, "but I think that sometimes we make it out to be more of a problem than it is. For example, they told me that Mrs. Fleming was the terror of the coaches. And we got along fine. I was very patient with her. Although I may have become less patient over the years, I keep reminding myself that the parent does have certain rights. In the Eastern countries the parents have virtually no say, but that's because their skating association pays for everything. The United States Figure Skating Association pays for virtually nothing. The parents are the ones who pay my bills, often at great financial hardship, and I do feel a certain loyalty to them. And the skating mothers are here at 5:15 in the morning, sit on a cold bench for a couple of hours, take their kids to school, and then bring them back to the rink at 3:30 for more long hours of waiting. They deserve a lot of credit, as well as some attention.

"Some coaches have their telephone numbers unlisted so parents won't be able to reach them," says Fassi. "I don't do that. You just have to make it clear that you don't want them calling every day for nonsense. And if you explain it to them, they don't do it."

One of the oft-repeated words in Carlo Fassi's vocabulary is patience. I wondered why. He laughed, "Well, I'm getting old now and one of my greatest problems is losing it. In the last two or three years I've been getting upset for nothing. The coach should really keep his cool and not get upset if the judging is rotten. Sometimes it *is*, but getting upset doesn't help." Despite occasional outbursts, Fassi loves his profession. "I think coaching is one of the best businesses," he says, smiling. "For one thing, we make lots of money. But the best part of the job is that although I'm fifty-two years old, I'm still working with kids who are fifteen. Sometimes they're a pain in the neck. But most of the time their vitality and enthusiasm is invigorating. They are such nice, healthy, happy, crazy young people. Working with them keeps me young."

The bond between coaches and athletes forms loosely, but tightens into interdependence, trust, and affection. The relationship is an important one, not simply for the shaping of athletic talent but also for the shaping of the athlete's personality. Gayna Grant's exuberance is passed almost osmotically to her fledgling skaters; Bill Sands's forthrightness produces hard-working, resilient competitors; and Carlo Fassi's hot-blooded temperament, melded with his years of experience, provides the final psychological boost to skaters verging on greatness. Coach and parents thus become the two strongest links in the child's developing career. Together they plot the course that the career will take. And the first major decision that must be made concerns education.

# 7

# The
# Education
# of the
# Superstar

**A**t the beginning of an athletic career, sports and school coexist peacefully. The serious eight-year-old swimmer or skater is nudged awake at 5:00 or 6:00 A.M. and is in the pool or on the ice for a two-hour practice session half an hour later. Every early-morning moment is precious. As the mother drives from arena to school, the child changes from athletic gear to school clothes. Although the child may miss a homeroom period, interference with academic life is minimal, except for the fatigue that sets in toward homework time at the end of the day.

But once the child enters the realm of competition the two worlds collide. Attendance at distant meets and tournaments requires that weekends must be stretched; training hours will also need to be extended. Requests are then made to rearrange the child's school schedule. Often teachers and school administrators are willing to comply because a successful competitor reflects well on the school. Many teachers go out of their way to make up special assignment kits to help gifted athletes keep up with their schoolwork when their schedules keep them away from school. Some schools even give competitors gym credits, thereby allowing them to leave school an hour or two early for an afternoon practice session. But occasionally school officials bristle at the disruption in the status quo or what they believe to be a challenge to their authority.

When Lynne Lederer was ten and living in Chicago, her first gymnastics coach told her mother, Gloria, that Lynne could be an Olympian. But five years later, when the family moved to Palatine, Illinois, and Lynne enrolled as a freshman at Fremd

High School, Fremd officials became angry when Lynne, who was then a member of the U.S. National Gymnastics Team, began missing classes to practice for the 1980 Olympic trials. According to her mother and her coach, Lynne was harassed by some teachers, who felt that athletic activities weren't good enough reasons to be absent. An A student in junior high, Lynne felt torn between academics and gymnastics. She became ill with one cold and sore throat after another. "She was sick about 90 percent of the time," her mother says. "The doctor said the strain was too much. He said to get her out of school."

The tension at school showed up in Lynne's performance at the Olympic trials. She finished twelfth, and in the course of the competition fell off the balance beam — one of her best events— and missed her handstand on the uneven parallel bars. The final straw came after the Olympic trials, when some of her teachers refused to allow her to make up the final exams and failed her. By the end of her freshman year Lynne had dropped out of Fremd. Her parents hired a private tutor who could work around Lynne's training schedule.

As the number of competitions grows and the hours of training increase, many young athletes opt for Lynne's private tutoring solution. In the months prior to winning the Ladies' National Figure Skating Championship in January 1981, fifteen-year-old Elaine Zayak's hectic competition and exhibition schedule forced her away from her small parochial school for weeks at a time. There was no solution aside from private tutoring, but her mother grew increasingly upset at the situation. "It bothered me that Elaine didn't have any communication outside the skating rink," says Jeri Zayak. "I felt that mentally it would be better to put her in a school environment so that her life would be a bit more normal."

The nuns at her parochial school were not receptive to a part-time arrangement, so Elaine became a student at Paramus High School. Not a full-fledged student, for she attended only three classes — acting, typing, and health — from 8:00 to 10:00 A.M. She continued to study her major subjects under the aegis of a private tutor. But Mrs. Zayak hoped that this dip into the public school system would keep her daughter's life in balance.

The taste, however, proved extremely palatable to Elaine. "She likes it too much, that's the problem," said Jeri Zayak at the time. "I'm happy I did it, but unhappy because she's realized there is another life out there. She's a year older and she's more developed since last year. Now the boys are interested in her. She was asked to go to the Senior Prom next week and she can't go because she is committed to skate in an exhibition in England. She moaned, 'Oh ma, do I have to go to England? I'd rather go to the prom.' I had to tell her, 'That's too bad, Elaine. You have your commitments and you have to stand by them.'

"And now that she's been in school, she wants to run around more," Mrs. Zayak continues. "Last year she'd skate from eight to three and watch soap operas for the rest of the afternoon. She didn't do much else. She was under my nose and I knew she wasn't going to get hurt. But now she makes me nervous. She has a moped and she'll go riding off with her friends from school. And she'll want to go to the high school wrestling matches on Friday nights with her girlfriends and then go out to get something to eat afterwards. Then she has to get up early the next morning and skate."

Elaine began to take her social life more seriously and her skating less so. She was, after all, the national champion, and heavily favored to defend her title. She entered the 1982 Nationals with a cavalier attitude but fell three times and finished third. "I knew I hadn't trained as hard as I should have. I realized no one would make it easy for me. I'd have to give up my social life if I wanted to make it to the Olympics," she said.

In the next two months Elaine Zayak trained harder than she ever had before. She shut out all distractions and focused on the upcoming World Championships. She got off to a terrible start at the Worlds. After a fourth-place finish in the school figures, she sank to seventh place after the short program by falling on the same combination double flip/triple toe loop jump that had cost her the Nationals. Before going out on the ice for the free skating she was in tears, almost too embarrassed to perform. But then her resolve returned. She says, "I thought to myself, 'I can't make a fool out of myself again. I'm not going to give anyone the satisfaction of saying I'm a quitter. I'm going to go out on that ice and not miss a single thing. There's no way that I'm going to fall during this program.' "

And she didn't. The entire American team held its breath when Elaine came to the ill-fated combination jump in her routine. The arena shook with applause as she executed it perfectly. "I didn't fall, I didn't fall," she cried to her coach as she came off the ice. "But I learned my lesson," she told me later. "I can't get too involved with my friends and still expect to be a champion."

Whereas for Elaine Zayak public school was a novelty, for youngsters who start in public school and remain there, school may become a sanctuary, a constant in their otherwise tumultuous lives. By the time Tracy Austin was a high school junior, she already owned the most coveted tennis title in America, that of the U.S. Open. But adjusting to the tennis tour had not been easy for the sixteen-year-old pro. At her first press conference at Wimbledon, a British reporter began to grill her about rumors that she didn't have many friends on the tour. She began to answer, but her voice faltered and her eyes filled with tears. It wasn't easy to explain that as the youngest on the tour the older kids didn't relate to her, that she was not old enough or mature enough to go discoing and drinking with them, or that they particularly disliked losing to a ninety-pound, pigtailed prodigy who was not much taller than the net.

Her high school guidance counselor remarked, "School is about the only place left where Tracy can still be a teenager." Tracy agreed. "At school, I get no special attention," she said. "After all, I'd been going to school with those kids for a long time. About the only thing I can remember is a 'Welcome Home, Tracy' sign when I won the U.S. Open. After that, I was just another student. They joked a lot with me. They always wanted to borrow money or trade cars — especially after I won a Porsche in my first pro tournament at Stuttgart."

The conflict between school and sports has increased as the age at which children enter competition has dropped. Sixteen-year-old Andrea Jaeger and fourteen-year-old Kathy Rinaldi belong to the new generation of assignment-toting tennis pros who have shown the ability to maintain their tennis game while keeping up in school. Foreign tennis prodigies like sixteen-year-old Catherine Tanvier often have to sacrifice their education when they join the American tour. "In France you cannot continue school and play professional tennis," says Catherine's mother. "So I try to take her to museums and galleries when we are traveling. I try to make her aware of things. But it is very difficult for a young tennis player to motivate herself to study."

One solution to the problem of mixing sports and studies has been the establishment of specialized sports academies, a movement that began several years ago with the development of summer sports camps. Clusters of promising youngsters began to follow their coaches home for the winter, and these enclaves became tremendously successful. Many of the families of the country's top swimmers have relocated in Mission Viejo, California, where the Natadores swim team trains under Mark Shubert. The Natadores, who have won an unprecedented nine national titles, have included such Olympians as Shirly Babashoff, Brian Goodell, Jesse Vassalho, and Olympic diver Greg Louganis.

Informal arrangements like Mission Viejo have given rise to more formal academies where children live, train, and study. These academies include the National Gymnastics Academy in Eugene, Oregon, where America's two top female gymnasts, Julianne McNamara and Tracee Talavera, train under Dick Mulvihill and his wife, three-time Olympian Linda Methany; the Hunterdon Academy in Pittstown, New Jersey, where equestrians — including Paul Newman's daughter Clea — flock to train under George Morris; and the Stratton Mountain School in Stratton, Vermont, where skiers may pay up to $17,000 for tuition, board, and travel in a ten-month period.

The atmosphere of the sports academy depends to a large extent on its leadership. According to headmaster Peter St. John, the Stratton Mountain School was founded by "historical accident." Warren Hellman, an investment banker, and Donald Tarinelli, a building contractor, both lived in Fairfield County, Connecticut, and had children who were promising ski racers and excellent students. They knew their children could become even better skiers if they could spend more time at the family ski chalets in Vermont, but the parents didn't want to sacrifice their children's education. The ideal solution, they figured, would be to move the kids up to Vermont and have them tutored there during the winter. Their newspaper ad for qualified teachers and coaches yielded more than a hundred replies. In 1971 the Stratton Mountain School — two teachers, one coach, and twelve students — was officially founded. The boys lived at the Hellmans' house, the girls at Tarinellis'.

The idea worked. Deborah Tarinelli completed her homespun high school education, made the U.S. Olympic Team, raced on the World Cup circuit, was accepted by Dartmouth, raced on its women's team (and was the school's Athlete of the Year), finished college, and now has earned a master's degree in urban studies from Harvard. Her brother Donald became a college racer, and after a stint coaching at Williams is now training to become an architect. Frances Hellman was Eastern Junior Champion, graduated from Dartmouth summa cum laude, and is now working toward a Ph.D. in physics at Stanford. Her sister Tricia graduated from Williams summa cum laude and Phi Beta Kappa, received the college's scholar-athlete award, and is now attending medical school.

In 1977, as the school began to be a real force in U.S. ski racing, Hellman and Tarinelli negotiated a donation by the International Paper Corporation of much of the land on which Stratton's trails are located to the U.S. team's Ski Educational Foundation (USSEF). Under the terms of the donation the USSEF leases the land to Stratton Corporation and a part of the proceeds from the lease goes to the Stratton Mountain School, which currently consists of sixty-six skiers, six full-time (and six more winter or part-time) teachers, and twelve of the best ski coaches in the country.

The skiers now live two or three in a room in the former Hotel Tyrol, a dark wooden lodge at the base of the mountain. A long low, sloping porch over the main entrance disguises its size, but in the back (called "the high-rent district" by the skiers), large windows provide expansive views of the slopes. Inside, the place has the look of a comfortably abused fraternity house. The entire school was carpeted in the late 1970s in gray-brown tweed. After several years of teenage trampling, however, the carpet has worn thin in places and is brightened by orange patches. Down the road is a spacious new gymnasium, fully equipped, and adjacent to the slopes a small private home has been converted into a training building for coaches' offices, ski tuning and storage, and race headquarters. A large ski chalet nearby was donated to the school by the Hellmans for staff and student housing in 1982.

Headmaster Peter St. John, a lean, young former banker, Outward Bound instructor, and dean of students at a large private boarding school, is himself an avid marathoner and cross-

Courtesy of Stratton Mountain School

Students, teachers, and coaches at the Stratton Mountain School.

country skier. He has nurtured the healthy mind/healthy body spirit with which the school was founded (and, like most of the staff, he serves as an important role model for the students). "There's a very creative tension in the school," he says. "Not in terms of people being at each other's throats, but simply because of the enormous demand on the kids' time and energy. The academics are tough and we want to keep them that way. The physical training is grueling. And on top of that we're very much interested in having these kids develop into fine, altruistic people. In the long run what we're trying to develop is not just ski racers or kids who go to Dartmouth, but people who are thoughtful of others and self-disciplined."

Stratton's academic record is impressive. Since the school's founding nearly half its graduates have been accepted by four top academic institutions — Dartmouth College, Williams College, the University of Vermont, and Middlebury College (schools which also have some of the best ski teams). On the skiing side, recent graduates of the academy have included Richie Woodworth, the U.S. top pro racer in 1980 (and now a ski commentator for NBC Sports), and Heidi Preuss, who finished fourth in the downhill of the 1980 Olympics. Sixteen Stratton students or alumni are currently on U.S. Alpine or Nordic teams.

In the winter, classes are held in the afternoon so the skiers can take advantage of the morning light for training. They are up by 6:30, running and doing stretching exercises in time to rock music in the gym. Breakfast is served at 7:30 and by 8:30 the students are on the slopes. They ski for three hours, eat lunch at noon, and spend the rest of the afternoon in classes. Dinner is at 6:00, followed by an evening study hall. Lights go out about 10:30. In the spring and fall, classes are held in the morning and early afternoon. By 2:30 the students are running or playing soccer, working with weights, running up and down the mountain, playing tennis, or going for long bicycle rides.

The atmosphere is invigorating. After working alone at home toward a distant Olympic goal — and often feeling alienated from their peers as a result — exposure to similarly motivated youngsters energizes everyone. "Before I came here I never did anything 100 percent," says Kate Knopp, a recent graduate who is now a student at Williams. "The first morning, we had early training and we ran over to the gym and I thought I was going to die. Then, on top of that, we went on an eight-mile run. From that day on, I decided I was going to get in shape. I had to, to keep up. Here, if you don't try, it just doesn't work. If someone's sloughing off in school or in training, the kids themselves get right on your case. . . . They do it because they care, and somehow they know you're driving the whole group down. When I go home and go to parties and look at all the giggly girls, I feel like throwing up."

Adds headmaster St. John, "When you have only fifty or sixty kids, everyone really knows each other. They share a dedication to a degree that few people outside of monasteries and nunneries experience. They all have similar goals, values, and interests. We give them the responsibility to take care of their lives, in terms of managing their classes, study, and race schedules. What we find is that very few people choose to laze through the day."

Because the students decide when to study and when to train — and if they are behind in one area they sometimes try to let the other slide temporarily — sometimes the tension between skiing and studying is more than "creative." Said Kate Knopp, "You do get torn between the coaches and the teachers. The teachers want you to give 100 percent to your schoolwork, and the coaches want you to give 100 percent to athletics. If you stay up late doing your homework, you get it from the coaches. If you're off racing or training, you get it from the teachers. It's hard on you personally. The kids are doing schoolwork and training and cleaning the building and the latrine. It's like every second of the day is taken up." She then confessed, "It's hard, but it's good."

The financial costs are also high: $9,700 for ten months of room, board, tuition, and training for high school Alpine racers (seventh and eighth graders, who are usually enrolled only for the winter term, and cross-country skiers, pay less); an extra $1,000 for books plus meals and hotels at distant races; a four-week $1,600 winter training trip to Austria for the top Alpine racers; and a four-week, 3,200-mile cross-country summer bike trip to give the top Alpine boys a solid training base for autumn dry land training and winter races. In addition, those who are on the National Junior team must pay at least part of their expenses, the amount depending upon the annual funding philosophy of the U.S. Ski Team. Sometimes funds are spread among several junior skiers to build up a large pool of promising talent; other years, only a few skiers will be sponsored. In 1980, for example, being on the team tacked another $8,000 in expenses on the basic tab.

To help defray these enormous costs, about a third of the students receive some sort of scholarship aid. The school has a half-million-dollar-plus budget, roughly a quarter of which is provided by fund-raising events and donations, including a $15,000 to $20,000 yearly donation from the U.S. Ski Educational Foundation. Manufacturers frequently help student/racers with loaned racing equipment. A top racer may need new training and racing skis for slalom, giant slalom, and downhill — a total of six pairs — every year.

If a youngster is the product of a good skiing program, he may find it surprisingly easy to get into the Stratton Mountain School. Most applicants first make contact by telephone. Says Peter St. John: "We usually have a fair idea if the child is a likely candidate for our program from the initial phone conversation, which is sometimes with the parent, and other times with the skier himself. If a parent calls and says 'I have a kid who loves to ski fast and would love to go to Dartmouth' we know in a couple of minutes that they don't have any idea of what's involved in coming here, so we usually advise them not to apply. Often we can judge the skiers ability by finding out about his points [a novice skier starts with 500 points and then, with successful race results, eventually works his way down to zero] and comparing his points to others his age. Or, if he or she is a member of a racing program, we will often know the coach and can find out more through them. If a skier hasn't had a lot of racing experience and isn't a member of a well-established program, we suggest that they come to see us during the winter months for an on-snow interview, where our coaches will run him or her through some gates and do motor-skills testing in the gym to determine present and future physical capabilities. We also consider academic transcripts, teacher recommendations, and ski results in making our admission decisions. Our main goal is to get kids who will be happy here and their happiness is often predicated on their ability to keep up academically and athletically in this competitive environment. Of the people who call us for information, we encourage about half to apply and then accept roughly two thirds of the applicants."

Although the school is demanding in every conceivable way — financially, academically, physically, and socially — almost every student and parent waxes lyrical about the rewards. Nina Armagh, mother of Juli Furtado, the national thirteen-and-under girls' champion, and now a member of the national junior team at fifteen, told Holcomb Noble of the *New York Times*: "I simply can't discuss the school without getting very emotional. My daughter has grown up so much, has learned at 13 how to travel around the country; she's getting all A's; she's developed so well. We couldn't have done it without full scholarship help, and none of this would have happened without the school."

Richard Jaeger, associate director of admissions at Dartmouth, also told Noble, "Stratton is producing super kids academically — and the kids are also great skiers. It's the frame of mind — skiing requires a dedication and perseverance that very often carry over into the academics to produce students who are very strong intellectually."

Young skiers come to the school dreaming of making the U.S. Ski Team and participating in the Olympics. At some point during their stay at the academy, many are forced to realize that they will not be skiing in Yugoslavia in the 1984 Olympics. Says Peter St. John: "Most of them have a pretty good idea of where they stand and what they can do. Occasionally we have to say, 'Hey, be a little easier on yourself.' We have to let them know it's okay if they don't make the national team."

The majority of the skiers go to college and race on their school ski teams. Some make it to the Senior National team; several may reach the Olympics. Although there is a professional skiing circuit, after college most of the skiers choose a different profession. Perhaps because they know their competitive careers will be short-lived and they have role models in the diversity of the adults in the school, Stratton students do achieve the triad of goals set for them. They take their studies and their friendships, as well as their skiing, seriously. Their camaraderie is evident in the joyful confusion inside the old Hotel Tyrol and during the ski races themselves. At a race before Valentine's Day, the whole Nordic team, including three national team members, painted lipstick hearts on their faces — and proceeded cheerfully to dominate the race.

The atmosphere at an academy in which the goal is not college but the professional ranks is quite different. The largest, fanciest, and most competitive of all the academies is Nick Bollettieri's Tennis Academy in Bradenton, Florida.

"Get those feet moving, Chip. Arc it up, arc it up. Roger,

you've got to be hitting chest high. Take an extra step, don't lunge, Carling. Fanny, look at your fanny, Raffi. RAFFI! We're going to send you back to Sicily." No one bats an eye when Nick Bollettieri imitates Raffaela Reggi, the fourteen-year-old Italian national tennis champion, hitting a volley with her derriere extended or when he wails at her like an Italian matron urging her bambina to eat her spaghetti. It's vintage Nick, who is perhaps the most unorthodox tennis professional the world has ever known.

Bollettieri arrived at his tennis academy through a long and circuitous route. An army paratrooper during World War II, he went on to the University of Miami Law School, dropped out, and supported himself by picking up any tennis coaching job he could find. He found a plum. The Rockefeller family made Bollettieri their personal teaching pro, and he spent his summers at their Pocantico Hills estate in Westchester County, New York, and winters at their Dorado Beach Resort in Puerto Rico. He then founded the All-American Sport Camp and cofounded the Port Washington Tennis Academy (where Vitas Gerulaitis and John McEnroe trained). Then Bollettieri's life fell apart. His second marriage failed. He lost his job at Dorado Beach. He lost $100,000 in a tennis-camp venture. He and Hy Zausner, co-owner of the Port Washington Academy, had a falling-out. He was left without a court to teach on.

Bollettieri finally got a job teaching at the Colony Beach and Tennis Resort in Longboat Key, just outside Sarasota, Florida. While there he invited a top junior player, a young West Virginian named Anne White, to live and train with him. His house then became home to several other promising youngsters — Kathy Horvath, who at fourteen was the youngest female to play in the U.S. Open; Jimmy Arias, at fifteen the youngest male pro; and eleven-year-old Carling Bassett, Canadian champion and daughter of millionaire industrialist and sports entrepreneur John Bassett. The word spread. More students arrived, including

Paul Annacone, then the top sixteen-year-old in the East, and Pam Casale, who now is one of the best young players on the women's professional circuit. These newcomers were housed in a former hotel converted to a dormitory.

When ABC-TV's "20/20" did a special on Bollettieri's junior tennis mecca in Longboat Key, more interest was generated. So many teenagers arrived that there was no longer anyplace to put them. Bollettieri began looking at sites for a larger academy. When he found a suitable spot in Bradenton, he approached the First National Bank of Florida to put up part of the $2.8 million needed to build the academy. They examined Nick's plans, the site, and his success at Longboat Key and signed on for $1.2 million. Then Bollettieri went to a longtime friend and wealthy patron of tennis who had voiced great belief in the academy concept. This friend also thought Nick's plans would make a good investment and agreed to loan the remaining $1.6 million.

In September 1981 the Nick Bollettieri Tennis Academy was completed. Its spacious brown stucco housing units, swimming pool, weight room, and twenty-two tennis courts make it look like an idyllic retirement community, but it has been called "the sweatshop with nets." Its purpose is to produce tennis champions. Some stay only a week or two; others, such as Jimmy Arias, Paul Annacone, and Carling Bassett, have spent years with Bollettieri. Although the faces may change, the routine doesn't. A typical day begins at 6:00 A.M. when the alarm clocks go off in ch eight-person, two-bedroom apartment. The 150 players-in-residence clean their rooms before eating breakfast at 7:00. By 8:15 the majority of them are out on the courts for three hours of practice. (Only 20 percent of the players attend school. The rest have either graduated from high school, are taking a semester off, take correspondence courses, or are foreign students with no academic requirements to fulfill.) Those who attend the private school down the road return at lunchtime and

136

join the others in the spanking clean and slightly antiseptic cafeteria. By 1:00 they are back on the courts, where they practice drills and play until 4:30 or 5:00. The next hour is usually devoted to Nautilus weight training, running, or calisthenics. Dinner is served from 5:30 to 6:15, with the following two hours reserved for academic study. Those who aren't in school watch television or play video games in the rec room or socialize around the pool. The supermotivated play more tennis on the lighted courts. At 10:30 everyone must be back in the apartments. Lights must be out by eleven, when Julio Moros, the academy's manager, checks in. He shines a flashlight at the band of reflecting tape on the front of each bunk and then at the head resting on the pillow, to insure that the name on the tape and the body in the bed are identical.

There is no smoking, no drinking, and no visiting other students' rooms. Anyone who arrives by car surrenders his keys. Players are chauffeured to tennis tournaments, doctors' appointments, and the social event of the week — the Saturday night movies at the local shopping mall — en masse. When asked whether any of the youngsters feel they are giving up part of their adolescence by following such a spartan regime, Bollettieri sputters savagely, "I hear that word sacrifice all the time and I think it's an absurd and erroneous notion. Hell, it's 90 degrees here today and it's 40 below in New York. The kids have a wonderful place, they're exchanging cultures from 32 countries, they're getting good schooling. I don't think that they are giving up a thing. Hell, [Tracy] Austin's worth two or three million dollars, [Andrea] Jaeger's making $600,000 a year. Why the hell is that a sacrifice? I mean, you got people down here in Florida who can't make a living. You got GM laying off 130,000 people. And then you got athletes making a million dollars a year. Sacrifice? They're fortunate. They should try to go out in the world today and try to make a living outside of sports. They'd run back to tennis saying it's the greatest opportunity they ever had in their life. And besides, these kids are happy as anything. Sure, they're giving up their parents somewhat, but they're also learning a lot about themselves, tennis, and life. I think it's a good exchange."

Carling Bassett has no complaints. At thirteen, she is already beautiful. Her long, blonde hair is neatly tied back in a ponytail. Her flawless skin is golden, perpetually tanned. Canadian National Indoor and Outdoor Champion, she whips two-fisted backhands with her big Prince racket like an angry princess wielding a flyswatter, a long sigh of exertion accompanying every stroke. At nine Carling was already playing in national tournaments in Canada, but she had several other interests. Tennis was something her father, a former Davis Cup player, wanted her to do. At eleven she was sent to Bollettieri's. She lived in his house then, and still is one of the privileged few who reside there. "It wasn't until I came down that I really started to enjoy the game," she says. "There are so many good people to play with and so much to work on that it never gets boring. There aren't really other things to do, just going to the movies once a week. But you're not here to go out, you're here to concentrate on tennis.

"Nick has taught me discipline. Living with him isn't like living in a normal house. You're not allowed to goof around, like you can in your own house, because goofing off affects you on the tennis court. It's really strict — *very* strict," she says, rolling her eyes. "But you have to be *very* competitive to make it in the world of tennis. And you have to work very, very hard. But I love it here. Especially when I win. My goal? That's easy. I want to be number one."

Her father is producing a movie called "Spring Fever," starring Carling. "It's a funny story, but it's really touching," Carling says. "It's about a rich kid and a poor kid. The poor kid is the number one tennis player in Las Vegas but her mother never had the money to take her to the Nationals. The rich kid always wanted to be a ballerina, but her father wanted her to be a championship tennis player. She doesn't have the nerve to tell him she doesn't want to play because once she did, and her father had a heart attack, which she thinks she caused. Anyway, the rich kid and the poor kid get to be good friends. Then they meet at the Nationals, where the rich kid is the number one seed. Everyone wants to be part of her because she's rich and famous. But nobody cares about the poor kid. Of course, the poor kid wins. It's to show that tennis isn't all fun and glory."

The rich kid sounds like her. Is that part of the story based on her life? "No," she replies, sounding puzzled. "Everyone down here is the same. Nobody is rich or poor. Everybody just wants to win."

After a morning of tennis practice, the players adjourn to the cafeteria. A line snakes from the adjacent rec room to the serving window. Sloppy Joes are plopped onto trays by the kitchen staff. Some of the students pass up the Sloppy Joes for chicken salad sandwiches, or decide to make their own peanut-butter-and-jellies. Salad and fruit accompany every meal, which is planned by a trained chef and approved by Julio, the manager. No junk food is allowed, except for occasional cake and ice cream at the 9:00 P.M. snack.

Most players are eating healthy, though not gigantic, portions. Some are given a special low-calorie meal. These dieters — players who have chosen (or been ordered by Nick or Julio) to cut back their calories — are weighed in weekly, sit at a separate table, and try to convince themselves and each other that this temporary deprivation will help their games.

In the far corner of the room, visiting ten-year-old player Susan Sloan is distraught. "This is yucky!" she proclaims to the others after one bite of her Sloppy Joe. "Hey, what's that?" she asks, eyeing her neighbor's sandwich.

"Chicken salad."

"Let me try it," Susan says, and takes a hefty bite.

"Gee, I sure wish this chicken was tuna fish," Susan says.

"This is better than tuna fish," replies the other girl.

"No it's not," replies Susan decisively.

"Yes it is," storms the neighbor, waving her half-eaten sandwich furiously.

It is competitive here, both in the cafeteria and on the tennis court. "In practice, the kids are just as tenacious as in the tournaments. Many simply can't stand to lose; competitiveness seeps out of their personalities," says former student Paul Annacone. "The potential financial rewards only add to the pressure. From the minute you arrive, everyone is competing for endorsements, rankings, and college scholarships, and the money to be made in the pros."

On the lesson court, called Nick's Court, Bollettieri conducts mass drills that seem more like mass executions. On one side of the net stands Bollettieri and a shopping cart full of yellow tennis balls. On the other side of the court six of the finest young tennis players in the world jog in a semicircle and one after another step up to return Nick's shot with a forehand volley. Crisp shots ring through the hot air like artillery fire. Sweat drips from the brows of the youngsters. Jog, jog, jog, hit. Mutters of frustration erupt when a player muffs his shot. Roger, a big blond kid, is caught not jogging and condemned to one hundred kangaroo hops, exhausting knee-to-chest leaps on the sidelines. He laughs good-naturedly and does his hops with zest. Then the drill switches to one forehand approach shot followed by a quick volley. Both of Roger's drives fall into the net. "Dammit!" he shrieks. Bollettieri sentences him to twenty-five more kangaroo hops; this time Roger isn't laughing. The drill continues until the shopping cart is empty and the balls lie scattered like lemon drops on Bollettieri's side of the court.

Throughout the drill Bollettieri's eyes rove to other courts, picking up laziness and small errors. His attention wanders to the new shrubs around the court, which appear to be dying. "Hey, Mike," he yells to one of the assistant coaches, "where's our maintenance man? These things are drying up. Tell 'em they should be watered every day. We've got to keep after this." Bollettieri is loud and stoop shouldered, with inexhaustible nervous energy. His small, wiry body is the color of a bronzed coconut. Like the rest of the boys, he is shirtless. His only apparel is a pair of thin white nylon jogging shorts, Pony sneakers, three gold chains around his neck (of which at least two have pendants that read "#1") and a pair of Porsche sunglasses. The glasses sit on a red blade of a nose. His hair is thinning and turning gray. His bottom lip often juts out petulantly. The accent is New York suburban by way of Miami. Good shots are "be-you-tee-full." The weak game has "floors" (flaws). Subtlety is not known to Bollettieri. Discipline is. Once, when Jimmy Arias missed a shot and dropped his racket to the ground in disgust, Bollettieri grabbed the racket and hollered, "You want to bounce your racket, you bounce it right." He smashed the racket, shattering the frame, as Arias looked on in shock. It was his favorite racket.

Although youngsters like Arias may be annoyed when they become the object of Nick's wrath, they are not surprised. In the initial interview required of everyone who hopes to spend a year at the academy, tennis skills are evaluated and the disciplinary code is fully outlined. Only about 5 percent of those who come to be interviewed are turned away, although some find the regimen too intense after a month or two and decide to leave. (Almost all of those who want to visit the academy for less than three weeks and are beyond the beginner level are accepted.)

Bollettieri believes that an important element of the training he gives is lessons in court behavior. Academy manager Julio Moros, a longtime friend of Bollettieri's and a former Venezuelan champion, concurs. "Even ten years ago, this was a gentleman's game," he says. "If there were any children on the court, they were well behaved. You'd never see any tantrums from a Rod Laver or a Pancho Gonzalez. And the spectators didn't say a word. Now it's like a football game. Everyone screams and throws things on the court. It's a disgrace to the game. We want to prevent that here. I want the kids to know if they don't behave on a tennis court, they don't belong on a tennis court. I do want them to stand up for their rights. If they feel a bad call has been made they should call it to the attention of the tournament director. But no kid is entitled to make obscene gestures and to call the umpire an imbecile. I think John McEnroe could have really used a place like this. But now it's too late. The boy got away with everything and now he feels he can do whatever he wants because he's number one.

"A lot of kids come here lazy. Many of their parents send them here because they are too much trouble at home. We have one boy who's a great player. But he has the mind and manners of a six-year-old. We like them like Raffaela. She's all business. She would slam the ball down your throat if you gave her the chance. When she's out on the court, she's there to beat you. But off the court, she's a wonderful kid."

A courteous Jimmy Arias and Chip Hooper, another former Bollettieri product, are visiting the academy. At six feet six and 210 pounds, Chip Hooper, the best black tennis player since Arthur Ashe, cuts an impressive figure simply walking to the court. When he unleashes one of his 150-mile-an-hour serves — perhaps the fastest in all of tennis — the youngsters on surrounding courts gape. He first came to Bollettieri's in 1980 while taking a semester off from college. In six months, he says he improved 50 percent. Now, after an eye operation on his cornea, the twenty-two-year-old has been at Bollettieri's for six weeks, getting ready to rejoin the pro tour. Although his ranking is only 230 on this day, by the end of the year, with impressive victories in the French Open and Wimbledon, it will skyrocket to 23. "It's like the army around here," says Hooper, as he fits his large frame into a small chair by the pool. "What I try to do most for the kids is to provide an example of what can be done by working hard. I'm not as good an athlete as one third of these kids. But between the ages of seventeen and eighteen, I really got on the stick and started working."

During the Arias-Hooper match, most of the kids who are supposed to be practicing keep close tabs on the proceedings out of the corners of their eyes. Most of them dream of becoming pros. Some 98 percent will get college scholarships, but most consider college a way station, a place to bide their time until they achieve professional-level skills. Most seem to be like Paul Annacone, who take their studies only seriously enough to pass their courses. Also like Annacone, if they go to college, many will drop out before graduating. Unlike the students at the Stratton Mountain School, they have decided — perhaps as early as age ten or eleven — that tennis will be their life.

Everyone loves the hard-nosed Bollettieri. Under the gruff exterior lies a gentle, generous man and an excellent tennis coach. When Rodney Harmon, the other black pro on the tour, came to Bollettieri's in 1977, he was, according to Chip Hooper, "very, very bad. When he served the balls rolled into the net. His forehands screeched into the fence. His backhand was nonexistent." Harmon "got with the program," as Bollettieri calls his instruction, and moved up to fourth in his age group and won the NCAA doubles title. "I owe everything to Nick Bollettieri," Harmon says.

Barrett Powers, now a premed student at Rutgers University, attended the academy for one semester two years ago. He is now spending his Christmas vacation honing his game. "When I came down here two years ago, I saw myself improving daily. I came here ranked 30th in my section and when I went back a semester later, I was fifth. I got two consecutive national rankings, whereas before I had never even *been* to the nationals. Nick runs a tight ship, but a lot of the kids need it. They come down here with big heads, but then they quickly learn that there's always someone down here who can beat you. It'a a very humbling process. You come out of here with a lot of respect. I think Nick's the greatest." Seventeen years after Bollettieri saw nine-year-old Brian Gottfried on a public court in North Miami Beach and moved him into his home, Gottfried, who ranked as high as fourth in the world in 1977, still turns to Nick for advice. In Gottfried's mind he remains "the greatest teacher."

Perhaps it is possible for a tennis player today to stay at home and compete locally (thus saving $1,350 a month in academy fees). But Bollettieri's philosophy is that it is time we Americans duplicated the programs used in Communist countries like Czechoslovakia (which has produced Ivan Lendl and Martina Navratilova), programs with a centralized system under the direction of one person. Bollettieri has nominated himself director. "Through dedication and discipline to sport the children here are given the opportunity to develop great capabilities if they have it. It is here that they find out how deep their talent is."

Taking cues from their parents' subtle messages, children are deciding earlier and earlier whether their futures lie in sports or in school. The personalities of those in charge of sports academies further influence that decision. Peter St. John has devoted much of his life to teaching; Nick Bollettieri dropped out of law school and made tennis his profession. St. John believes in the need for education for all his students; Bollettieri believes that the ones who aren't Hoopers and Ariases need an education for security. The tennis academy's competitive atmosphere, however, sweeps most of the youngsters along in the belief that they *will* be Chip Hoopers or Jimmy Ariases. Education is given lip service; tennis is given almighty respect.

Yet the sports academy offers a sheltered world where youngsters need conceive of no other reality. For some, this protected life becomes stultifying. For others, the womblike environment allows the nurturing and refining of intricate skills far from the distractions of the workaday world.

# 8
# Sportspolitik

**L**ee Gargel wears the Aspen trademark of high health. Freckles march across the nose of his permanently tanned face. Clear blue eyes, the color of the mountain sky, peer from beneath a swatch of brown hair casually parted in the middle. He speaks in measured, deep tones and when he smiles, he seems to do so in spite of himself. Quiet, almost unemotional, his jock swagger nonetheless exudes self-confidence, even cockiness. On the mountain, skis on, his reserve slips. His body hurls down the slope, his skis hammering at the snow as he streaks through gates at speeds in excess of sixty miles an hour. His movements are economical, his weight superbly balanced. He is a study in confidence and grace. His father once asked Lee what he thought about at the start of a race. Replied Lee, "I say to myself, 'These people better watch 'cause they're going to see the most incredible run they've ever seen.' "

At age thirteen, Lee Gargel is "hot," the term used by Aspen locals to describe an up-and-comer. He cannot remember a time in his life when he didn't ski. When he was two his father, Doug, then a skiing instructor, took him out to the slopes. When Lee wasn't on the mountain he was practicing in the living room or driveway on special roadrunners that his father attached to the bottoms of his plastic skis. Lee started running slalom gates at age eight as an Aspenaut, a member of a weekend ski program sponsored by the Aspen Ski Corporation, owner of three of the four mountains that comprise the Aspen complex. To encourage the children of Aspen, the corporation provided instruction and lift tickets free of charge.

The next year Lee was enrolled in the Aspen Ski Club age-group program. Three afternoons a week at 3:30 one of the club coaches arrived at Lee's school in a big van and shuttled the club's skiers to nearby Buttermilk Mountain. Although the lifts officially closed at 4:00, the Aspen Ski Corporation — at considerable expense — kept the lifts open for the young skiers to practice until 5:00. Lee soon dominated the local Aspen Cup races. Aspen Ski Club coaches began to take Lee and other qualified juniors to race against other western ski clubs. Thanks to his own determination and the efforts of his father, his coaches, the Aspen Ski Corporation, and the Aspen Ski Club, Lee was already a winner by age ten, placing third in the Junior Olympics and catching the eye of the U.S. Ski Team's coaches.

Every sport has its hierarchy. In sports such as swimming, children progress through age-group categories; in skating they are grouped by ability as determined by standardized tests; in wrestling they are matched by weight. Whatever the classification system, the top competitors in regional events qualify for national championships and then international competitions. But perhaps the most important level is the grass roots — the local clubs — where the youngsters get their starts.

Soon after its founding in 1937 by two land surveyors, the Aspen Ski Club made racing a priority. The first race took place in 1938 to celebrate the newly opened trails on Aspen Mountain. In the 1940s Andre Roche, one of the club's founders, established the Roche Cup, an international race that would bring the best skiers in the world to Aspen every year. Within a few years Aspen changed from a mining to a skiing town. In the 1950s local skiers placed on the Olympic team; since then, Aspen has raised many of the country's finest racers, including Bill Marolt, current director of the United States Ski Team.

Beyond the tourists in fancy snowsuits who pack the bar of the Hotel Jerome is a town deeply committed to junior racing. The Aspen Ski Club revolves almost completely around its 110

United Press International Photo

U.S. team at the 1980 Winter Olympics.

junior racers. Between the ages of nine and thirteen they compete in two-year age divisions: those fourteen and over are grouped in an "ability" class. The nine- to thirteen-year-olds cut their competitive teeth in the local Aspen Cup series of ten races, in which ribbons are awarded to the first five finishers in each age category. And at the end of the season silver goblets are given to those with the most points in the slalom, downhill, and giant slalom.

"The Aspen Ski Club is a nonprofit organization and the fees for the racing program* do not come close to covering their expenses," says Doug Gargel. "They get a lot of the local businesses kicking in — restaurants, ski shops, even radio stations. The club also sponsors fund-raising events that get the whole community involved. Last year's Las Vegas Casino Night made over $25,000. They also sponsor local bike and foot races. And they sell adult memberships, which really are little more than donations to the junior program."

The money raised annually has enabled the club to hire three full-time top-level coaches (all of whom have been with the club for more than three seasons, giving continuity to the racing program) and four part-time coaches; to buy two fifteen-passenger vans to bus the youngsters to the slopes after school and to regional competitions on the weekends; and to run the Aspen Cup races. The Aspen Ski Corporation and the Aspen Highlands Company, owners of the four local mountains, lend their support to the program by keeping lifts open for after-school training, donating season lift passes, and reserving and grooming trails for the Aspen Cup races. The racers in the fourteen-and-over ability class also receive psychological assistance in periodic goal meetings with the ski club coaches. Discussions with each skier indicate whether the racer's goal is a college

---

*Four hundred dollars for a November-to-April ski season for nine- to thirteen-year-olds, which includes six days a week of coaching and training, lift tickets, and transportation to regional races.

scholarship or a place on the national team. The coaches then help the racers design an appropriate individualized training program.

A thirteen-year-old Aspen skier like Lee Gargel travels to approximately fifteen races against the seven clubs in the Rocky Mountain Division. Those who do well in the regional races qualify for the end-of-season Junior Olympics, a competition that brings together the best skiers in the West and Alaska. Skiers over fourteen who place in the Junior Olympics then qualify for the Nationals, an event scouted by U.S. Ski Team coaches. A coach enters the names of top young racers into the team's computer, where a file on individual race results will be kept for the next few years. The coach may also invite the racer to come to one of the ski team's one- to four-week summer or early fall training camps, where he can train with the best skiers his age from across the country.

"Lee is already being tracked," says Doug Gargel. "Last season he had good results in all the regional races. But in the Junior Olympics he crashed in the downhill and hurt his leg, which blew him out of the competition. The Aspen coaches invited him up to the U.S. Ski Team's summer training camp in Mount Hood, Oregon, anyway. He spent a week and a half there, and when I went to pick him up, the ski team coaches told me they were definitely impressed with his ability."

When the racer reaches sixteen and seventeen years of age, he competes in only one national Junior Olympics. The skiers who excel qualify for the North American Trophy Series (the Nor-Ams), a group of races held at venues across the United States and Canada. The best Nor-Am racers are invited to attend further training camps, and a few are then selected to compete in the Europa Cup abroad. As members of the National Junior team, the Europa Cup skiers are only one step below the senior-level "B" and "A" teams that compete on the international World Cup circuit.

Skiers who are eliminated from one training camp are given the opportunity to go to another training camp and try to make the team again. For example, the twenty girls eliminated between the first training camp in June and the Europa Cup selections in the fall can return to camp in the United States in December. The top one or two skiers from that camp are then allowed to join the Europa Cup team in January.

Most sports have one central organization with one board of directors and one set of sponsors to help pay for the national team's expenses. In skiing, the central organization for the various ski clubs across the country is the United States Ski Association (USSA), which organizes regional and Nor-Am races. Because top-ranked skiers spend so much of their time on the international Europa and World Cup circuits, the U.S. Ski Team, although technically part of the USSA, functions independently. Each organization has its own board of directors and corporate sponsors. The United States Olympic Committee (USOC), which distributes funds to each Olympic sport for the development, training, and travel of competitors, sends skiing's allotment ($725,940 for both Alpine and Nordic skiing between 1977 and 1980) to the USSA. The lion's share of the funds is then passed on to the U.S. Ski Team.

But the travel and training costs for each member of the U.S. Ski Team are so high that USOC's contribution is not sufficient. Fund-raising is the main goal of the U.S. Ski Educational Foundation, a branch of the U.S. Ski Team. With high-profile businessmen and politicians (including former Vice President Walter Mondale) as trustees, their formal affairs (such as the $175-a-plate 1981 New York Ski Ball held aboard the U.S.S. *Intrepid*) raise $1.5 million annually. Most of the funds are used to meet the ski team's travel and living costs, but some go to ski academies like the Stratton Mountain School for development of future champions.

The U.S. Ski Team has also received corporate sponsorship

| December | On-snow training, Arnoldstein and Kannertal, Austria (DH). Domestic training in western U.S. |
| Nov. 9 – 26 | On-snow time trials, Killington, Vermont (GS/SL) |
| Oct. 18 – Nov. 4 | Home dry-land training |
| Sept. 18 | On-snow training and time trials, Hinter Tux, Austria, and Val Senales, Italy (SL/GS) |
| Aug. 27 – Oct. 7 | On-snow training Laax, Switzerland. Wind-tunnel testing, Buffalo, New York (DH) |
| Aug. 10 – 21 | On-snow conditioning camp at Mt. Hood, Oregon |
| July 25 – Aug. 2 | Physical conditioning and motor skills testing at Olympic Training Center, Colorado Springs, Colorado |
| June 1 – July 24 | Home dry-land training |
| May 1981 | On-snow conditioning/technical camp and testing at Mammoth Mountain, California |

DH = downhill      Men's Team Training
SL = slalom
GS = giant slalom

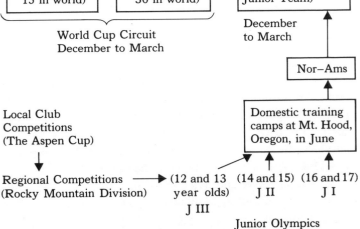

**THE SKIING LADDER**

from the United States Tobacco Company for a special sports-medicine program. "We have several ongoing research projects," explains Bob Harkins, the U.S. Ski Team's assistant alpine director. "Dr. Mike Holden of Buffalo, New York, is doing wind-tunnel testing with the downhillers to determine the best aero-dynamic positions and the drag effects of different materials used in racing suits. Our trainers, who have degrees in physiology, have made great strides in the area of conditioning. They've found that our skiers can't just do a few push-ups or ride an exercycle to stay in shape when they aren't skiing. They need training exercises that closely replicate on-snow situations. And to find out how highly athletic ability correlates with ski results, we've been doing a lot of motor skills testing. These tests will then help us evaluate the specific physical capacities needed for racing. Also, we've hired a psychologist who comes into the training camps and is available to talk to the athletes if they have any anxieties, whether they relate to racing, their personal life, or their relationship with the coach."

In 1981 Phil Mahre won the World Cup, the first time an American had earned ski racing's highest achievement. The same year eighteen-year-old Tamara McKinney captured the women's world slalom crown. American ski racers, who had long been hopelessly outclassed by the Europeans, have come into their own. "When you look across the pond and see the level of competition in Europe it's frightening," says coach Harkins. "Over there, skiing is the national pastime. If a kid makes the Austrian national team he's a national hero. The Austrian coach is regarded like football's Bear Bryant. Our kids' viewpoint has typically been that if they don't win an Olympic medal, they haven't done well. So until recently they've been disappointed a lot of the time.

"But judging by the success we've attained in the past few years, it now appears that our system is working. I think a lot of that success has to do with getting the U.S. Ski Team better organized. With the qualifying system that has been developed in the past three years, the kids know where they stand. There is good, open communication between the central U.S. Ski Team office and the kids who are out on the mountains, trying to make the team. And they know that making the team isn't a one-time shot. If they are eliminated and don't make the team, they can come back to another training camp and try again."

Overseeing all amateur sports organizations, including the USSA, is the United States Olympic Committee (USOC). Started in 1896 by a small group of American athletes who wanted to enter the first modern Olympic Games in Athens, the committee's budget for 1980–84 is $77 million. With no government support, funds are generated through individual and corporate direct mailings; media campaigns: the sale of posters, art prints, stamps, and coins; and special events organized by volunteers in each state. Perhaps the largest single promotion campaign for the 1980 Olympics was Toyota's "Million Dollar Dash for the Olympics," in which the Toyota Corporation donated money for every Toyota car and truck sold by June 1978. Each car purchaser was eligible for a sweepstakes with Olympian prizes: a $100,000 condominium in Aspen; his-and-hers Toyotas; a $5,000 AMF sporting goods shopping spree; $1,000 worth of Levi clothing; a three-week trip to Munich, Montreal, and Moscow; a Sony color TV; a Nikon camera and $10,000 in cash. Through this campaign Toyota contributed more than a million dollars to the USOC.

As the USOC has been able to generate more funds, its function has expanded from merely sending athletes to the Olympic Games to earmarking funds for junior development, making and enforcing rules on amateur standing, operating the Olympic Training Center in Colorado Springs, underwriting expenses for the Olympic Trials, organizing the National Sports Festival (an annual competition in non-Olympic years used by some sports to select their national or Olympic teams and by others simply to introduce younger athletes to Olympic-style competition), and representing American athletes on the International Olympic Committee. Through the years the USOC has become a vast organization that rivals the U.S. government in its complexity. Its main branches include a House of Delegates (which sets general policy); an Administrative Council (which supervises the daily operations of the USOC); an Executive Board (which handles the business affairs of the USOC); specialized constitutional and standing committees (such as Development, Eligibility, Sports Medicine, and Games Site and Preparation); and an Athletes' Advisory Board (which allows athletes currently training for the Olympics or recently retired to have a voice in the Olympic Committee).

Major representation on the committees and boards comes from the thirty-three National Governing Bodies (USSA is one), which are the national organizations for each Olympic sport. Each sport also elects one athlete to serve on the Athlete Advisory Board. And every state is represented in the USOC by state chairpersons appointed by the USOC president. Several individuals, most of whom are former athletes, are also prominent fixtures in the structure: Executive Director F. Don Miller, the six United States Olympic Committee officers, and Bob Mathias, Director of the Olympic Training Center.

Twice Olympic decathlon champion, Bob Mathias is a mountainous man. The short sleeves of his polo shirt barely contain his biceps. On the left side of the navy blue shirt that spans his large chest is a small Olympic insignia. His brown hair has receded slightly since 1952, when he won the Olympics for the second time, but his physique is that of an athlete still in his prime. Fast on the heels of the first impression, which is strength, comes a second — understated pride. Mathias is proud to have been an Olympic champion and is equally proud to be director of a program that began in 1978 and was unforeseeable back in 1952. His large desk at the Olympic Training Center in Colorado Springs is only a hop, skip, and a long jump from the National Sports Building, where several of the national sports organizations have their offices, and from Olympic House, administrative home of the USOC.

Says Mathias, "The Olympic Training Center is used by teams and individuals selected by the National Governing Bodies, which have jurisdiction over their sports. Each NGB requests time at the center. For example, the U.S. Volleyball Association will meet independently and decide to send 50 volleyball girls along with the best volleyball coaches to train at the center for two weeks. Once we have given our approval, we meet the athletes at the airport, give them free room and board during their stay here, and provide transportation to the athletic facilities if necessary."

For many sports, facilities are located at the training center, a thirty-four-acre former Air Force base. Hundreds of runners have used the 400-meter outdoor Chevron track, which is equipped with special electronic testing and timing equipment. (Speed skaters and skiers also use the track for dry-land training on roller skis and skates.) Soccer and field-hockey players, long jumpers, high jumpers, and pole vaulters train on the track's Super-Turf infield. Triple jumpers and shot-putters practice in areas to the north and west of the track. There is also an indoor rifle range, a building for weight training, a sports medicine building, and recreational squash and racquetball courts. In September 1982 a new $4 million gym was opened for all indoor sports — gymnastics, judo, boxing, basketball, volleyball, weight lifting, and wrestling. Although the training center has a twenty-five-meter pool, plans are underway for a larger swimming and diving complex. Swimmers who require a longer pool, skaters, hockey players, cyclists, and hammer, discus, and javelin throwers use the facilities at the nearby Air Force Academy, local

Eric Heiden . . .

. . . with members of the U.S. Speedskating Team
at the Olympic Training Center, 1979.

parks, or, in the case of the cyclists, simply the surrounding country roads and mountain passes.

Athletes usually stay at the center about ten days, although permanent programs have been established for judo, weightlifting, boxing, cycling, and racewalking. (Athletes in these sports arrived in 1981 and will be staying through the 1984 Olympics, living semipermanently in Colorado Springs, where they go to school or hold jobs.) The majority of the visitors are housed in three dormitories — simple, whitewashed brick buildings bearing the names Oslo, Innsbruck, and Cortina to conjure up images of previous Olympics. A maximum of 550 athletes share rooms that are comfortable, though not luxurious. They dine in a similarly spartan cafeteria in the St. Moritz building.

Several hours a day are devoted to training, and every athlete undergoes extensive physical testing. Different muscle groups are tested for strength, flexibility, and endurance. The cardiovascular efficiency of the heart and lungs is measured by the amount of oxygen the athlete consumes while running on a treadmill or riding a stationary bicycle. Another set of tests determines the athlete's optimum weight and proportion of body fat to muscle. Athletes whose sport involves the execution of one complex, integrated motion (such as a discus throw) or a series of specific technical feats (as in figure skating) are also studied by computer for errors in technique. A coach uses a high-speed movie camera to shoot the athlete in practice. The film is fed frame by frame into a Talos Digitizer, an electronic grid embedded in thick glass. Each frame is then analyzed with an electronic stylus, which pinpoints every joint in the body. Taken together, the frames produce a stick-figure electronic image of the athlete's motion. "After testing the muscles, cardiovascular capacity, body fat, and personal technique of each athlete, we can tell who needs help in specific areas," explains Bob Mathias. "We can compare a young speed skater's record to the profile of Eric Heiden. We can then say to him, 'Look, if you want to be as good as Eric

Heiden you have to do more exercises with a certain exercise machine to strengthen your thighs.' Or we can look at the computer image of a shot-putter and see that his right knee is bent at the moment of release and say, 'You're losing the power of the thrust. Keep that leg straight.' "

Not all — not even most — of the athletes who come to the center will ever walk behind the American flag at the Olympics. In fact, less than 10 percent of the 19,000 athletes who came to the Olympic Center between 1978 and mid-1980 are considered elite, or world-class, athletes. Like that of the ski training camp Lee Gargel attended at Mount Hood, one of the center's main purposes is to inspire young talent. "Many who come here won't ever get a chance to go to the Olympics or Pan-American Games," says Mathias. "But just bringing them together to compete with one another makes them want to excel. Although most of the schools or private clubs do the actual training of athletes, we can bring together ten of the most promising young decathloners and get them to know each other and compare notes about the problems of doing a decathlon. While a boy is here he can practice the events and perhaps, after having the biomechanics of his javelin-throwing technique analyzed by the computer, we may detect a small hitch in his motion, which the coaches can help him iron out. He can learn about new advances in the equipment, such as the latest fiberglass pole for the pole vault. And he can participate in a seminar given by a sports psychologist on managing competitive stress. During his stay the decathloner can also meet athletes from other sports and learn what they go through. This interaction broadens his scope and brings a closeness between sports. It's an incredible opportunity. And the athletes don't have to pay a penny for it.*

*The Miller Brewing Company, corporate sponsor for the Olympic Training Center, has provided $4 million to prepare athletes for the 1984 Olympics. The rest of the yearly $1.5 million budget is provided by individuals and other corporations. Surprisingly, the daily cost of training, housing, and feeding an athlete is only $12.61.

"I remember when I was a decathloner," laughs Mathias. "But then we were track and field athletes who would go out for individual events. At the end of the season our coach would try to coax us to compete in one decathlon. We never trained for it. But now a boy can compete in fifty decathlons a year. Everyone is a decathlon specialist. The training has advanced light years since 1952.

"We really needed this program," Mathias continues. "If you're going to be good in sports today, you have to devote much of your time to training. In other countries where the athletes are subsidized by the government, the teenager has nothing else to worry about. That's not true here. And once an athlete gets out of college it's almost impossible for him to get a job and still train enough hours to make the Olympics. And then he can't get off his job to compete. So he quits his job or we lose an Olympic athlete. The United States Olympic Committee has responded to this problem by developing a job opportunities program. We have contacted the Fortune 500 companies and asked them to hire athletes with Olympic potential with the stipulation that they can have time off during their competitive season. So far we've placed 100 athletes with these companies, and they've been paid when they leave to compete. We've gained 100 potential Olympic athletes that otherwise would have quit. And it works out well for the companies. The athletes have somehow managed to sandwich in their education with the training, and usually because they are such highly motivated individuals, excelled in school. So the company is getting a diligent part-time worker who will eventually become an even more valuable full-time employee when his athletic career is over. And should the athlete do well in competition, it reflects on the company.

"The Russians have 75 or 100 training centers," Mathias points out. "East Germany has a training center and sports medicine program in almost every city. They have almost unlimited funds, whereas the United States Olympic Committee gets no federal funds. We are limited in how much we can do by the amount of money we raise. But we're doing the best we can."

Besides establishing the Olympic Training Center, the USOC's other special project in recent years has been junior development. The USOC coffers, which suffered a serious shortfall in 1980 despite the successful Toyota campaign, have already received generous corporate support toward 1984. This has allowed the USOC to allocate $15 million for development over the period 1981–84, an increase of $6 million over the past four years.

National sports organizations receiving funds from the USOC usually give part of the money to top athletes to help them defray training and travel costs (grants sometimes labeled "scholarships"). Part may be given to athletes who are exceptional students to further their education, and part is used to send promising juniors to the Olympic Training Center. In years when the USOC allotment is high, sports associations become particularly eager to send their top prospects abroad for greater international exposure. But although the association subsidizes the athlete, parents and coaches are left to fend for themselves. This can pose a serious financial problem for the families of competitors who need adult supervision.

"The figure skating association wanted to send Elaine to Japan when she was fourteen, and I wouldn't let her go," says Jeri Zayak. "Because I had to go and I'd have her coach go, too. It would have cost us about $2,600 in plane tickets. If you figured another $1,000 or more for accommodations and food, it would cost about four or five thousand dollars for Elaine to go to Japan for one week. And that was in October, and all the national competitions started in late October, where we have to pay for Elaine, me or my husband, and her coach, Peter. But one week later they called up and asked if Elaine could compete in Skate

161

Canada. I agreed, because though Canada is expensive, it's nothing like Japan would have been."* The Zayaks felt it was important to stay in the association's good graces and they realized the trip to Canada would smooth things over. They knew too well what happened to Lisa-Marie Allen when she displayed too much bravado. Although the Zayaks felt the limits of their budget, maintaining a favorable relationship with the association was all-important — not only to ensure Elaine's $1,500–2,000 annual "scholarship," but also to improve her chances for the 1984 Olympics.

Sports politics eventually influence personality. To be the darling of the coach, the club, the association, is to emerge with a clearly defined sense of self. To have been chosen to visit the Olympic Training Center is to be given an enduring psychological boost. The athlete with less talent, the competitor who remains unrecognized by club or association officials, is often left with a pervasive sense of self-doubt. Mark Eid is a skier who is trying to succeed without the backing of the skiing establishment. He is envious of youngsters like Lee Gargel, a fellow member of the Aspen Ski Club's "ability class." Like the prospectors who arrived to search for gold and silver in the Aspen hills, six months ago Eid came to Aspen from Anchorage, Alaska, to seek his skiing fortune. Inhabiting a trailer fifteen miles out of town, he lived until recently on earnings from previous summer jobs as a garbage man. (For the moment his father, a retired pastry chef, is supporting him.) A rawboned twenty-one-year-old with close-cropped blond hair and a genial smile, he gave himself this year to either make it in skiing or get on with his life.

Although Eid began skiing at age five, he didn't start racing until he was fourteen. He had none of Gargel's advantages. His

*Since the Japan incident, the association has been more sympathetic to the financial plight of parents. It now distributes a questionnaire in advance, polling what competitions the top skaters are most interested in attending.

father, although an avid sportsman, was not as interested in skiing as Doug Gargel. The racing program at Mount Alyeska, thirty-five miles from his home, was limited to weekends. It was prohibitively expensive to go "outside," as Alaskans call the lower forty-eight states, to compete. Mark started improving rapidly only when he reached college. It was then that, on the suggestion of his coach, he decided to spend a year training in Aspen.

Gargel has the luxury of letting his career unfold over time; Eid is enrolled in a crash course. From December to April he competed in forty races, or four races a week. He also practiced four to six hours on the days he didn't compete, ran in the mornings, and lifted weights. "You get burned out and want to just free ski or stay off your skis for awhile," he says. "Skiing is fun and that's what it's all about, but after awhile you want a little change. But if you want to get somewhere, you have to do it."

The highlight of Eid's year was competing in the World Cup race in Aspen. Sixty of the world's best racers transformed Aspen into a kind of Olympic village. "It makes you really tentative because you see a lot of big-name guys and all their coaches," he says. "Everyone is fussing over the skiers. Photographers are running all over the place, people are out on the mountain working the course, and the tourists ski along the sides, getting into their tucks and pretending to be Joe Downhiller."

The first day of the competition, Mark was a forerunner, one of about five skiers who *schuss* down the course before the competition to pack down the snow. When fellow forerunners, younger skiers from the Aspen Ski Club, were asked to enter the competition the next day, he was momentarily jealous. But then he too was invited to race. "Strangely enough, I was really nervous forerunning, but the day I got to race I felt very confident," he recalls. By the time Eid got his turn, however, fifty-one racers had been down the course. The snow looked like something between a bad case of acne and the surface of the moon. He fell.

"It was a silly skiing mistake. My ski got caught on the outside of a rut and got shaken around. Instead of putting more pressure on my downhill ski, I stupidly shifted more pressure to the inside ski, something you're never supposed to do. So my outside ski caught and I flipped over. My skis were bent, but I wasn't hurt. I was disappointed not to have finished, but at least at the start I felt more confident than the day before."

Eid's goal is to compete in Europe with the U.S. Ski Team, but he worries that he may not get the chance. "I don't know if there is a peak skiing age, but nowadays they are picking the younger skiers to go to Europe. The age to excel seems to be between seventeen and nineteen. If you're winning a lot of races, the coaches can't look past you. But they also are looking for the kids who may not be getting results now but have the potential. They feel that they can work with these youngsters to mold a champion. It makes me think that maybe if I had started racing earlier . . ." he says, his voice trailing off in frustration.

Ranked twenty-fourth nationally, Mark Eid had a fair, but not great, year. A lot of younger skiers did better, pressing past him in the rankings. He is now waiting to hear whether he's been chosen to train at the U.S. Ski Team spring training camp, which would be the first in three steps to Europe. He is not overly optimistic. "I'll be disappointed if I don't get to go to the camp," he says. "But I don't blame them if they don't pick me. I didn't ski super well. I'd really like to be picked because I think that if I were given the opportunity, I could show them something."

Eid realizes that he is nearing a turning point in his life. Despite his cheerful demeanor, he is tense. He hasn't been given enough time. "My Dad's a strict German and he decided on his career when he was young," Mark explains. "He'd like me to do the same. The deal was that I'd have this year off to ski and

164

see how well I'd do. I feel I'm still in a bind within myself because I'm really close to being there. I'm right on the verge. I don't want to quit ski racing. But my age is making it difficult. I've learned a lot about skiing both mentally and physically this year," he adds. "Every time I see something new I think, 'Wow, I could really work on this during the summer and fall and then I'd be that much more ahead next year.' Skiing is largely a matter of miles. The more miles you've logged, the more experience you have, which means you can see more and realize what you have to do."

When Lee Gargel was asked what his goals were, he did not miss a beat. "I've got my small goals and I've got my big goals," the thirteen-year-old declared. "Next year I want to do really well and be in the top three in all my races. Then I want to make the Olympic team and go to the Olympics and then be the number one racer in the World Cup." Mark Eid, as he admitted himself, is more tentative. His goals are strictly short-term. "I had a hard time deciding if I wanted to come to Aspen or stay up in Alaska where it's cheaper. But I thought I'd come down here and get the exposure. One of my goals for the season was not only lowering my points to get a better ranking, but being able to race in the World Cup. I don't know if I'll ever ski well enough to ski in a World Cup race again, or if it will be the first in a long series. I'll just have to wait and see."

# 9

# Growing Up: Physiology and the Role of Sports Medicine

Childhood lays the foundation of a sports career, but it is during the rapid physical and psychological changes of adolescence that the career truly takes shape. At this time, the pool of young athletes expands. Those whose talents lie in team sports enter the sorting system out of which some will emerge as potential professional baseball, basketball, and football stars.

It is also during this time that many young athletes drop out. Inevitably, as children begin competing at younger ages, more will drop out before they reach their teens. A twelve-year study by Dr. H. Harrison Clarke, research professor emeritus of physical education, found that only one in four children who were star athletes in elementary school were still exceptional three to four years later in junior high.

Biology plays a part in this sifting process. We all have biological limits placed on us by the length of our bones, the percentage of "slow-twitch" and "fast-twitch" muscle fibers we possess, the tightness or looseness of our joints, the capacities of our hearts and lungs, and our unique hormonal profiles. At adolescence our genetic blueprint is revealed. A girl who becomes buxom like her mother or finds that her weight has settled around her hips won't be able to be an Olympic gymnast. The small, slight boy who is a marathon runner suddenly may acquire the heft more suitable to a middle linebacker. Girls who have competed successfully with boys in childhood now find themselves surpassed in sports that place a premium on upper-body strength.

It is in adolescence, too, that injury rates rise. In contact sports like football and hockey, the greater size, strength, and speed of the high school athlete places him at a much greater risk of muscle tears and pulls than the preadolescent, whose smaller size doesn't allow him to generate much force. A child's bones are springy and flexible, fracture infrequently, and repair quickly, but they grow harder and more brittle over time. The child's ligaments (ropelike sinews that link one bone to another at the joint) are also highly elastic during childhood but become tighter in adolescence.

Those destined to become superstars are much more prone to injury than normally active adolescents. Their training schedules, which may have been leavened with other activities in their early years, become more onerous as the athlete nears the world-class level. A minimum of two hours a day is usually set aside for practice, but some athletes work out for as long as eight or nine hours. (Ironically, marathon running, which in some quarters is considered almost synonymous with child abuse, requires an hour or two each day, while the male and female world Frisbee champions both practice six to eight hours a day.) Moreover, as athletes progress, they become more wary of taking breaks from their training regimens for fear of getting out of shape. Even finely-tuned athletes can lose their conditioning rapidly. If muscles are not stressed, they lose their ability to use oxygen efficiently. According to Dr. Gabe Mirkin, author of *The Sportsmedicine Book,* the muscles begin to lose their tone after a few days, and after three to four weeks most of the muscular strength and endurance built up through exercise is lost. Perhaps a greater fear is psychological. Most young athletes feel that if they don't train hard every day, their competitors will surpass them.

Usually practice is not confined to the sport itself, but includes additional weight training to build strength, jogging to boost endurance, and calisthenics to increase flexibility. Fifteen-year-old Tiffany Cohen, a champion long-distance swimmer for the Mission Viejo Natadores, swims thirteen miles a day for six days

168

Howard Zryb/SPORTS FOTOFILE

a week, forty-eight weeks a year, and also runs several miles three times a week and has twice-weekly workouts on a strength-building Nautilus machine.

But training only gets the athlete to the starting block. Exhibitions and competitive schedules have extended many sports seasons to twelve months a year. The competitive figure-skating season officially begins with regional competitions in November and ends with the World Championships in March, but like emergency room physicians, the top skaters must be on call year-round. "I'm tired," admitted fifteen-year-old Elaine Zayak as she flopped into a rinkside seat after rehearsing for "Super-skates," an annual benefit for the United States Olympic Fund. The previous day she had flown in from China, where she and a handful of America's top skaters had been sent by ABC-TV to introduce competitive skating to the Chinese. The week before she had competed in "Skate Canada" in Calgary. And the "Superskates" exhibition in New York would be followed by performances in Boston and Colorado Springs. All this traveling took place in the autumn of 1980, before the major national and international competitions. Somehow Elaine fought off jet lag and fatigue to win her first national championships in January and place second in the world championships six weeks later. She was lucky. Most injuries occur when an athlete reaches the point of physical exhaustion. With longer training hours and the stresses of year-round travel and competition, more young athletes are placing themselves in danger every day.

Youngsters may push themselves too hard not only out of their own desire to win, but also to impress the coach. Becky Muelhausen's swimming career ended with shoulder surgery at age thirteen. Her training regimen had consisted of four hours of swimming a day plus lifting weights. Her coach suggested additional upper-body strength training in the form of push-ups, but he did not specify a number. Becky thought she would impress him by doing two hundred a day. When Becky and her

170

father appeared on the Phil Donahue television show two years after Becky's shoulder surgery, the two experts on the panel— sports physician Dr. Richard Dominguez and swimmer Diana Nyad — squared off.

Said Dominguez: "Fifty percent of all competitive swimmers at Becky's level get shoulder pain. Becky's problem was that she drove herself very hard, ignored the pain, and thought, 'Well, Vince Lombardi is right, I've got to play with pain. Pain is good for me.' And as a result she developed very severe tendonitis in her shoulder."

Countered Nyad: "I grew up in swimming and I know that if you want to reach a sophisticated level in the sport you're going to have to do a tremendous amount of shoulder work. Which means a lot of pushups. At ten years of age, I also was doing 200 pushups. And there were swimmers who were in excellent physical condition *because* of the 200 pushups."

Becky's father, Walter Muelhausen, then entered the fray: "I don't think Becky was physically ready for that at age 13. A lot of the kids were; a lot of the kids handled it with no problem at all. But I think this particular coach was used to handling older kids. Becky was one of the youngest he had." Because Becky kept the pain to herself, she pushed her shoulder beyond its limits to the point where surgical intervention was required. Two years later Becky still can't swim, "because of the pain," she says. "It still hurts too bad."

The physical dangers of training several hours a day year-round are perhaps greatest in sports like running, tennis, and skiing, where the legs are constantly pounding against an un-forgiving surface. "We're going to have to change the winter tour," said Jerry Diamond, executive director of the Women's Tennis Association, after a 1982 winter season that saw three top players — Chris Evert Lloyd, Tracy Austin, and Andrea Jaeger — sidelined with lower-body injuries. "We need to move to some outdoor tournaments in the winter and maybe have a

171

rest week or two. When a player plays on a carpet* laid over a hard surface, the muscle gets two hits for every stop. That's okay for three to four weeks, but over the long haul it has to take its toll."

Injuries are eliminating competitors in several other sports. The growing popularity and competitiveness of gymnastics and figure skating have resulted in the development of complex new maneuvers that threaten many competitors with serious injury. For example, a young gymnast practicing ten to fifteen routines twenty or more times a day is not new. What is new is the nature of the stunts. Gymnasts used to use their hands for support while upside down, as in walkovers and handsprings. Because the force of the jump was generated from the hands, the gymnast's momentum rarely reached dangerous levels. But these moves have given way to feet-to-feet moves like the Tsukahara and the double back, in which double rotations are performed in the air. Even when the gymnast performs flawlessly, the force of the landing is much harder. And if she doesn't land properly, the strain on the joints is maximized because the body is still twisted during the attempted landing. Jim Corrigan, head coach of the advanced girls' team at Kathy Corrigan's School of Gymnastics, believes that the new physical demands have been a major cause of accidents and chronic injuries. "Just look at the Federation of International Gymnastics updated Code of Points," says Corrigan. "All of last year's superior moves have been devalued. These kids have to be superstars just to meet the bottom requirements!"

In figure skating, too, as the complexity of the movements has risen, the injury rate has climbed. Especially dramatic was the eleventh-hour groin injury that prevented Randy Gardner and his partner Tai Babilonia from competing in the 1980 Olym-

*The "carpet" is Sporteze, a polypropylene-fiber surface covered with a vinyl cushion. Sometimes the carpet is laid over a cement or wood floor; when the tour plays in hockey arenas, the carpet is laid over ice.

pics. Perhaps even more distressing was the 1981 Ladies' National Championship in which Lisa-Marie Allen skated with her severe ankle injury. Three of the other top four skaters were either in acute physical distress or had been sidelined from the competition with injuries. Only winner Elaine Zayak was not among the walking wounded. The culprit was the triple jump, attempted by many, completed by few, and capable of causing chronic bone, muscle, and ligament injuries.

"A short while ago a young girl who showed great promise was referred to me by the United States Figure Skating Association," says psychologist Dr. Bruce Ogilvie. "I had a bone analysis done which revealed that the girl's skeletal age was sixteen months below her chronological age. Here we were expecting this girl to do triple jumps with consistency and thinking that she had some psychological problem when the real problem was that her little body was a year and a half below the standard and just couldn't handle all the triple jumps."

A movement is now underway to eliminate triple jumps from all but senior-level events or to give credit only for a limited number of them. Dr. Tenley Albright, a Boston surgeon, 1956 Olympic figure skating champion, and mother of a competitive figure skater, believes that most of the damage is done in practice, by coaches who demand that the skater rehearse the same jump again and again. She suggests that children be limited in the number of times they can practice a triple jump each day.

In sports such as skiing, in which athletes strain to cut hundredths of seconds off their times, injury has become almost a way of life. When he was seventeen, Phil Mahre sat out the 1974 season with a broken leg suffered in an avalanche. He was unable to compete in 1975 when he refractured the same leg. In 1979 he shattered his ankle. In a bold display of courage, he competed in the Olympics the next year with his ankle held together by a steel pin and won a silver medal in the slalom. For the past two years, Mahre has been uncharacteristically healthy. Each year he has won the World Cup, the first American to bring the trophy across the Atlantic.

One of the youngest members of the U.S. Ski Team, seventeen-year-old Beth Madsen, has already fractured her ankle twice. After the 1982 European tour, at the downhill of the Nationals, she tore the interior cruciate ligament in her knee. She was surprised to find the other two local members of the ski team back home in Aspen also recuperating from knee injuies. They commiserated in the trainer's whirlpool. Says Beth, "I'm used to ankles, but knees are sort of scary. They're more painful and it takes up to a whole year for them to recover. I'll probably recuperate for six more weeks and then go up to the training camp on Mount Hood and try to ski again."

In team sports, youngsters' injuries have occasioned great debate. Coaches usually say that injuries are infrequent and minor. They contend that if children are matched with opponents of similar size and weight, organized sports are less dangerous than skateboarding, bicycling, or unsupervised sandlot games. According to critics, injuries are often ignored and underreported. It is true that even the best-intentioned Little League and high school coaches may unconsciously be leading their players toward injury. Most coaches are not trained in biomechanics, and often use warm-up exercises that are contraindicated — instead of relaxing the muscles, they strain them. According to Dr. Vern Seefeldt, director of the Youth Sports Institute at Michigan State University, many football coaches advocate exercises called neck bridges to strengthen the necks of their linemen. These warm-up exercises can injure the soft bones of the neck. Similarly, double leg lifts — done to strengthen the abdomen — and push-ups — aimed at building up the arms and shoulders — can lead to chronic back problems.

Worse, in their zeal to win, many coaches encourage or condone the violent behavior that children have seen used successfully by their professional idols. Filmmaker Barton Cox has produced a filmstrip on youth sports that begins with a real-life situation: a youth hockey coach addressing his team. "When you see a man against those boards let him have it. Don't ever miss that opportunity. If he's got the puck, you can let him have it as hard as possible. Put him out of play. That's one less guy you have to worry about." Utilizing major-league techniques, many youngsters are beginning to suffer big-time injuries. Football helmets, designed for protection, are being used to spear opponents. Nearly one in five Minnesota high school football players reported symptoms of cerebral concussion in 1977. Butting the opponent with the helmet was cited as the cause of head injuries by 33 percent. But only 57 percent of those injured said they had been told by their coaches that this technique was illegal.

Even if these players return to action, the long-term effects may be devastating. "In youth football, 50 percent of the athletes who are referred for neck injuries show bone abnormalities. And those are just the ones who are referred to physicians," says Dr. Bruce Ogilvie. "I was a football player when I was young and I had an undiagnosed neck fracture that didn't bother me until later in life. In a few months I'm going to have surgery to fuse my spine because of the pain. I wonder how many youngsters are going to have to suffer the same pain?"

The increasing incidence of sports-related injuries has led to the new specialty of pediatric sports medicine. These orthopedists, internists, and gynecologists are studying the implications of growth, reproduction, and injury on young athletes whose bodies are physically stressed for several years, beginning before puberty. They are focusing on heart and lung capacities, bone strength, muscle power and endurance, ligament and tendon elasticity, and maturation rates — factors that determine the relative stress the systems can bear without injury. For example, it was originally thought that strenuous sports might place excessive demands on children's hearts. Most of these fears have been quelled. Studies have shown that although children do have smaller hearts than adults, when exercised to the point of exhaustion few show any cardiac abnormalities (some may become nauseous, however, and take a few hours to recover). Says Canadian sports physician Donald Bailey, "True, there have been cases of sudden death and cardiac arrests in young athletes during or immediately following games or practices, but in most of these cases congenital factors were probably involved. The physical stress of the contest may have precipitated the event, but it is probable that the affected individual had previous damage to the cardiovascular system unrelated to physical exertion."

Early training in endurance sports can, in fact, increase the size and efficiency of the heart and lungs. In a study of Swedish girl swimmers aged twelve to sixteen who had trained twenty-eight hours a week for several years, not only was their oxygen intake (the best measure of total fitness) significantly greater than that of their peers, but the components of their oxygen transporting system (heart and lung volume plus total hemoglobin, the part of the blood that carries the oxygen) were significantly larger.*

Another widespread fear that has prompted study concerns the possibly adverse effect of vigorous training on maturation and growth. Male athletes tend to be more advanced physiologically than their nonathletic peers, especially in sports and other endeavors in which size is a factor. Similarly, females who mature early may have an athletic edge in some sports. But data derived from college-age female athletes suggest that de-

*The results from a follow-up survey on the same swimmers ten years later were quite different. All of the young women had stopped training and most did not engage in any specific physical activity in their spare time. Their lives were filled mainly with domestic and professional work. Although the dimensions of their hearts and lungs remained larger than normal, their aerobic efficiency, which had been 20 percent higher than untrained girls their age, had dropped to 15 percent below the mean for Swedish females the same age. In other words, by turning off to the sport after college, they had forfeited their cardiovascular fitness as adults.

layed maturity is related to successful performance in running, swimming, gymnastics, and figure skating. Many young girls who begin rigorous training in long-distance swimming and running before puberty are likely to start menstruating as much as three years later than their peers. And menstrual disorders are likely to continue as long as the athlete trains hard. In a study of thirty-eight college swimmers and runners in Boston, 83.5 percent of the women who had begun training before puberty had irregular or no menstrual cycles, but only 40 percent of the women who began training after puberty experienced irregularity. For menstrual periods to be present, a critical level of body fat is required, a level the competitive swimmer or runner may not reach. The tension and stress of competition also may affect the menstrual cycle. But when athletic training is over (or if the girl can gain more weight), the regular menstrual cycle usually resumes. More frightening is the fact that weight loss is now deliberately being used to delay maturity. "We are seeing that more mothers of gymnasts are depriving their daughters of food so that their bodies will remain immature and thus better suited to the sport," reports Dr. Lyle Michaeli, chairman of the sports medicine program at Children's Hospital in Boston.

The effects of extensive training on growth are less predictable. Jolting and wrenching of the knee, hips, and ankles can injure the growth plates, the tissues near the ends of the bones where actual expansion of the bones takes place. According to Dr. Burton Berson, director of the sports medicine program at Mt. Sinai Hospital in New York, "In children the ligaments surrounding the joints are stronger than the growth plates. So when there is sudden jarring of the joint, the force is absorbed by the growth plate, rather than the ligaments. By adulthood, the reverse is true. The bones are more resilient than the ligaments, so ligament tears and ruptures become more frequent."

Only 6 percent of injuries in preadolescents involve the growth plates, however. (Most mishaps are cuts, bruises, sprains, and strains.) Nor does a growth-plate injury mean permanent deformity. Usually the plate is simply displaced and can be relocated by gentle pressure or traction. More dangerous than jolting are repetitive actions of the shoulder (pitching in Little League baseball, serving in tennis, or using a freestyle stroke in swimming) and the knee (jumping in basketball). Cumulative wear and tear on the joints often leads to chronic injuries. Those suffering from overuse syndromes such as "Little League elbow," "swimmer's shoulder," and "jumper's knee" experience pain, tendonitis, and sometimes changes in bone structure that can last a lifetime. Because children have only recently become seriously involved in marathon running and weight-resistance training, the long-term effects aren't yet known. Although it is unlikely that such activities will inhibit a child's growth, several experts believe that young athletes may be susceptible to premature arthritis in their hips, knees, shoulders, and ankles.

One of the best ways to prevent injury is a thorough physical screening that examines the athlete's strength, flexibility, and body type. The physical profile yields important information to help parents select sports suitable for their children and make them aware of any anatomical weaknesses that may require special conditioning programs. For example, everyone's ligaments will tighten after childhood, but the degree of tightening can vary considerably. In some people the ligaments remain rather loose around the joint; in others they bind the joint more compactly. The loose-jointed individual will have a great range of flexibility* and is naturally suited to sports that emphasize agility (diving, gymnastics, figure skating) and endurance (bicycling and swimming). At the same time, these people are susceptible to shoulder dislocations, sprains, and loose kneecaps. The tight-jointed person is best suited to explosive sports such

*Flexibility is often tested simply by noting the ease with which the athlete touches his toes, rotates his shoulder, and bends back his thumb to meet his forearm.

as basketball, hockey, squash, soccer, and racquetball. Although tight-jointed individuals can generate speed faster, they are more susceptible to muscle tears and ruptures.

Just as we are all born with different degrees of flexibility, we are also born with a unique ratio of fast-twitch and slow-twitch muscle fibers. Slow-twitch fibers contract slowly and are better suited for endurance sports: a world-class marathon runner like Bill Rodgers has 80 to 90 percent slow-twitch muscle fibers, while champion sprinters Carl Lewis and Evelyn Ashford have about 70 percent fast-twitch.*

Biology is not necessarily destiny, because once anatomical weaknesses are noted, specific training can often compensate for them. The late Dr. John L. Marshall points out in *The Sports Doctor's Fitness Book for Women,* "An extremely loose-jointed and physically slow tennis player like Chris Evert Lloyd makes up for this by her extraordinary anticipation, reaction and movement time. She's been trained to be right where the ball is, and in the end, that's what counts." On the other hand, an athlete like Billie Jean King, whose muscles are more powerful and faster firing, must train to develop stamina and must carefully stretch by doing flexibility exercises before and after each match. "Your inherited body type by its very definition is something you simply can't change no matter what you do," wrote Dr. Marshall. "But if you're armed with the correct information about your muscle-fiber type and know whether or not joints are loose or tight, you can figure out how best to compensate for what you lack, how to avoid injuries you're susceptible to through the right kind of training, and how to take advantage

*Rodgers, Lewis, and Ashford were studied by physiologists David Costill and William Fink at Ball State University. By means of muscle biopsies they extracted pea-size bits of muscle and examined them under a microscope. Biopsies, however, are not usually necessary, because physiologists have detected a correlation between muscle-fiber type and joint flexibility. Loose-jointed individuals tend to have a higher proportion of slow-twitch fibers whereas tight-jointed individuals have more fast-twitch fibers.

of your natural gifts by choosing the activities that make the most of them."

A physiological profile can educate the parents as well as the athlete. "A sense of what sports the child is good at should be picked up along the way, either by the youngster or the parent," says Dr. Burton Berson. "But the problem is that parents often see the child through themselves. Fathers, especially, see what they want that child to be — and they may look right past any physical problems. Although the sport physician can only advise the parents, his recommendation, if followed, can help prevent injury and may lead to greater success and satisfaction for the child."

Dr. Berson believes that it is also the responsibility of the parent to be sure the athlete is using properly fitted equipment rather than hand-me-downs from an older brother or sister, and that practices are adequately supervised. Parents should also oversee the conditioning program used by the coach to ensure that the teenager is adequately strengthening the specific muscles used by the sport before competing, but at the same time not pushing himself too hard. "I'm convinced that parents shouldn't be pushing sports on their children, but rather de-emphasizing them," says Dr. Lyle Michaeli. He advises that parents remain alert to signs of physical and psychic tension — irritability, sleeplessness, problems in school, unaccounted weight loss or gain, persistent soreness in the muscles and joints — symptoms that may indicate that the sport has become too stressful emotionally or that the child is training too hard.

Injuries can also be prevented by a warm-up period before and a cool-down period after each workout. Although as a rule children and teenagers are more flexible than adults, they can still tear or rupture muscles by jumping into combat before stimulated blood circulation has raised the muscles' temperature and made them more pliable. According to Dr. Gabe Mirkin, the athlete should begin by exercising the muscles slowly in the same way they will be used during competition. Runners should jog, tennis players should rally for ten minutes, and hockey players should skate around the rink. Cooling down too quickly after a workout can lead to stiff muscles that are more prone to injury during the next session. All athletes regardless of age should walk for a while after running long distances and then do some stretching exercises while the muscles are still warm.

Parents should also be on the lookout for signs of nutritional faddism and drug abuse. Drugs are endemic in the youth culture, and athletes are no exception. In fact, they may be particularly vulnerable because as a group athletes are often desperately eager to improve performance. Some stuff themselves with vitamins, thinking that if one vitamin tablet will keep the doctor away, a handful will make them superhealthy. Conversely, wrestlers who have to "make the weight" and appearance-conscious gymnasts and figure skaters often embark on unhealthy crash diets or simply consume too few calories. After noting how the Soviets and East Germans swept Olympic and world meets by using anabolic steroids (drugs derived from the male hormone testosterone), American track and field athletes, wrestlers, and football players were quick to jump on the steroid bandwagon, believing that these drugs would increase their muscular strength. Many football players and long-distance cyclists use stimulants like amphetamines to give them added speed and keep them alert, while football and basketball trainers may inject their top athletes with painkillers to help them play with known or suspected injuries.

Rumors about special "energy-packing, performance-boosting" foods and drugs have seeped down from the pros to the high school level. The American Academy of Pediatrics was concerned enough to issue an official statement in 1974:

Young people today grow up with the notion that there is a drug to hasten recovery from practically every illness and that a healthy person can be even better off if he has something special in his diet or his manner of living.

The results of these beliefs is a host of misconceptions about ways by which a healthy individual can be improved by a miracle drug, a special diet, a vitamin, a hormone, particular exercises, or some other procedure.

There is no scientific basis for any such practices, although they are usually not actually hazardous. However, a number of drugs, including those allegedly capable of increasing performance, may indeed be harmful.

Nutritional myths have circulated widely not only because star athletes have been quick to extol their "secret" formulas (ranging from wheat germ oil to raw eggs), but also because there was until recently virtually no well-documented research in the area of sports nutrition. As more research has been done, scientists have found that although intensive physical activity does increase the need for calories and fluids (especially in growing children), there is no single nutrient that when taken in greater than normal amounts will enhance athletic performance.

Vitamins are perhaps the greatest area of nutritional faddism, largely because most people don't know what they do. Vitamins are *not* a direct source of energy but only components of enzymes that are needed in tiny amounts to regulate chemical reactions in the body. Simply popping a handful of vitamins won't make up for the nourishment lacking in a 600-calorie-a-day diet. Nor will massive doses of vitamins improve a healthy person's strength or endurance. In fact, megadoses of certain vitamins can be extremely dangerous. Because vitamins A, D, E, and K are fat soluble (which means that they must attach themselves to fat molecules to move through the bloodstream), excessive amounts of these vitamins can accumulate in the fat tissues within the body and produce at first unpleasant side effects (headaches, nausea, dizziness, and blurred vision) and then more serious signs of toxicity. Megadoses of the water-soluble B complex vitamins — the vitamins usually heralded as energy boosters and fatigue fighters — are less likely to cause bodily harm because amounts in excess of what the body needs are simply excreted in the urine.

Although young athletes are likely to experiment with food fads, in time most will recognize the merits of a well-balanced diet. Moreover, many sports psychologists and physicians believe that young athletes who have spent most of their lives honing their talents are *less* likely to experiment with drugs that may interfere with their ability to compete well. But if an athlete's performance starts to decline, susceptibility to drug-taking may increase. This is especially true when there is pressure from peers or coach to indulge in drug use.

The most controversial drugs used widely by athletes today are anabolic steroids. The steroid craze began when an American physician who happened to be a weight lifter reasoned that if anabolic steroids (synthetic derivatives of testosterone) could heal torn muscles quickly and add muscular bulk to men who had low testosterone levels, then if healthy men used steroids, they would become even stronger. To find out, he began injecting himself with steroids. Soon he was satisfied that he had gained considerable muscular strength, more than he could have gained with weight lifting alone. He reported his observations in a popular weight lifting magazine, and within a short time the craze had spread through the ranks of weight lifters and body builders to football players and athletes in power sports (javelin, discus, shot put). Next, national rivalries fanned the flames. At the 1960 Olympics the Russians were rumored to be using steroids widely to increase strength. By 1964 male athletes were so convinced that steroids were the Russians' secret weapon that they began to feel the need for pill parity. The practice spread to American women in 1973 when East German swimmers showed up for the World Swimming Championships in Belgrade, Yugoslavia, considerably huskier than the year before. (Some also had a light growth of hair on their upper lips and voices that had mysteriously deepened.) The Germans swept the swim meet, winning ten gold medals.

It has not been confirmed that steroids actually build stronger muscles in healthy individuals. Some scientists speculate that much of the weight gain could be water retention; others believe that the real performance-boosting quality of the drug may lie not in its anabolic effect (that is, its direct effect on the muscles), but in its androgenic effect, the effect the drug has on the hormonal balance. Because of the additional testosterone, the athlete may become more aggressive and therefore train harder. It is this psychological desire to train hard, to progressively stress the muscles so that they gain strength, that could cause improved results, rather than the steroid's direct action on the muscles.

Yet many coaches believe steroids work, and are introducing high school athletes to these drugs. Anywhere from 10 to 50 percent of women in track and field use them, with body builders, weight lifters, cyclists, and speed skaters also toying with the drug. Middle-distance runner Kathy Scatena took steroids during the 1976–77 season as a member of the Naturite Track Club in Northridge, California. Coach Chuck DeBus told Kathy not to talk to her teammates about steroids, but in *Women's Sports* magazine she explained, "The main thing people have to understand is that I had a coach who was a really good talker, and he knew his stuff. I grew up in a small town. I didn't know questions to ask, and I'm not a person to doubt my coach's word — DeBus is about the best coach you'd ever come across as far as workouts and training. If he's going to tell me something is good, I'm not going to say, 'You're full of shit.' " Coach DeBus denies Kathy's story. "There was absolutely no steroid use at Northridge," he says.

According to Dr. Gideon Ariel, member of the Olympic committee on sports medicine and a former Olympic discus thrower, anabolic steroid use among male athletes in the power sports has reached 100 percent. Although the drugs are officially banned from Olympic competition, there are several ways of escaping detection in the postcompetition urinalysis test. (The most common, Dr. Ariel says, is curtailing use of the artificially produced derivative and substituting natural testosterone supplements from a bull or other animal several weeks before the competition.) Dr. Gabe Mirkin believes that more high school football coaches are also dispensing steroids to their athletes, often without realizing the physical consequences. "Many youngsters do not stop growing until they are out of their teens. Medical scientists have known for years that anabolic steroids cause premature closing of the epiphyses [the site of the growth plates] of growing bones and stop growth forever," Dr. Mirkin explains. Also, because tendons aren't affected by steroids, if a muscle grows and the tendon (which attaches the muscle to the bone) doesn't, the tendon may become inflamed and rupture. Further, some researchers believe that long-term use of steroids can predispose an athlete to heart attack, liver cancer, or sterility.

Beyond the danger of physical damage lies the overreaching issue of fair competition. "To go into a competition *au naturel* against someone who is chemically prepared is not fair," complained Canadian pentathlete Diane Konihowski when a Russian pentathlete who had been banned for steroid use was reinstated a year and a half later and went on to win the 1980 Olympics. But is being "chemically prepared" being better prepared? And is a gold medal worth physical side effects that may be severely damaging, perhaps life threatening? These are some of the questions sports physicians are now trying to answer.

Myths concerning enhanced sports performance are starting to fade as research results are passed from the labs of the sports physician to the coaches and on to the players. It is a slow process in which the various specialties have only recently begun to work together. Studies of the long-term effects of intensive training on maturation and growth and the effects of drugs on athletic

185

performance are only beginning. Physical profiling, which is routinely administered at sports medicine centers in virtually every Russian and East German city, is not handled with any accuracy in our schools. Parents interested in a thorough physical screening must take their children to a sports physician or a sports clinic associated with a major university or hospital.*

Yet strides are being made. Nutritionists are now measuring athletes' body fat to devise sport-specific diets — that is, diets with enough calories and nutrients to meet the demands of a particular sport without making the athlete either over- or under-weight. Physiologists are studying muscle function and helping coaches devise training programs that develop muscular efficiency without overtaxing the fibers. Trainers are developing rehabilitative techniques to allow young athletes to maintain overall fitness even after a leg fracture or knee surgery has put them in a cast. With new techniques that simulate the actual athletic activity in speed, power, and strength, trainers are better able to judge when a player is ready to return to action. And orthopedic surgeons are developing techniques such as arthroscopic knee surgery, which means that repair of torn cartilage (one of the most common athletic injuries) is a less painful, less traumatic, and less complicated operation requiring a shorter rehabilitation period.

"The future of sportsmedicine is bright," says Dr. James A. Nicholas, director of the Institute of Sports Medicine and Athletic Trauma at Lenox Hill Hospital in New York City. "In the future, more children will be matched by maturation rather than age. There will be new techniques such as radioscopic scans and ultrasound to diagnose contact and overuse injuries. Preventative physical fitness testing should become part of our daily medical practice. And an understanding of the risks of contact

*These physicians and clinics can be located through your local medical society, the nearest medical school, the American Orthopedic Society for Sports Medicine (430 North Michigan Avenue, Chicago, Illinois) or the American Medical Association (535 North Dearborn Street, Chicago, Illinois).

sports as well as knowledge of the movements of sports will come as all the specialties work together."

Adds Dr. Tenley Albright, a surgeon who won the 1956 Olympic figure skating title and now specializes in sports injuries, "When I was competing, everything was done by trial and error. Now the field of sports medicine is necessary for maximum health of the athlete, particularly because there are so many chronic injuries as we expect more and more of these young bodies. One of the things we haven't gotten to yet is being able to set firm guidelines — to say that it isn't wise for a body of a certain age or a certain type to train at a certain rate. I think we're going to be looking for guidelines from sportsmedicine that are going to be hard to give, but are going to be crucial to the welfare of our young athletes."

# 10
# The Sift

Fear is a powerful natural force, and the great athletes use it, control it, and they make it work for them. Fear gives them extra strength. The adrenalin makes the heart pump faster, which brings more oxygen to the body, then more energy. But fear is like fire. If you don't control it, it will destroy you and everything around you.

—Cus D'Amato, former
boxing manager

**I** am thirteen years old. Tomorrow I will be taking my third skating test. From the previous tests I know what to expect. Three stern-faced judges bundled in overcoats will stand less than two feet away, staring while I skate each of the eight figures. They'll watch to see that my body is straight, my legs steady. After I trace each figure three times, trying to make each tracing fall on top of the last, the judges will get down on their hands to inspect the tracings. They'll put down red markers to be sure that the circles are aligned, and check to see that there are no flats or premature changes of edge when I turn backward or forward. Then they will furiously scribble their remarks on their clipboards.

I know what to expect, but still I am nervous. For from the third to the eighth test, the highest, the skater must not only execute variations on the figure eight, but also skate devilish little figures called loops, which are about one sixth the size of the figure eight in diameter. With so little room to maneuver, the slightest wobble spells disaster. One goof on a loop and six months of practice go down the drain.

As I walk into the arena the next morning, the silence is eerie. The ice, usually chalky and rutted by the end of our daily practice sessions, lies gray and unblemished. My mother helps me put on my special test dress — a navy blue skating costume with a touch of lace around the neck and sleeves — and fixes my long hair into a neat bun. I lace up my newly polished skates, my coach wishes me good luck, and finally one of the judges summons me onto the ice.

On the loops my legs start shaking. No commands from my

*head can get them to stop. After the test the man and two women emerge from the judges' room and deliver the verdict. "I'm sorry," one says, her voice soft with sympathy. "You failed."*

*They have better news for my friend Dorothy Hamill, who has recently passed her second test and has also taken her third today. She passed. We had agreed that whatever happened, she would sleep over at my house that night. Unlike most eleven-year-olds, she does not gloat over her victory. For the rest of the day, she steers us clear of any activity that is remotely competitive. But later that night, as Dorothy sleeps on the other side of the room, I toss in my bed. One thing is clear: Dottie is fearless and I am not. But the causes of my fears are unknown and unnerving.*

*One month later I fracture my leg and ankle in a skiing accident. My Olympic hopes are dashed. But I am secretly relieved. For I have already come to the conclusion that I cannot pass the test unless God miraculously intervenes and banishes my fears. My broken leg gives me the ready-made excuse I've been looking for to quit.*

I don't know why I failed the test that day. The loops were difficult, but I had done them flawlessly hundreds of times before in practices. Perhaps it was the sight of the judges. Perhaps it was my desire not to disappoint my parents and coach. Perhaps it was my fear of being surpassed by Dorothy Hamill. The accident prevented me from ever knowing whether I had the emotional stamina to make it to the top, and I was beginning to sense that succeeding in skating was less a measure of athletic ability than of psychological toughness. Deep down I knew, and was embarrassed and saddened by the knowledge, that I probably did not have what it takes.

With the onset of adolescence comes the first major sifting process for the young athlete. Besides the changes brought about by physical maturation and development, a host of new pres-

sures is brought to bear on the competitors. Many of them fail
to withstand these pressures and drop out.

"A very young athlete often must face in hours or days the
kind of pressure that occurs in the life of an achievement-
oriented man over several years," write sports psychologists Bruce
Ogilvie and Thomas Tutko in a *Psychology Today* article entitled
"Sport: If You Want to Build Character, Try Something Else."
"The potential for laying bare the personality structure of the
individual is considerable. When the athlete's ego is deeply invested in sports achievement, very few of the neurotic mecha-
nisms provide adequate or sustaining cover. Basically, each must
face his moment of truth and live with the consequences."

As my experience shows, many young athletes drop out because they are unable to withstand the psychological pressures.
For in sports, as in other aspects of life, those who survive tend
not only to be the fittest, but also those with stronger personalities. Psychological studies indicate that successful athletes in
all sports consistently show fewer signs of psychopathology and
lower levels of anxiety, neuroticism, and depression than less
successful athletes and the general population. Although personality types among competitors vary widely, successful athletes share one common characteristic — emotional stability.
Those without strong self-assurance simply aren't strong enough
to perform well consistently.

The problem for many young athletes today is not so much
facing the moment of truth but waiting around for it. In many
junior tennis tournaments competitors may have to play for days
to qualify for a spot in the main draw. And the main draw may
still be so crammed with competitors that in order for the tournament to fit into a weekend, competitors must often play two
or more matches a day, with long stretches of boredom and/or
anxiety in between. The player seldom has the luxury of suffering alone, since the locker room is likely to be crammed with
other players and their coaches and parents (as well as his own),

all in a state of high tension. Representatives of sporting goods companies, prospective agents, college recruiters, and tournament sponsors are outside, waiting to persuade the top juniors to use their equipment or management services, attend their universities, or appear at their tournaments.

"It's like a zoo," says Paul Annacone. "During the last year of high school, the politicking gets especially intense. When you're out on the court you're thinking, 'Well, maybe I should go to this college, but that coach wants me more.' There are so many factors that can fog your views and affect your game."

The pressures have become so great and so diverse that even the strongest personalities are liable to succumb. "Stress increases as the child progresses because of the greater number of people who have invested in that talent," says psychologist Bruce Ogilvie. "When the child is young, sports are a very innocent thing. The demands are there, but they aren't that important. The child starts doing something because he or she has some aptitude and finds joy in it. But then the parents start getting their needs involved, and then the neighborhood, school, community, state, nation, and world enter in. When children reach the age of about 16 they begin to feel social responsibility. Their performance has to be of a certain order or they feel they have disappointed their parents, coach, fans, or the press. The pressures magnify almost geometrically as you go up the sports ladder."

A certain degree of selfishness is needed to dispel these pressures. Those who feel too much responsibility to others may become too nervous to compete well. At age ten, Meredith Rainey defeated more than 300 girls her age to capture the quarter-mile event at the Colgate Women's Games, a track and field championship for 22,000 inner-city youngsters. As she posed for pictures at the finish line, she threw her arms around her two sisters, Schuyler and Ellen, then twelve and seven respectively, and handed one her trophy and the other a bouquet of flowers.

A victorious Meredith Rainey at the Colgate Games.

"I didn't feel that I should be getting the flowers and the trophy while they got nothing," she explained. "I wondered if I would be able to put up with it if they were off doing something else and Mommy had to be with them."

"We've all been very proud of Meredith," said her mother, Carol. "But at times it's been hard on her sisters. It isn't easy for them when Meredith flies off to competitions in Florida, California, and Arizona. To her sisters, that's very romantic and glamorous. But they don't envy the work part."

Even though Schuyler and Ellen openly admitted that Meredith's training regimen was not for them, they sometimes became angry when people asked, "Are you the runner?" And their mother and sister usually didn't come home from track practice until 7 or 8 P.M., and by that time Schuyler and Ellen were hungry, lonely, and bored. They weren't complainers, but Meredith knew how they felt. "I always used to feel sorry for them," she says, "knowing that they had to be home by themselves. I know how much I hated it the few times I had to be cooped up at home and my mother wasn't there."

She was also aware of the sacrifices of her coach. To Meredith, whose parents are divorced, coach Fred Thompson of the Brooklyn Atoms was godlike. Indeed, Thompson's commitment to his runners, both on and off the track, has earned him the nickname "Freddy the Saint." From the time Thompson founded the Atoms twenty-four years ago, he has struck an agreement with each of his runners. If they work hard in practice and in school, he will get them to the competitions. One year, for instance, Thompson paid airfares for fifteen girls, including Meredith, to attend the Nationals in Arizona. Although the youngsters later sold raffle tickets and sponsors pledged their support, Thompson was never fully reimbursed for his $7,000.

Thompson's dedication was not lost on his young runners, but his generosity created another pressure for Meredith. "I enjoyed traveling to different places," she says. "But the best time for me was after the competition was over. When I got there I couldn't stop thinking about how nervous I was. I wished the day I was scheduled to run wouldn't come or wouldn't come so fast. At the Nationals in Arizona, especially, I felt that if I didn't do well I would have let Freddy down, because he'd paid all that money for me to get there."

At the Colgate Games the next year, Meredith placed sixth. The following year, she failed to qualify for the finals. By the next year, she had quit. "It's less of a strain on my family, now that everybody isn't following my schedule," says the thirteen-year-old. "I was relieved when I went to see the Colgate Games this year because I didn't have to feel nervous. I missed competing, but it wasn't a sad kind of missing it. It was diff-er-ent," she says, drawing out the last syllable, trying to define the change in her life. "It was hard seeing everybody I used to compete with. But I didn't long to be running."

By the time the athlete reaches Olympic level, the demand for achievement is compounded by the pressure of national pride. "Not only must they perform well, the Olympic athlete must also be a positive example to the world for a national ideology. The Olympic Committee indoctrinates athletes with feelings that their performance will reflect directly upon how other nations view their country. This represents the height of human exploitation in sport," says Dr. Bruce Ogilvie. "Forty percent of our Olympic team members experience a level of emotional stress sufficient to cause them to seek some psychological intervention prior to the event."

Dr. Ogilvie discovered much about the stresses of elite athletes almost incidentally, while addressing a group of Olympic-bound figure skaters at the Olympic Training Center in Colorado Springs. "I was making a presentation about what the behavioral sciences had to offer the figure skater and the type of psychological preparation required at the national level. One of the things I talked about was the emotional cost of success — how no child is ever really prepared to handle it. And then I gave some case histories. This is when they all had a chance to measure me — my methods and my sincerity. I told them that while I was at the training center I would never approach them. But if there was anything they wanted to talk about, they could just grab my elbow and pull me away. And that's what they did. One skater said, 'Let's go away and have a glass of wine.' Another wanted to sit in her room and talk. About 90 percent of the skaters came up to me and wanted to talk."

The sports psychologist is a new kind of specialist who has emerged to help competitors eliminate mental blocks and slumps. Using visualization and relaxation techniques, the sports psychologist helps the athlete train the mind in much the same way that the coach helps build the muscles. Mental exercises fortify confidence and exclude distractions. Dr. Bruce Ogilvie is one of the field's founding fathers. Over the past thirty years he has counseled eight professional basketball teams, fourteen major league baseball teams, five National Football League teams, and the national gymnastics and figure skating teams. Sixty years old and pencil thin, he speaks in a slow, soothing, almost hypnotic voice.

After hearing Dr. Ogilvie speak at the Olympic Training Center, figure skater David Santee telephoned the psychologist and was invited to come to his California home. David stayed for three days of marathon talks. "David had a series of bad performances in a row, which built up in intensity," recalls Dr. Ogilvie. "His self-confidence was shaken to the point where he was skating defensively. He was so anxiety-ridden that he'd work himself into a frazzle before he even got on the ice. Instead, we wanted him to ride on the sharpest edge, on the most self-enhancing edge, of what I knew to be his vast physical talent. So together we rummaged around his nature to find things that really made him feel light, expansive, and most important, totally in control. We made tapes out of his consciousness, using his own nurturant images and cognitions. They had to be his own thoughts, and very personal. For I know what will elevate me, but it wouldn't work for David or anyone else."

One of the things that elevated Santee, Ogilvie discovered, was the movie *Rocky*. Drawing parallels between Santee's and Rocky's struggles, Ogilvie redefined David's approach to skating. At the 1980 Olympics, David listened to his relaxation tapes before competing and then skated to his beloved "Rocky" theme song. Santee turned in the finest performance of his career, raising his fist in the finish, in true Rocky style, as he placed fourth. In the world championships a few months later, he placed a close second.

David had become hyperaroused before competition because he feared he might not do his best. In some sports, where the physical risks are greater, fear of pain and injury can intrude even at the top echelons of competition to increase the level of anxiety. In equestrian events, for example, horses and riders have become so technically accomplished that selecting a winner is very difficult. The only way the judge could choose among the 182 eighteen-years-and-under qualifiers at the national 1981 Maclay championship was to construct what was, in the opinion of some trainers and owners, a frighteningly dangerous course. First there was the "in-and-out" — two fences set so tightly that the horse could take only one stride between them, with the second fence set so close to the corner that the horses could barely clear the side wall. Then there was the "bounce," an obstacle that allowed not even one stride between jumps. After clearing one solid wall, the horse immediately had to lift itself and its rider up to clear another, a maneuver seldom required of professional riders, let alone teenage amateurs. The course was so tricky and so dangerous that some felt it was clearly more a test of survival than of riding skill. A judge has claimed that "the course is not dangerous. It was merely ill-executed by children who weren't properly prepared." However, most of the horses either cantered thunderously up to the two jumps and stopped dead, or else attempted the jumps and stumbled, tripping and sending their riders flying.

Neil Ashe, a young rider from Tennessee, made the mistake of thinking harder about clearing the corner than completing the "out" part of the "in-and-out." Because he jumped too early, his horse's feet got caught in the fence, and the animal somersaulted through the air. While the horse was airborne the girth snapped, releasing Neil and the saddle. The young boy crashed to the ground, landing flat on his back. A hush fell over the thousands of spectators in New York's Madison Square Garden as the boy lay unmoving on the ground. As Neil was carried away on a stretcher, more than one young rider's dreams were revised. Nine-year-old Janet Kovak, a spectator who had been training seriously for a year to perhaps compete one day, turned to her mother and whispered, "Mom, I don't think I want to ride in the Maclay after all." As it turned out, Ashe miraculously suffered only a chipped vertebra. And Janet Kovak is still jumping. But such events do leave lasting mental scars, both on those who suffer serious spills and on those who merely watch.

Lee Gargel, the thirteen-year-old Aspen skier, took a serious fall in a downhill race when he was ten. Only lately has he been able to put it out of his mind. "In downhill, once you take a bad fall and hurt yourself, you're afraid of speed," says Lee. "And in downhill, speed is the name of the game. If you don't go fast, you don't win. After that real bad fall, my results in slalom were still okay, but my downhill results were terrible. I've just come over that this year. But it's taken three years to put it behind me."

Most athletes who are training and competing hard will experience some degree of physical pain, ranging from occasional black-and-blue bruises to perpetual muscle aches. "We trained until we hurt," recalls Meredith Rainey, who ran two hours a day, five days a week. "I came home with my knees aching and my back and arms sore. I discovered a lot of muscles I didn't know I had."

In fact, improving in a sport means stressing the muscles to the point at which they are mildly injured. Healing strengthens them and gives them an improved capacity to store glycogen, the muscle fuel. This is what the training effect is all about— stressing the muscles, giving them time to recover, and then stressing them again. But, if the muscles are stressed before the fibers have adequately healed and the stores of glycogen and potassium have been replenished, the fibers will become more severely injured rather than strengthened. Well-trained athletes therefore get into the practice of alternating heavy training days with slower, easier workouts.

Top athletes, who are totally familiar with their bodies and capabilities, usually recognize the warning signals. They can distinguish between temporary muscle aches and pain that signals torn muscles, ligaments, or tendons. They know when to ease up and when to push themselves. But younger competitors often think of themselves as invulnerable. They are usually less aware of how their bodies function, nor are they encouraged to dwell on the source and nature of their pain by overzealous coaches. They may well be told to ignore the only means by which nature can tell them something is wrong. Sports psychologist Thomas Tutko, for one, is incensed by this attitude. "The injustice is that the child cannot be honest; if he said it did not hurt, he would be lying. To train a child to lie about pain, and have him play regardless of injury, is foolish and just short of criminal," says Dr. Tutko.

Some children choose to quit after experiencing high doses of fear, pain, or injury. Others simply lose their motivation. Those who have had a physical head start thanks to early maturation often lose their interest when others start to catch up. "Maturation is the single most important variable in early athletic success in children," says sports psychologist Rainer Martens, author of *Joy and Sadness in Children's Sports.* "The child who starts early and excels early becomes the big star and gets lots of attention. But other kids' biological clocks then start ticking and they may bypass the prodigy. This can cause problems, not only for the young athlete who has become used to the spotlight, but also for coaches and parents who mistakenly attribute the fall from stardom to the erroneous belief that the early maturer is no longer putting forth the needed effort rather than to the improvement of the other youngsters."

Often the child's loss of interest is the result not only of a slowdown in improvement, but also of the burgeoning social attractions of the teenage years. Girls who have spent seven to ten years in narrowly focused intensive training suddenly become aware that their classmates are going to school basketball games and dances while they are going to bed at 9 P.M. Before, the dedication may have defined them as special; now, more interested in dating or "hanging out," they may view their training as a sacrifice. Perhaps for the first time they realize that they can make decisions concerning their careers. The athlete begins to ask crucial questions: Who am I doing this for? What does it all mean? And the most important question: Do I want to continue? Some renew their commitments and make a final run for the top. Others decide they do not have the desire to continue training.

Fifteen-year-old Torrance York, a student at the prestigious Spence School in New York City, remembers her early interest in gymnastics. "You know these kids who you always see hopping around and can't sit down? Well, that's what I *used* to be like," she laughs. Early on, a gymnastics coach at Spence spotted Torrance doing cartwheels and said, "Hey, you oughta get into gymnastics." So, at age seven, her gymnastics program began. Three times a week after school her mother, Janet, drove Torrance to Schnaar's Gymnasium, a $1\frac{1}{2}$-hour commute each way

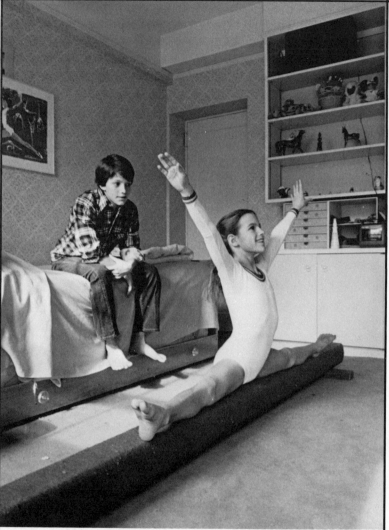

Torrance York practices in her room as brother Clifton looks on.

to Farmingdale, Long Island. For seven years her day ran from 8 A.M. to 11 P.M. And on the days she wasn't training at Schnaar's, she practiced at Spence, where she quickly became the star of the gymnastics team.

At age ten Torrance was the all-around gymnastics champion of New York City. She had competed nationally and internationally. She became a minor celebrity when Jill Krementz documented her life in a book entitled *A Very Young Gymnast*. And yet both Torrance and Janet York began to have doubts. Mrs. York was particularly disturbed by the ferocity of the competition. "Because I didn't go to all the practices, I was pretty much unknown to most of the other mothers," she says. "But one competition, when Torrance was nine, I'll never forget. The woman behind me whispered, 'See that little girl down there? Don't you wish she'd break her neck?' Then I realized she was pointing at Torrance."

At the same time, Torrance began to doubt her perseverance. "I never considered myself as good as the girls at Schnaar's. Sometimes I beat some of them, but I couldn't really compare myself to them because somehow they were different. I was going to what I considered was a better school and told myself that maybe I was working harder in school while they were working harder in gymnastics. I did know that after a long day at school and not liking snack dinners and not eating much of the stuff my mother packed for me, that by the time I got there I was often hungry and had a headache. I'd always looked forward to going during the day, but once I got there I wasn't really in the mood.

"The routine began to get to me," she added. "Since I was used to practicing every day, if I went away — even for a weekend — I'd get out of shape. My hands would rip and bleed when I returned to the bars. But I couldn't stand always staying in the city during vacations when all my school friends went away."

Torrance hit a plateau. Janet York went to the coaches at

Schnaar's, telling them she was considering stopping further training there and just continuing gym at Spence. "No, no, no," they said. "She's just on a plateau right now. She'll pull out of it. She's one of the best on our team." But Torrance didn't improve. "I feel I could have gotten out of my rut, if I had enough willpower," she says. "But I don't think I wanted it badly enough. When I was little I'd try a new trick a few times and get it. If it took too long, I wasn't interested. Now I've reached the point where all my basic tricks are pretty decent. But to go above that, I'd have to do double backs and double twists. When I go to do them, it's terrifying. I think if I worked at it a lot, I could do it. But I just don't feel it's worth it anymore."

Torrance left Schnaar's, and with it the fast track of regional and national competitions leading up to the Olympics. "I'd just like to maintain my skills, so that I can teach while I'm in college," she says. "I probably won't be a professional coach, but I like teaching people and making up routines. It's hard seeing my friends compete and not being there. I'll always have a few regrets I suppose. But in the end, I'm glad I quit."

Says gymnastics coach Bill Sands, "The dropout rate in gymnastics, as in most sports, is high. But I don't think that's unnatural. We've invented a word called burn-out when the kid has lost interest and brand him or her with it like it's some kind of scarlet letter. We tend to forget that the typical adult changes jobs five or six times." Adds Dr. Tom Bassler, who presides over a family of ultramarathoners: "Deciding to leave a sport that one has been doing for ten years is usually a sign of maturity, not cowardice. In *Runner's World* magazine, track coach Bill Delinger described runner Rudy Chapa's decision to give up a superlative running career to go to law school as 'losing his desire to excel.' And this from a college coach, who supposedly should value education! When Rudy decided to switch his efforts from running to earning a law degree he should have been congratulated, not criticized in a national magazine. The only thing damaged by the maturation of age-group champions are the careers of collegiate coaches who must now find new material to work with."

Indeed, quitting is similar to defection or revolution for those who must shoulder the ambitions of parents and coaches. A well-known swimmer recalls that when she was in high school the team coach, an Olympic swimmer himself, needed her to make the Olympic team more than she did. "Every day for eight years he'd hold me with tears rolling down his face and say, 'Baby, you're going to be on that Olympic stand. You're going to make it. We're going to be the best in the world.' " She dropped competitive short-distance swimming to pursue marathon swimming. But one of her teammates killed himself. "He did his best," she said. "But our coach kept telling him that his life wasn't worthwhile unless he became an Olympic champion."

Knowing the havoc that adolescence can wreak on a sports career, some coaches try to tiptoe around it by keeping the athlete as isolated as possible, as was the case with Debbie Meyer. Other coaches try to subvert it by building up an athlete's dependence on sports early on. The coach of a world champion figure skater admitted, "I tried to get Maria [a pseudonym] sucked up into the world of international competition at an early age so that when she hit adolescence she would be so wrapped up in world-class competition, and so famous, that she couldn't justify getting out."

But even winners like Lisa Castellucci, who eventually triumphed over 181 competitors in the 1981 Maclay championship, feel torn by the trade-offs. Before the finals, she told Linda Bird Francke of *New York* magazine: "I never had the time to play school sports or make any friends or just hang out. I always had to worry about a horse show." Of the horse show circuit she said, "They are not normal people. They are just a big social clique. All you talk about is horse shows, because no one knows each other outside of the horse shows. It's all so fake."

After the finals, tears of relief welled up in her eyes, and for the first time that day, she smiled. But she still wasn't sure the trophy was worth the cost. "I guess so," she said slowly. "I guess it is."

Success, in addition to reinforcement from parents and coaches, sometimes helps quell the teenager's doubts. "The most sincere test of the parent/child relationships occurs when the sports career moves from the introductory stage of pure joy to the level where there's not as much improvement, the increments of success are smaller, and there is a greater incidence of failure," says psychologist Thomas Tutko. "The child is under great strain. If the teenager can openly discuss the doubts with the parent and the parent can still be accepting and encouraging, that's great. But it's also very rare, especially considering the generally stormy nature of adolescence."

Close parent/child bonds are also often loosened by the financial sacrifices parents have made over the years. Although the sport may have started as a hobby, by adolescence it has become an investment. The teenager is often acutely aware of the money that has been spent to subsidize the career, in some cases because in the name of motivation parents may harp on their financial sacrifices. Either the child or the parents may decide that the rate of progress is no longer keeping up with the cash outflow. For example, at age ten Priscilla Hill became the youngest skater ever to pass the eighth test. She seemed destined for greatness. But somehow, over the years, she was surpassed — first by Dorothy Hamill, then by Linda Fratianne, and finally by Elaine Zayak. At age nineteen, as she competed in her second World Championships, she entered the final free-skating program in sixth place. Moments before she took the ice her father, Ralph, summed up Priscilla's plight, "If she bombs tonight, I'm afraid I'm going to have to pull the plug on her," he told a reporter. "I'm afraid there will be no other alternative but to tell her it's over. And that's going to be the hardest thing I've ever done in my life."

205

Many families are finding it increasingly difficult to finance a competitor. When athletes reach national prominence, the sports organizations pay for international travel and in some sports, equipment manufacturers supply athletes with free gear. But reaching this level requires years of scrimping to pay for travel and equipment, lessons, club memberships, tournament entry fees, and the daily cost of using a sports facility for training. Indeed, the costs of competing in individual sports like skating, gymnastics, skiing, and tennis are comparable to the costs of an Ivy League education. Dom Annacone estimates that while Paul was chasing a national ranking and attending Nick Bollettieri's Tennis Academy his expenses exceeded $13,000 a year. Before Elaine Zayak won the national championship, her father, Richard, paid $25,000 a year to subsidize her career.

Elaine Zayak has been able to become a world champion with a father who owns a bar, but had her sport been riding, she would have needed the resources of a corporation president. All parents of young riders will have to pay $10,000 to $50,000 a year for travel, clothing, and lessons for their equestrians (expenses that rise to approximately $70,000 in the year preceding the all-important Maclay junior championship), but parents who can top off these initial expenses with the purchase of a fine thoroughbred are more likely to see a successful return on their investment. Those children whose parents cannot afford an already trained $100,000 thoroughbred face not only the difficult task of breaking in a green mount, but also the psychological pressure of knowing that the horse may buckle in difficult situations. Most riders who enter shows fearful of being outclassed leave the ring without ribbons, and eventually leave the sport altogether.

Blonde, green-eyed Susanna Schroer made it to the "A" circuit on a shoestring budget. On her family's Fayre Horse Farm in Bedford, New York, she began riding before she could walk. At age three she competed in her first show, and over the next

Scarborough Fayre and Susanna Schroer are both happy as
the mare wins Grand Champion Hunter honors, 1981.

twelve years, as she showed the ponies she and her mother raised on their farm, Susanna's love of horses grew. But as she was winning shows, she was learning the economics of riding. While some of her competitors rode well-schooled thoroughbreds, had daily lessons, attended riding academies, had closets full of breeches and boots, and showed up at the stables only to ride, Susanna took shortcuts by buying her first horse, a three-year-old named Razmataz, for a rock-bottom $5,000 and taking only one lesson a week. She raised funds by joining her mother in the business of buying and selling ponies and by exercising and showing other people's horses. She cut corners further by driving to the weekly shows with her mother in their own van, braiding and grooming her horse herself, and staying in inexpensive hotels.

When Susanna bought her horse, the first thing she did was to change the horse's name from Razmataz to Scarborough Fayre, in keeping with the Fayre Farm tradition. But developing the mare's potential proved more difficult than changing her name. Her jumping technique was all wrong, her stride needed improvement, and her mind needed sharpening. "Young horses like to spook and play," explains Susanna. "Their concentration span is short. It's like trying to reach algebra to a four-year-old. You've got to start at $1 + 1 = 2$ and then work up the line." The learning process worked both ways. Susanna had already become a champion showing ponies, but she had to start all over when she decided to show horses. The fences were bigger and the other riders older and more experienced. Balancing a green thoroughbred, moreover, was much more difficult than controlling the shorter strides of a pony.

For three years Susanna and her horse worked together, trying to make Scarborough Fayre into a top show hunter. "There were times when I felt like I wasn't getting anywhere," Susanna recalls. "I'd go back to the barn and cry. But you've got to pick yourself up and keep working at it." One of Susanna's greatest difficulties involved developing faith in her horse. "I guess since Scarborough Fayre didn't cost as much as a 'good' horse, I didn't think she was one. At one of the shows George Morris, one of the country's top trainers, was in the warm-up area coaching one of his best junior riders. And then there was my horse, spooking a little at the strange fences," says Susanna. "At times like that I'd catch myself wishing we could have afforded a made horse."

Junior-level riding ends at age eighteen, and the final year is known for its competitive frenzy. Susanna graduated from high school early and put off college for a year to concentrate solely on her riding, joining the other prospective champions on the winter circuit in Florida. She would need four blue ribbons to qualify for the two major indoor shows in the fall, the Medal at Harrisburg and the Maclay in New York. In addition, her horse needed twenty-five blue ribbons in junior hunter competitions to qualify for these championships.

In April she returned to New York. Although she was weary from the horse-show-a-week routine, Susanna and Scarborough Fayre were making a name for themselves. At the important Farmington, Connecticut, show, she was the first rider ever to win both the equitation championship and a special equitation class, the Governor's Cup. "As the season went on, I began to learn the ropes," Susanna says. "I knew my horse lacked the composure of a seasoned campaigner. I knew I had to be particularly careful so the strange sights and sounds at a new show didn't upset her. But I also knew that her attitude was wonderful. She might spook a little, but she'd never stop or get nasty. She didn't even seem to care if I got left behind and caught her in the mouth. As I realized that Scarborough Fayre was holding her own despite her greenness, I straightened up and rode into each class in a way that let the judges know I was going to win it. Not flashy, but confident."

While living at home, she drove her van to Nimrod Farms in

Westport, Connecticut, once a week to receive additional training from Ronnie Mutch and his assistant, Timmy Kees. One of the best trainers in the East, Mutch also met Susanna at each show and schooled her and Scarborough Fayre before each class. By the end of the summer, she had qualified for both the Medal class and junior hunter division at Harrisburg and the Maclay.

In the first junior hunter class at Harrisburg, Scarborough Fayre rode like a dream. Well enough, Susanna thought, to win. But the judges placed her sixth. It was the same old story, she muttered to herself. A green horse that didn't cost a lot of money. A third place in the hack class the next day didn't do much to alleviate her disappointment. Only one junior hunter class remained: the stake class, a special jumping class in which riders dress formally in long black tail-coats, flowing white ties, and bowler derbies. "Are you feeling all right?" Dana Douglass, who had also helped train Scarborough Fayre, asked Susanna before she entered the ring. "No," the young rider answered through clenched teeth.

Again Scarborough Fayre performed beautifully, but by now Susanna assumed that even the best wasn't good enough. Leaving the ring, she took her horse to the schooling area, beyond reach of the loudspeakers. Only when she saw her mother, in the distance, leap into Dana's arms did she realize she had won. Susanna jogged into the ring with tears running down her face. "I knew I could do it," she thought. Three years of hard work had gone into making Scarborough Fayre a quality horse.

The culmination of the year, she hoped, would be the blue ribbon at the Maclay. Susanna had amassed more points than any junior rider in the country. Now, after winning at Harrisburg, she was fully confident. But to accommodate all the qualifiers, the Maclay began before dawn. As the day wore on, the commotion around the schooling area increased. Susanna sensed that her horse was unsettled. When she got into the ring, Scarborough Fayre refused to jump the bounce. Susanna was disqualified. Once out of the ring, she burst into tears. Losing was bad enough, but that very weekend Scarborough Fayre was sold. Susanna was going off to college in the fall, and at least during freshman year, she wouldn't be able to take care of a horse. Only one horse in the country had scored more points in shows that year. Now Scarborough Fayre could command the highest price and help pay for Susanna's tuition.

The Maclay is the climax of a junior riding career. Most riders go to college after the junior championship and leave competition. Susanna, however, has long-term goals in riding. She is a student at the University of Vermont, where she is majoring in animal science. During the summers Susanna plans to improve her riding by working with several professional riders and trainers. After college she hopes to return to riding full-time, and if all goes well, to ride for the U.S. Equestrian Team before becoming a coach and trainer.

Despite her loss in the Maclay, Susanna was named the Professional Horseman's Association Junior Rider of the Year. Her initial disappointment at Madison Square Garden has been eased by a reevaluation of her junior riding career. "It's no fun sometimes to train your own horse and look after it, but to me it's all part of the experience. You start to understand your horse; you learn how she thinks. Sure, I sometimes felt like I was knocking my head against a brick wall, thinking I would never get anywhere and feeling, 'Oh, there's another kid who just popped out with another $100,000 horse. Of course she's going to beat me.' But I just had to keep going and saying, 'I can do it.'

"In the Maclay," she continues, "the horse can be so much of the whole act. My horse might have been a little more difficult and maybe it proved a disadvantage. But the best rider and horse will eventually rise to the top. And what I did all year means a lot more to me than winning the Maclay. Scarborough Fayre and I both learned a lot from each other. We both peaked at the same time. And working together, though frustrating at times, was also a lot of fun. In the end, I'm glad I did it my way, rather than being handed a $100,000 horse on a silver platter. I think the other kids missed out on a lot. There's so much more to it that they'll never see."

If biology has a fluid hand in setting absolute limits at different stages of development, parents, coaches, and athletes themselves serve as biology's interpreters. A coach decides who will be the first-string quarterback and who will be cut from the team. Parents decide whether the child's progress continues to merit expenditures of so much time and money. Children conclude whether fear and injuries are worth overcoming and whether sports continue to be number one in their pantheon of interests.

The sift thus operates at all levels of amateur competition, from the Little League to the Olympics. The long-term psychological effect of dropping out of sports seems to depend largely on the point at which the leave-taking occurs, the degree of success and self confidence attained, and whether the impetus is internal (personal fear, loss of interest) or external (pressure from parents and coaches, injury, or insufficient funds). For those like Meredith Rainey and Torrance York, whose decision to drop out of sports was made individually relatively early, motivation and ambition are easily channeled elsewhere. They already see their sports experience nostalgically, trading memories of long hours of training for the memories of the exhilaration of winning, the bond of working with an inspiring coach, and the wonderful freedom of movement they experienced.

Those who are eliminated from sports at higher levels by forces beyond their control may also eventually look back on the experience as a positive one. But at the moment of elimination (and for months and possibly years later) they are hounded by questions. Could I have won the World Championship if my father had let me compete one more year? Could I have done better in the Maclay if my horse had been a fancy thoroughbred rather than a green mare?

There have been no studies of those who fall through the competitive sieve and fade away. The only research to date looks at Olympic gold medalists. Dr. Bruce Ogilvie, who has conducted many of these studies, reports, "The Olympic gold medalists turn out to be very special young men and women. They talk about the travel, the people, learning to be socially gregarious, making contacts so when they finish they can get into careers. If you make the gold, it opens many, many doors. But what about the youngster who spends 12 or 14 years of his or her life at a sport and ends with no rewards or recognition? Do they feel their growth has been stunted? The ones who win the gold medal certainly don't feel that way. But the ones who don't place we never hear from again. They join the rest of us."

Competitive careers in amateur sports such as swimming or track and field are self-limiting, usually coming to a close at the end of the athlete's college years. Other sports, such as gymnastics, skiing, figure skating, and squash, extend beyond college but have limited professional circuits. But for those in golf, tennis, basketball, bowling, hockey, soccer, baseball, and football, the culmination of their careers comes when they join the professional ranks. And it is here that the athlete's world expands still further as another sifting process takes place.

# 11
# Turning Pro

**F**ebruary 1976. I am twenty-two years old and a member of the International Holiday on Ice. After recovering from my broken leg at age thirteen, I had regained my interest in skating, changed my specialty from free skating to ice dancing, calmed my fears, and had progressed to the highest (gold) test level by the time I finished high school. During college I kept one foot in the skating world by teaching at a local rink. I had wanted to travel after graduation, and becoming a chorus skater with an international ice show seemed like a perfect solution. I applied, auditioned, and was told that I would be starting in Nîmes, France, two months later.

Life as a professional figure skater has not been quite what I expected. Upon my arrival in Nîmes, I was told that my first assignment was to be a skating carrot in "La Revue de Bugs Bunny." In the same show I was also a scantily clad seductress, a rhinestone-studded rock star, and a sword-wielding Roman soldier. As the troupe zigzagged through Europe, I found the work physically exhausting but also a lot of fun. It seemed the perfect interlude between the rigors of college and getting on with my life.

The show has now crossed the Atlantic and I am sitting around in costume backstage in Buenos Aires. I hear a knock on my carrot. A face peers through the peephole and a voice tells me that Dorothy Hamill has just won the Olympics. I feel a rush of joy. She did it! In front of millions of people, she came through. I'm immensely proud of her accomplishment and self-satisfied too, for I've known all along that she could become great.

I am also, I must admit, jealous. Now she will sign a million-

*dollar contract with the Ice Capades, while I make a measly $110 a week — before paying my hotel bill and food expenses. She will skate two numbers as opposed to my eight, and I doubt either appearance will be inside a cockroach-infested carrot. She'll have a separate dressing room with her name on the door, while I sit at a long table with thirty other girls, with naked light bulbs strung overhead and makeup, skates, and costumes strewn all over the place. If there is any glamour to be found in an ice show, Dorothy will undoubtedly find it.*

But I was wrong. A few months later, when I returned home, she sent me tickets to a performance of the Ice Capades at Madison Square Garden and invited me to visit her backstage afterwards. We met at the employees' entrance. Her ponytail was gone, long since styled into her famous haircut. She wore a lush full-length fur coat. Behind her designer eyeglasses were her familiar blue eyes. But they looked tired and dispirited. I wondered what was wrong. A few months later I read a story in *Esquire* magazine called "The Exploitation of Dorothy Hamill." It said that Dorothy had become a pawn of Madison Avenue, her agent, and television producers.

"How much control do you have over your own life?" asked the story's author Philip Taubman.

"None," she replied.

Taubman went on to describe that all Dorothy had wanted before the Olympics was to become a college student afterward. But national heroism changed all that. So did the offers from ice shows, the cosmetics industry, and television producers. Her parents had sunk deeply into debt to finance her career. She owed it to them, if not to herself, to cash in. But Dorothy had spent the past eleven years in the deep freeze of the skating rink. Her parents, too, were greenhorns when it came to the world of big business. She signed up with Jerry Weintraub, a big-time agent who promised her big-time bucks.

He delivered. She signed a million-dollar, two-year contract with the Ice Capades. Clairol signed her to endorse a shampoo called Short 'n' Sassy. The Ideal Toy Company came up with the idea of a Dorothy Hamill doll. And American Optical capitalized on her squint by hiring her to promote their glasses.

But what wasn't written into the contracts was that Dorothy would lose her freedom. Weintraub lined up several television specials for her. In one, the producers insisted that she leap through the page of a dictionary on which the word "winner" appeared. She had never skated through a dictionary. "I was scared to death," she told Taubman. He then described the fiasco that followed:

As she prepared for the stunt, a prop man noticed no one had scored the thick paper. Through negligence, the crew was ready to send Dorothy Hamill flying into a piece of paper that might not have torn easily. The problem was corrected. Dorothy took off down the ice and burst through the pages. No good, announced director Stan Harris. She was off-center. A backup page was brought onto the ice. Dorothy blasted through again. No good. This time she was not smiling. A third dictionary blowup was rolled out. By this time she felt like an animal in a circus act. The scene had to be right, the director told her. The take was the opening of the show. Dorothy obliged, hitting the paper on center with a smile.

She was a skater who had done nothing more than win an Olympic gold medal, but she now had to become an actress as well. "An Olympic performance is one thing. There's real tension and competition there. It grabs people. It's like the Miss America show. People are vying for something," explained the special's producer, Frank Brill, to Taubman. "That's not the case with these specials. We are now an entertainment vehicle competing with two other shows."

Taubman describes how Dorothy grew more frustrated. The Ice Capades, too, dictated her every move. They picked her music, set her choreography, and padded her costumes so her breasts would appear bigger. She was used to whipping around the ice in her own inimitable way; now they were making her do little mincing steps. They were robbing her of her fire. They were making her boring.

The article went on to say that she asked for an accounting of the television show's expenses. The ledger wasn't itemized. There was no way to tell if Weintraub was paying himself a salary as executive producer. She knew that the going rate for hosting a TV special was $100,000. As a guest star she could have asked for $30,000, yet she told Taubman she had not seen a penny. "I don't get paid," Dorothy said, "and I don't know why." Weintraub told her that all specials lost money. "I know Jerry Weintraub doesn't lose money making TV specials," she told Taubman. Yet she was afraid to confront her agent. Taubman asked her why. "Jerry Weintraub is like God," she said. "I hate to go and see him. I'm afraid he's going to yell at me."

She developed a bleeding ulcer. Her friends and family had trouble reaching her by telephone. As I suspected back in Buenos Aires, she did merit special accommodations and plane tickets, but her isolation from the rest of the troupe — indeed the world — was not welcome.

Taubman completed his *Esquire* article with this depressing summary:

Not yet twenty-two, she is frightened, defeated, and resigned. She has been overwhelmed by forces she does not comprehend. She has been ripped free of her moorings and swept away by the Big American Entertainment Machine. Theoretically, she could still walk away from it all, cut her losses, and regain control of her life. But that requires a toughness Dorothy finds difficult to muster. That's asking her to buck the weight of an entire culture, to be a martyr rather than a millionaire. The middle course, to make money and be master of her career, seems beyond her reach.

After the *Esquire* article appeared, Dorothy issued a statement that read:

"I am announcing today an extension of my management

contract with Jerry Weintraub for a renewal term of three years. The original three-year contract expires on April 15, 1979.

"I am taking this action as an expression of my faith and confidence in Jerry Weintraub. Frankly, I am prompted to do so by the appalling article concerning me that has just been released by Esquire Magazine. This article portrays me as 'uncomfortable' and 'distrustful' towards Jerry Weintraub.

"Nothing could be further from the truth. I regard Jerry Weintraub as a close personal friend whose professionalism and integrity have been indispensable to my career. My action in renewing my contract at this time is an expression of my friendship and respect for Jerry Weintraub which I am proud to proclaim.

"The theme of the Esquire article is that I have been exploited by all the people and organizations with whom I have had a business relationship during my professional career. This is their side not mine. I am associated with honorable people who have treated me fairly, and I resent Esquire's unfounded charges against them."

Dorothy Hamill has since acquired a new agent and has signed a new contract with Ice Capades that stipulated that instead of traveling nine months a year, she would travel only twelve weeks, to the cities of her choice. She repaid her parents by buying them a larger home in Riverside, Connecticut, and she married Dean-Paul Martin, the son of Dean Martin, who is a former professional tennis player and could understand her pressured and transient life-style. Although her life on the road is still hectic, she now feels secure with a home base in Beverly Hills.

For Olympic champions, college all-stars, and Wimbledon winners, the process of turning pro is similar to the way a major private corporation goes public. Agents are selected, million-dollar contracts are signed, press conferences are called, and sporting goods manufacturers outbid each other to see who can pay thousands of dollars to have the star endorse products he or she had been grateful to receive free. The publicity surrounding the event suggests to everyone — not least of all the athlete— that this pro career will be among the few that lasts a decade or more.

Most athletes, however, do not enter the pro ranks with the eyes of the world upon them. They are chosen in the later rounds of the hockey, football, baseball, and basketball drafts, or — if not drafted — show up at training camps as "walk-ons" and try to make the team as free agents. In racket sports and golf even the collegiate star must start at the bottom of the rankings and work his way up. Some of the best college tennis players — John McEnroe, Jimmy Connors, Gene Mayer, Chip Hooper — have quickly worked their way to the top, but the majority soon realize that junior-level or collegiate success doesn't necessarily translate to success in the pros. They scale down their expectations. While the superstar is launching a career, the lower-ranked player or second-stringer often thinks of his tenure in the pros as a job — a way to earn a living without working nine-to-five until he can no longer win enough to pay tour expenses, he grows tired of the transient pro life, or his contract is not renewed by management.

The gulf separating the superstars at the top and the crowds who flow into and out of the pro ranks is a relatively recent phenomenon. Pro golf, tennis, racquetball, and bowling tours until a few years ago could support only a limited number of male competitors. Ten thousand dollars was a large purse for an event. The pros were a coterie of superbly talented athletes, usually presided over by one superstar like Arnold Palmer or Rod Laver, whose supremacy was enduring. In team sports, too, the number of teams was limited and available positions were few. More attention was paid to college sports, in which play was spirited if sometimes a bit sloppy.

Then professional sports boomed. In 1970 professional football spilled over from Sunday afternoons to Monday nights and successfully competed with other prime-time television programs. The team of hyperbolic Howard Cosell, "Dandy" Don Meredith, and forthright Frank Gifford heightened the sense of drama and conflict, and in the process turned broadcasters first into personalities, then celebrities. Aided by new technologies such as slow motion, the instant replay, on-the-field directional microphones, and spectacular camerawork (a wide-angle shot of 100,000 fans from the Goodyear blimp, a zoom showing the pitcher's face contorting as he releases the ball), directors successfully transformed simple motions into visual magic. Sports programming was so successful that by 1980 all-sports cable TV channels were bringing fans an ever-expanding variety of sports contests.

Meanwhile, attendance at pro games swelled as spectators became fiercely loyal to their local teams. Car manufacturers, cosmetics firms, and liquor distillers were only a few of the industries that saw their sales figures take off as they got into the business of sponsoring bowl games and tennis tournaments. New teams, leagues, and circuits were added. The players' salaries skyrocketed. In many sports it became possible for the top athletes to earn more than $100,000 a year. The Professional Bowler's Tour, for instance, began in 1959 with three tournaments, 33 competitors, and a total purse of $49,000. By 1981 more than 2,600 bowlers competed on the $4-million, nationally televised, thirty-five-stop tour. Five bowlers earned more than $100,000, with Earl Anthony heading the list at $165,000. In tennis and golf, the top players can earn $40,000 or more in a weekend, while lower-ranked players can earn more than $100,000 a year without winning a major tournament. In racquetball, skiing, and rodeo top male competitors also earn more than $100,000 a year in prize money alone.

Boxing and the team sports hold promise of even greater riches. In only two bouts against Roberto Duran, Sugar Ray

Leonard raked in more than $16.7 million — more money than Joe Louis, Sugar Ray Robinson, and Jack Dempsey earned over their combined careers. In baseball the average player's salary jumped from $35,000 in 1970 to more than $143,000 ten years later, while the hardest hitters have been able to demand far more. In 1980 Dave Winfield signed a $20 million, ten-year contract with the New York Yankees. The next year Earvin "Magic" Johnson put his pen to the largest contract in sports history — $25 million over twenty-five years — with basketball's Los Angeles Lakers.

A professional sports career is now also a possibility for women. Since the creation of the Women's Tennis Association in 1973, prize money has increased 1,000 percent, from a million dollars on the initial Virginia Slims tour to the $10 million offered on the Avon and Toyota circuits in 1981. The $119,000 that Billie Jean King won in nineteen tournaments in 1971 would total more than $1.5 million today. By 1981 even the tenth-ranked woman, Mima Jausovec, earned a respectable $175,000. Prize money on the women's golf tour has sprouted from $1.2 million in 1975 to $6.4 million in 1982. Katie Monahan, the leading professional Grand Prix rider of 1982, earned more than $150,000 in money and merchandise — including two Mercedes-Benz cars. In the women's racquetball, squash, and skiing tours, which are newer, few of the female pros can support themselves solely on their prize money. Yet the total prize money in women's pro racquetball (which split from the men's tour in 1979) jumped from $100,000 in 1981 to $175,000 in 1982. Within the next few years, these less established sports should be able to support an increasing number of women.

Like Las Vegas gamblers, young athletes of both sexes and their parents are impelled toward professional sports by the high financial stakes. Boys who once memorized their idol's batting average can now recite his salary and contract clauses. Girls who once thought of sports as unfeminine have been stirred by such models as Chris Evert Lloyd, Peggy Fleming, Suzy Chaffee, Nancy Lieberman, Donna deVarona, Nancy Lopez, Cathy Rigby, and Robyn Smith. The dream of excellence is now partly a dream of striking it rich.

The process of turning pro varies with each sport. Some sports impose age requirements. To become a professional bowler one must average a score of 190 for two consecutive years in league play and also be eighteen or finished with high school. Pro hockey, baseball, and basketball leagues also require players to be eighteen or to have finished high school.* In professional football, a player cannot join the National Football League until he has graduated from college or until the year his classmates graduate.

In sports with no age restrictions (skating, tennis, racquetball, squash, and skiing), a player can officially turn pro simply by collecting prize money. But in order to enter major pro tournaments in the racket sports and golf, the new pro must play qualifying rounds. In tennis, where there are more than 900 male pros, it became necessary to establish separate satellite tours to determine eligibility for major tournaments. Hoping to be among the eight qualifiers in the 64-player main draw, the "qualies" arrive at major tournaments several days in advance and are required to play on inferior courts (often far removed from the center of town), dress in separate locker rooms, and play without benefit of referees. Worse, they must be able to foot the expenses of the professional tour, expenses that often run as high as $50,000 a year. Several of these players devote most of their time not to psyching themselves up for competition, but to pitching their talents to local friends and businesspeople as potential sponsors. With less worry about finances and more time to devote to their games, the pitch goes, their rankings will soar and the sponsors will soon be repaid in full. Sponsorship

*Major league baseball scouts often sidestep this eligibility requirement by signing youngsters from Latin America and Mexico, where the age requirements don't apply.

has put a few players, Tim Gullikson for one, on the tennis map, but in most cases, players who have failed without a sponsor fail to make it with one.

To prevent large numbers of aspiring players from joining the tour and then finding they can't meet the expenses, the professional golf association has limited the number of players who can turn pro each year. In October 1981, for example, more than 500 aspiring pros competed in six regional competitions. The 120 top scorers were then invited to play four rounds in a final qualifying contest. Of the 120, 72 survived the thirty-six-hole cut. At the clubhouse only twenty-five "cards" — the prestigious pieces of plastic that certify membership in the Touring Professional's Association (TPA) — were awarded. As if earning the card weren't difficult enough, the golfer must earn the right to keep it by playing within $2,000 of the total won by the 160th player on the money list during his first year, and then staying within the top 160 in all subsequent years.

Although the age at which players turn pro has recently dropped in several sports, the effect has been most dramatic in women's tennis. Most male pros keep their amateur ranking until they have had at least a taste of college tennis, but girls are now turning pro as young as age twelve. This is a function partly of maturation and partly of their respective games. Girls are physically mature by their mid-teens, while boys are still growing in their late teens and may not physically master the crucial elements of their game — the explosive serve and volley — until their twenties. Furthermore, boys are often deeply involved with other sports. John McEnroe, for instance, was not only captain of his high school tennis team but also a star in basketball and soccer.

Singleminded dedication to a sport, as well as a seemingly greater appetite for touring the country with a parent and/or personal coach, may also account for the influx of pint-size females into the pro ranks. Because success in the women's game

United Press International Photo

Stable of young pros: Andrea Jaeger (16),
Bettina Bunge (18), Tracy Austin (19), Susan Mascarin (17),
and Kathy Rinaldi (14), 1981.

depends as much on concentration and cognitive strategies as on powerful strokes, twelve- and thirteen-year-olds can often play competitively with girls several years older. When a girl who is thirteen can win her age division and also the one above, she may feel that the only true test of her talent lies in the pros. From a financial viewpoint her parents often find it difficult to justify her remaining an amateur. These thoughts can be fueled by prospective agents, who try to beat each other to the potential superstar's doorstep. One mother, whose tennis-playing daughters were invited by a prominent management group on an all-expense-paid trip to an exhibition match at a posh resort, reports that the real purpose of the excursion was not so much to play tennis as to give her daughters a good, casual introduction to the pro game. "The girls had a fabulous time," said the mother, "but when they got back I realized that there was a very strong pressure involved in this kind of thing, and that a kid would have to be exceptionally mature to see through it. And in a way, I don't blame the company. If one of my kids were going to turn pro, I'd probably have this company handle her. But that kind of campaign suddenly creates a lot of pressure on the kids and on the parents."

At age fifteen Kathy Rinaldi is already the fourteenth-ranked women's tennis player in the world. In 1981, after becoming the youngest player ever to reach the quarterfinals of the French Open and the youngest to win a match at Wimbledon, the fourteen-year-old gave up her amateur status. Turning pro was not an easy decision. True, she had zoomed through the junior ranks. Picking up her first racket at age four, by ten she had forsaken Girl Scouts, cheerleading, baton twirling, and piano lessons to become one of the top girls her age in the country. Two years later she swept all four national championships for her age group. She was starting to beat many of the seeded players on the professional tour by thirteen. But could a fourteen-year-old—

Le Coq Sportif

Kathy Rinaldi

even a mature girl like Kathy — juggle the rigors of the tour and her schoolwork? Was she ready for such a commitment?

Her parents, Lindi and Dennis, sat down with Phil de Picciotto, a young lawyer at ProServ, a marketing affiliate of Dell, Craighill, Fentress and Benton, a law firm founded in 1970 by former U.S. Davis Cup captain Donald Bell to handle the business and financial affairs of athletes. De Picciotto suggested that the move to the pros made good business sense. He outlined for the Rinaldis how much Kathy could expect to earn through endorsement contracts in one, five, and ten years — figures based partially on the earnings of Tracy Austin, another ProServ client whose development was comparable to Kathy's. The Rinaldis realized that they had not only a tennis star, but a potential million-dollar baby.

The groundwork for Kathy's relationships with ProServ and Prince rackets had been laid before Kathy won any major tournaments. Although ProServ agents shun what they term "ambulance chasing" (the active recruitment of young players by promising them lucrative endorsement contracts if they turn pro and sign with them), representatives of the company keep track of the top amateurs and regularly appear at junior tournaments in case the parents of a promising player want to talk to them. A year and a half before Kathy turned pro, Dennis Rinaldi did seek out ProServ. He knew the firm handled about three dozen top tennis players and he thought they might be helpful in finding a new coach for Kathy. He also wanted some suggestions on what tournaments Kathy should enter to pave her way to the pros. When Kathy announced she was ready to turn pro, virtually every sports agent contacted the Rinaldis and pleaded to represent the young star, but previous assistance and their respect for Donald Dell and his corps of attorneys made the Rinaldis choose ProServ. Although Kathy would officially become a client of the entire firm, Phil de Picciotto, an engaging twenty-eight-year-old University of Pennsylvania Law School graduate, was assigned to oversee Kathy's day-to-day needs.

Kathy's contact with Prince began after the 1981 Easter Bowl tournament when she lost in the finals of the eighteen-and-under division to Susan Jarrell, who had switched to the Prince Woodie two weeks before. Susan raved about the racket, and the results spoke for themselves. The next week Kathy called Tori Baxter, director of junior and collegiate tennis at Prince, and said she would like to try out the Woodie. Baxter immediately put Rinaldi on the "free list," where she joined 110 other top junior players who receive ten Prince rackets of their choice each year. Both parties were thrilled with the arrangement. After playing with the Woodie for only three days, Kathy entered the Amelia Island professional tournament and beat twelfth-seeded Anne Smith and 1980 collegiate champion Wendy White before losing a close match to Martina Navratilova. For Prince, adding Kathy to the free list was a minor coup. By building up an early association with the players, manufacturers of rackets, clothing, and shoes hope to establish lasting relationships. Indeed, seven months after Kathy turned pro, she signed an endorsement contract with Prince.

Although prize money may be the meat of the athlete's life, endorsements have become the gravy. As recreational athletes have become increasingly concerned with the quality and status of their sporting gear, the star whose name is embossed on the throat of a tennis racket or who bears a company's logo on her tennis togs in a televised match has boosted sales tremendously. Other industries have realized that they, too, can profit from athletes' fresh-scrubbed and familiar faces. As a result, when an athlete is winning big, endorsements can more than double prize earnings. In 1980 Bjorn Borg made more than $2 million on the tennis court and $3 million off it, endorsing everything from candy bars to cassette players. Golfer Nancy Lopez earned

$200,000 in prize earnings in 1981 and $600,000 in endorsements.

A player's endorsement potential is highest when he or she is ranked in the top ten, but when a talented and attractive teenager like Kathy Rinaldi bursts onto the scene, the endorsement potential is still staggering. After Kathy announced her decision to turn pro in a press conference on July 24, 1981, Phil de Picciotto's immediate task was to pitch the young star to prospective sponsors. The task was not especially difficult. Kathy is an agent's dream — a great tennis player *and* an intelligent, sun-bronzed, long-legged, blue-eyed blonde. In the hundred press interviews she granted within the twelve weeks after turning pro, she handled reporters' questions as if she were deflecting an opponent's volleys, responding with pat, pleasant answers. Nothing controversial. Nothing philosophical. Nothing more than could be expected or demanded of a fifteen-year-old who had yet to sport her first pimple. On the court, too, she oozed niceness. She played passionately, yet professionally. She often smiled, sometimes sulked, but seldom screamed or cried.

Her father, a dentist, was a former college baseball star. Kathy's three older siblings were equally attractive and athletic. At a time when the women's tennis tour was riddled with rumors of widespread lesbianism, Kathy Rinaldi and her family were a breath of fresh air. "Alice in Wonderland," Ted Tinling, the tour's unofficial public relations director, called her. "The model little Miss America," said de Picciotto.

The image was so good, in fact, that at first it outstripped her performance: her prize earnings for the first three months on the tour were a mere $10,413, yet within the first seven months she had signed contracts with Prince, Le Coq Sportif sportswear, and Lotto tennis shoes. According to industry reports, the latter two contracts were worth at least $250,000.

"It's a gamble," William Lawliss, marketing director of Le Coq Sportif told sportswriter Robert Johnson. "You gamble based on the personality. There are many players that rank higher than Kathy Rinaldi. There are few who have a more infectious personality."

So far, Kathy has appeared in two television commercials and numerous magazine advertisements. She has played in several exhibitions and made periodic public appearances at department stores across the country to model the products she endorses. (Under her three-year contract with Prince, for example, she is obligated to make four public appearances annually.) Seven authors have approached de Picciotto about writing a biography of the young star. She has also become affiliated with a tennis resort called Martin Downs in Stuart, Florida, her hometown. As the resort's official "touring professional tennis player" and unofficial goodwill ambassador, a luxurious new condominium there has been set aside for her use. Dennis Rinaldi sold their red brick home in Stuart and the condominium has become the family's home base. De Picciotto believes he has barely scratched the surface of Kathy's earning potential. "She doesn't have any cosmetic endorsements right now," he says. "But she will. She's still in high school, so she doesn't have much time for doing many things other than playing tennis or studying."

There have been other athletes — Bruce Jenner, Peggy Fleming, Suzy Chaffee — who have been marketed heavily for their athletic all-American looks, yet their advertising campaigns began after they were champions, not before. Simply clawing one's way up the tennis ladder while keeping up with schoolwork is taxing enough for a fifteen-year-old. If Kathy knew that thousands of dollars were riding on her looks and personality as well as her victories, the pressure could be overwhelming. De Picciotto insists that Kathy does not know or care about her financial status. "I don't think she has any idea how much money she's making, so it doesn't put any pressure on her whatsoever," he declares. "I have never discussed a financial item with Kathy since I've known her. Since she is a minor, everything is handled through her father. And to Kathy it's irrelevant. Endorsements are something that comes along with playing the game. Every major tennis player in the world has endorsements for tennis rackets, clothing and shoes, and many others are associated with a resort. So she doesn't view it as anything unusual."

In addition to negotiating the endorsement contracts and arranging personal appearances, commercials, and exhibitions, ProServ also prepares the athlete's income taxes and financial statements. When a player's bank account starts to swell, ProServ helps the athlete invest the money wisely. Tracy Austin, for example, is part owner of ten apartment buildings, shopping malls, industrial complexes, and office buildings. She is also an investor in thirty natural gas wells in West Virginia and Pennsylvania. "Right now Kathy's only been on the tour a year and she's earned about $60,000," says de Picciotto, who phones Dennis Rinaldi every day about business matters. "But her expenses are running about $40,000 a year, so most of her money now is in a high-yield savings and an Individual Retirement Account. But if Kathy lives up to her potential, if she continues to enjoy playing tennis, if she doesn't get injured and if we do our job right, Kathy should be financially secure for the rest of her life."

Financial security was virtually unknown to retiring athletes a few years ago. So was a firm like ProServ, which was founded in a one-room office overlooking an alley in Washington, D.C., in 1970. Now a multimillion-dollar-a-year business with fourteen lawyers and a corps of tax, financial, and marketing specialists, it occupies two floors of a select Washington office building, with branch offices in New York, Paris, Tokyo, and Sydney. Its clientele includes forty-five tennis players (including about half the world's top thirty), about two dozen of the top pro basketball players, figure skater Tai Babilonia, race car driver Mark Thatcher (son of Britain's prime minister), and former Olympic swimmer Shirley Babashoff. For allowing an athlete like Rinaldi to keep her eye on the ball rather than on her bank account, ProServ charges 10 to 25 percent of a client's earnings. Young lawyers like de Picciotto, however, are on salary. De Picciotto describes his as "embarrassingly low," yet sitting in his office, which is filled with pictures of Kathy Rinaldi and the dozen or so other athletes he represents, he concedes that he loves his job. "I've always been an athlete at heart, if not always on the field. This is the closest thing to being out there."

But what is it like being out there when one is simultaneously a high school sophomore and the fourteenth-ranked tennis player in the world? "It's exciting," Kathy said in her unaffected way soon after turning pro. "I don't know what's going on sometimes. I look up and I'm playing one of those players I've read about. Mostly, I try not to think about it. I try just to keep my mind on my game and not worry about who is across the net." And, indeed, her world has been structured so that excitement can filter in while many of the pressures are filtered out. Her supporting cast is large and strong. In one corner there is ProServ, handling all her business, public relations, and legal work. In the other, there is her family and coach. Virtually all of the teenage protégés on the tennis tour are accompanied by a parent, a coach, or someone handling both roles. These people provide companionship, become practice partners, offer match strategies, fluff up the teenager's feathers after a win, and pat her consolingly when she loses. Most important, the personal retinue lends a sense of order and continuity to a disjointed life. Kathy Rinaldi travels at least six months a year with one or both of her parents and her coach, Andy Brandi. Her college-age brothers Denny and Bill and her sister Tina come to every tournament they can. "We are trying to keep everything the way Kathy likes it when we travel," says Dennis Rinaldi, who has curtailed his dental practice to accompany his daughter. "She attends school when she is at home, and when we travel, she takes all her assignments with her. She still has lots of fun with her friends at school and loves going to parties with them. And the kids on the tour are a nice group. I don't see any negatives in having her turn pro so young, as long as we're with her and take care of her."

Some coaches contend that Kathy Rinaldi may have turned pro too young. If she begins losing, her self-confidence will flag and her endorsement companies won't renew her contracts. Although she may not care about her finances yet, in a few years her attitude is likely to change. It would be a pity, they say, if Kathy Rinaldi looked back and, like a child movie star, felt she had peaked at fourteen.

Phil de Picciotto, for one, believes Kathy will not fail or burn out. "In the developmental years it's especially difficult to maintain friendships at home when you've traveled around the world and have had experiences your classmates haven't had. It takes a special type of person to enjoy the tour, to be able to compete well, and then to integrate back into life at home. And Kathy is special. She's a delightful young lady who has the good fortune to have everything going for her and is intelligent enough to be making the most of it."


Black basketball players are also gravitating toward the pros at earlier ages, but without an enlightened and extensive support system like Kathy Rinaldi's, it is virtually impossible for them to attain the same success. A typical player emerges from the ghetto. Early in his life he becomes intoxicated by the speed and rhythm of the game. His heroes are superstars like Kareem Abdul-Jabbar and Julius "Dr. J" Erving. He knows that the average basketball salary in the National Basketball Association is almost $200,000 and thinks basketball — and only basketball — promises escape from poverty. The flames are fanned by high school scouts who roam ghetto playgrounds, looking for the twelve-year-old with the dazzling jump shot, the kid who can already dunk. The boy is handed a business card and dazzled with promises of a college scholarship — the doorway to the NBA. He is given a new address on school records — or in some cases actually moves to a different school district — so that he can play high school ball at a basketball powerhouse.

By high school the boy is a winner. As he leads his team through an undefeated season, his sense of mission increases. But the daily basketball practices are so exhausting he has no energy to study afterward. Luckily, he doesn't have to ask for anything. He receives. The coach has arranged for others to take tests for him, or his academic records can be fudged. The more prominent his name becomes, the more reluctant teachers are to blow the whistle on him.

The state championships are approaching. He feels the pull of anticipation. College scouts will be there, watching his every move. But in the first game of the championship he goes up for a shot and crumples to the floor. It's his ankle. It's either twisted, sprained, or broken, he isn't sure which. The trainer comes running onto the floor with a needle. He is shot with Xylocaine and the ankle is taped. The trainer tells him it's only a sprain. He doesn't feel a thing and is ready to play the second half. The team goes on to win the game handily, thanks mainly to his second-half scoring. The next game of the championships, however, the team loses. But it doesn't matter. College coaches are fighting for his ear, calling up his mother. His picture has appeared in the "Faces in the Crowd" section of *Sports Illustrated*. His ankle throbs whenever he twists to make a cut, but it doesn't matter. The season is over.

Within a few weeks, college stars fly in from the south, east, and west. They take him out for fancy dinners, and he listens to tales of championship teams, special fraternity housing, cars, cash, stereos, steaks, maids, and academic assistance. He'll be a starter and the star, showcased for the pro scouts. His high school coach, meanwhile, is being offered similar enticements to put in a good word for the colleges. Ten thousand-dollar bills fan out in the recruiter's palm. Or perhaps the coach would prefer a trip to Puerto Rico, a one-day-a-week summer job, a stay in a Mexican villa with the family?

Although colleges may virtually be subsidized by their athletic departments, the law of the land says the athlete must fulfill certain academic requirements. Our young star is totally unprepared for his new role as student-athlete. His curriculum is handpicked by the coach to include such courses as the The History of Basketball, Safety with Hand Tools, and Ceramics. His interest in more challenging courses is rebuffed with, "You're here to become an NBA star, not Albert Einstein." His transcript lists extension courses he never took. Others continue to write tests for him.

At this point the press may descend, exposing yet another college sports fraud, causing the school to be placed on proation and the player to be declared academically ineligible — in other words, athletically defunct. But even if no scandal erupts, he starts to question and to doubt his abilities. Maybe he won't make a million dollars playing for the Knicks, and what then? He realizes that he's not getting educated, that in fact he's almost illiterate. He panics.

Meanwhile, life at college is getting tougher. He's traveling constantly, in and out of classes, chronically exhausted from basketball practice and from trying to keep up academically. It's a crazy life, not at all the Eden portrayed by the recruiter. But let's suppose that he does somehow manage to keep body and soul together. Let's even go a step farther and imagine that he becomes the college basketball star he always dreamed he could be.

He doesn't earn his college degree, but he is drafted into the NBA. During practice he aggravates his old ankle injury. X-rays reveal it was originally broken, not sprained. And I played on it, a fucking broken ankle, he says to himself furiously. Now, after every practice — in fact after any extended activity — his ankle swells up like a balloon. He is cut from the team and sent home with a one-way bus ticket, a cup of coffee, a hunk of pie, and a permanently crippled ankle.

Consider, for a moment, the statistics. According to the National Federation of State High School Associations, every year close to 700,000 boys play high school basketball. Only 15,000 of them will play on an NCAA college varsity team. Of those 15,000 only 4,000 complete college basketball careers and only about 200 are drafted by the twenty-two NBA teams. It is statistically easier (and a whole lot safer) to become a doctor.

Sociologist Harry Edwards, himself a former basketball player from the ghetto, calls it a "cruel hoax." "Perhaps three million black youths between 13 and 22 are out there dreaming of careers as professional athletes," says Dr. Edwards. "The odds against them are worse than 20,000 to 1." The average professional basketball career lasts only three to four years, but the adulation of stardom bedazzles even the most directed individuals.

Isiah Thomas was one basketball player who knew there was an alternative to the NBA. He wanted to go to college and then earn a law degree. His desire for an education was instilled in him early by his mother, Mary, who was determined that Isiah, the youngest of her nine children, would rise above the poverty and brutality of the West Side of Chicago.

At three Isiah was already a basketball prodigy, the halftime entertainment at the neighborhood Catholic Youth Organization games, a tiny boy dribbling and shooting in an oversize jersey that drooped to his knees. He had catlike quickness and slightly protruding eyes that gave him exceptional peripheral vision. By the time he was in fourth grade, he was a standout on the eighth-grade team at Our Lady of Sorrows.

His older brothers took him on tours of the streets and pointed out the dangers — the dope, drinking, stealing, and killings. Four of them became victims themselves — two of them became her-

Isiah Thomas, as a freshman at Indiana University, 1980.

oin addicts, one a pimp, and one a chief of the Vice Lords street gang. But they knew Isiah had a way out, and they made sure he didn't dawdle on the streets on his way home from basketball practice. He got a scholarship to St. Joseph's High School, where he forged a lasting bond of friendship and respect with coach Gene Pingatore. His greatest asset, according to Pingatore, was his leadership ability. "We're more than a one-man team," explained one of Thomas's teammates, "but with Isiah out there we all have more confidence in ourselves."

Inevitably, the college suitors came calling. Thomas narrowed the pool to three — Indiana, DePaul, and Iowa. Although Mary Thomas met all the coaches and had strong opinions about each, she kept silent: the decision was Isiah's. "It's kind of strange," she said, "but I usually can tell right away whether they're putting me on. Isiah's kind of the same way. He can tell." Coach Pingatore agreed. "Isiah is a very level-headed kid, he knows you can't put all your eggs in one basket. It can't be all basketball. He has to go to a school that is interested in him as a person." And before his graduation the high school star said, "When I go out on the court now, I just go out and have fun. I hope it'll always be that way."

Thomas decided to attend Indiana, but told the frustrated DePaul coach that he would later attend his school — DePaul Law School, that was. His high school education had prepared him for college, but life still wasn't easy. Keeping up on both academics and basketball meant curtailing his social life. His two closest friends were on the basketball team, so they were able to cram conversations with Isiah into the sprint from classroom to basketball court. Nevertheless, Isiah became the star of the basketball team and maintained a B average. An especially sweet victory his freshman year was the 81–72 defeat of Northwestern in his hometown. His family and relatives, friends and neighbors, had all come to watch. The moment was special. "But basketball is still only a game. Like Monopoly," said the six-one guard in his slow, sweet voice. "I want to be a lawyer," he continued. "If I do get a chance to play pro ball, I'll still have a lot of life in front of me when my career is over. And while I'm playing I hope I'm smart enough to go to school during the summer."

By sophomore year Thomas was an All-American and led his team to a 63–51 romp over North Carolina in the NCAA finals. Scoring a game high of 23 points, he was named the tournament's Most Valuable Player. The pros liked what they saw. The opportunity to play pro ball had materialized sooner than Isiah had expected, with three pro teams dangling million-dollar contracts. He was torn. Playing in the NBA had been a lifelong dream. His mother's eyes were bad and her heart wasn't good. She had been working to keep the family together since her husband had left when Isiah was three. He wanted her to quit her job at the Chicago Housing Authority. In fact, he wanted to be able to buy her a new house in a safer part of town.

"But I know I'm a role model for a lot of people back in the ghetto," Isiah said. "Not too many of us get the chance to get out, to go to college. If I quit school, what effect would that have on them? And I had said I wanted to be a lawyer, and one day return there and help the people. They need it. I've seen kids who stole a pair of pants and got thrown in jail for five years because they couldn't get good legal assistance. I'm going to get my law degree, no matter what."

But first he would be a professional basketball player. He was flying high now, and who knew what next year's college season could bring? He needed that million dollars, for his mother's security and his own. He signed a reported $1.6-million, four-year contract with the Detroit Pistons. His family was skeptical when Isiah pulled up in front of the house in the new copper-colored Mercedes with gold stripes he had purchased before the ink on his contract was dry. "There ought to be a law against it," said his older sister Ruby. "Pro teams shouldn't be allowed to dangle that kind of money in front of a 19-year-old kid. I was hoping Isiah would stay in school. I feel sorry for him."

The exploitation and manipulation of young athletes takes many forms, but all stem from money. The $4,000 college scholarship granted to a promising athlete can generate hundreds of thousands of dollars in stadium attendance and television revenues. If a college game is televised nationally on ABC, the two teams split $1.1 million. ABC and CBS are also paying incentive fees of approximately $250,000 to schools that agree to switch the dates of football games to accommodate the networks. It is worth risking a possible recruiting or eligibility violation to ensure a championship team. Because the financial stakes are so high the universities are willing to go to great lengths — including arbitrarily revoking athletic scholarships — should athletes fail to produce.

Only a tough system of laws and penalties can break this cycle of exploitation. *Newsweek* sportswriter Pete Axthelm suggests that college scholarships should be frozen over five years for each athlete, so that if he hasn't graduated in that time, his scholarship money can't be awarded to an incoming freshman. Other possible remedies include sharper enforcement of recruiting violations and stricter policing of the university athletic departments so that it would be in the coaches' best interest to promote rather than undermine the athletes' education. Recruiting and eligibility violations could also be curbed by splitting the television pie into smaller pieces. If the $400,000 collected by a school that makes the NCAA basketball finals could be spread around the entire NCAA, the incentive to engage in illegal practices might be lessened.

As Axthelm puts it, "We are talking about a sick and sleazy atmosphere here." Perhaps the sickest part of this atmosphere is the noxious effect it can have on young people. Adults may understand and sympathize with Isiah Thomas's decision to postpone the rest of his college education and law school, but the kids only see that he's a pro basketball star and he left college two years early to get there. As long as the enticements are so powerful, young stars like Thomas are going to try to grab them. But if ghetto children grow up believing that the NBA is the only way, at age twenty they may find themselves with glorious memories of yesterday but no opportunities for tomorrow.

# 12
# The Pro Life

Travel disrupts the continuities of life.
Seasons of the year become merely months
of basketball games. Some day I'll wake up
in the same place every morning and that
will lend wholeness to my life. Flying away
to play and returning one week later destroys
that possibility, not because of what
happened to the place, but by what has
happened to me while away. When I travel
constantly the experience I have seems to
consist largely of observations and moments
of enjoyment — the 80-degree weather in San
Diego, the desert nights in Phoenix, the days
in the mountain ranges of the Northwest—
but never are they lived through and
absorbed. I miss that sense of sharing that
comes from people living together in one
place, over time. I miss permanence.

— Bill Bradley, *Life on the Run*

**P**am Shriver's eyes narrow to the clock by her bedside. 8:00 A.M. Slowly the world comes together. New York City. Winter. The St. Regis Hotel. The Toyota Tennis Championships. She stretches her long arms and legs. Feeling fine. It is amazing how the body recovers. Last week at this time she felt as if she had been hung upside down. A survivor, barely, of a twenty-seven-hour flight from Australia across sixteen time zones. Back at home in Lutherville, Maryland, she had gone to bed that evening and was wide awake two hours later. At 9 the next morning she was ready to go to sleep. What a mess. She always needed those few days at home to recover.

Going home represented more than a pit stop to recover from jet lag, deliver her dirty clothes to her mother, and visit her accountant. Home was also an emotional oasis. At home she could sleep in her own bed and be accepted simply as one of the family. She could go out late and not have to worry about being back early to play an important match the next day. She was far removed from airport terminals, press conferences, and locker rooms. Not that home was paradise, either. It was a lot different from the way it used to be, because her older sister and all her high school friends were away at college. Her forty-eight-year-old mother and eleven-year-old sister were not always on her nineteen-year-old wavelength. But it was a release. The week or two at home between stops on the tour was what allowed her to go back out feeling good, like a fighter raring to go at the sound of the bell.

In the past two months she had spent a week playing in

United Press International Photo

Pam Shriver reaches the final of the U.S. Open, 1978.

Brighton, England, had flown home for two weeks, played $3^1/_2$ weeks in Australia, then spent five days at home, and finally had arrived in New York last night by train. Each stop on the tour represented not only a change in time zone, but also often a change in culture and sometimes season. Last week in Australia it had been the middle of summer. Now it was coming up on Christmas. At first, jetting about had seemed glamorous; it still was exciting — sometimes. But playing more than three hundred sets of competitive singles and doubles in twenty-one tournaments a year had taken a lot of the glitter off. Having dinner in a nice restaurant with friends was almost the extent of her social life. In fact, her memories of a city were mainly those of its restaurants. In Chicago there was that place at the airport with the incredible salad bar, where you could load up your plate and not feel guilty because all the greens were good for you. Or Jim McMullen's in New York. That was another favorite.

The hotel made a difference too. This one was old and classy, a nice break from the ultramodern Hyatts and Hiltons that usually served as the tournament's "official hotels." The St. Regis was also right in the center of the action, smack in the middle of Manhattan's shopping district. She'd have to go out later and walk around, absorb the city's sights and sounds. Not necessarily its smells this time. Last night in the cab from the train station she had seen bags piled up in the street. The cabbie had told her coach, Don, that there was a garbage strike. Still, she looked forward to taking in a little of the city. Not too much, for she needed her physical and emotional strength for the tournament. Any hassle — a bad meal, a rude saleslady — could come back to haunt her on the court. But at the same time, New York was special. For it was here, a little over three years ago, that she had scored her first big triumph, reaching the finals of the U.S. Open.

She remembers that day. Fifteen years old and on top of the

world. She had lost to Chris Evert 7–5, 6–4, but she did get the tennis world buzzing. The headlines told of the six-foot-tall teenager with the rocket serves and the crisp volleys. She had been named the World Tennis Association's Most Impressive Newcomer of 1978. And at the end of her first year out of the juniors, she was ranked thirteenth in the world. After the Open, she decided to cut down on tournament play while she crammed her junior and senior years of high school into one, knowing that after graduation she could turn pro and devote all her time to tennis. The other kids at McDonough, a small private school on the outskirts of Baltimore, had never seen anything like it: trigonometry and calculus, psychology, studio art, the novel, the short story, black literature, the American dream, the personal essay, and more, all in one year.

But three weeks after graduation, while practicing for the Wimbledon championships in England, she felt her shoulder go. Just like that. A throbbing pain. She felt the pain every time she attempted to serve or volley. Stripped of her two weapons, her game fell apart. She withdrew from Wimbledon, and a year after reaching the finals of the U.S. Open, she lost in the first round to an unknown qualifier. Various physicians offered conflicting advice. Some told her to do stretching exercises, others advocated balms and ointments. Most, however, simply told her to rest the shoulder. So she stayed home, watching tennis matches on television, wondering when she would be able to play again. The rest didn't work. She still couldn't serve or volley. Depression set in. She feared she would never be able to play again and that her potential would never be reached.

Then she visited the late Dr. John Marshall, an eminent sports physician. He injected dye into the shoulder joint and watched the joint's movement as she went through overhead tennis motions. He told her that although the joint had a tendency to slip in its socket, it was generally healthy. But she had overstressed the tendons by suddenly playing strenuously after playing only sporadically during the school year. Now, after a five-month layoff, all the muscles that moved the shoulder had atrophied. She would have to do slow, heavy work with weights to build the shoulder back up.

In the fall of 1979 she had lifted seven to eight tons a day on her shoulder, three times a week. At the end of a day of weight training, she could barely lift a matchbox, but the strength in her shoulder returned. More important, Dr. Marshall's regimen had given her a sense of direction. She knew everything would fall into place again. She didn't have to quit. She began practicing in anticipation of the 1980 Avon Indoor circuit, which began in January.

At first she hadn't realized how tough the climb back to the top would be, for during her absence the tennis scene had changed. By 1980 Martina Navratilova had established herself as the tour's serve-and-volleyer. In the top ten there were some old faces — Billie Jean King, Evonne Goolagong, Chris Evert, and Wendy Turnbull — but also some new and quite determined young teenagers — Tracy Austin, Andrea Jaeger, and Hana Mandlikova. They were tournament-tough, while she was saddled by doubts about her shoulder. Time and again they beat her. Depression returned. Could the U.S. Open have been a fluke? She didn't think so. Before the Open, in her first tournament on the women's circuit, she had reached the semifinals. At the next, she became the youngest player ever to start at the prequalifying round and survive twelve consecutive matches to win the tournament. But why couldn't she win now?

Three months after returning to the tour, she won her first tournament as a pro — the Honda Civic Classic in La Costa, California. Toward the end of the year, her performance became less erratic. She would no longer post a strong showing in one tournament and then lose in the first round of the next. Doubts about her shoulder slowly faded. Although she had to be careful to apply ice packs after each match, she realized her shoulder was, in fact, stronger than ever. At eighteen, she was on the comeback trail.

The comeback year of 1980 was followed by consistency in 1981. She and her doubles partner Martina Navratilova won eight tournaments. She had upset Tracy Austin at Wimbledon in May, and then again last week at the Australian Open. She had reached at least the quarterfinals of almost every tournament she entered. She was now ranked sixth in the world and was proving that she was a force in singles as well as doubles. But the test of her real strength, she felt, would be this tournament, the Toyota Series Championship, the last and perhaps the most important tournament of 1981. Only the top eight players in the world were invited. Besides prestige, a $250,000 purse, and a 1982 Toyota Celica, the final computer rankings for the year were at stake.

Don Candy is waiting downstairs in the coffee shop. "Morning," she says, sitting down at the table. "Morning, Pammie," replies her coach, agent, and companion. Despite the fact that Don is a quarter century older, is married, and has grown children, they are like two peas in a pod — both tall, emotional, with a quick sense of humor and a deep love for tennis. She owes so much to him. He had identified her at fourteen as a potential champion and had helped her build her game. When her shoulder gave out, he had stuck by her, overseeing her rehabilitation program and giving her the emotional support she so desperately needed. In her typically impulsive way, she had wanted to be back at the top right away. Don had convinced her that it would take time. He was the one who had kept her in the sport when she felt like packing it in and going home for good.

And now, on the road, he is a wonderful companion. What would it be like if he weren't here? Waking up to eat breakfast, lunch, and dinner alone? She couldn't do it. At least, not for

249

long. He knows when she likes to eat breakfast and what kind of place she'd prefer for dinner. Fortunately, their tastes are similar. They have a great arrangement — Don takes care of the details of her life on the road, and she concentrates solely on her tennis.

They talk about the tournament. It will be run as a double elimination, which means a player has to lose twice to be out of contention. The first-round match-ups haven't been posted in advance but will be decided at the press conference this morning. Playing a good first match is always important. It sets your pace for the tournament. In most tournaments, she wouldn't be coming up against the likes of Chris Evert, Martina Navratilova, Tracy Austin, or Andrea Jaeger until she had already played two or three matches. Here she would be meeting one of the top four players right away. She hopes it won't be Martina or Chris. Her record isn't good against them. Whereas against Andrea Jaeger, she has won four matches and lost only one.

The press conference, as well as the tournament, is to be held at the Meadowlands, the huge athletic complex rising out of the barren marshes of New Jersey. Don hails a cab and zip, they are through the Lincoln Tunnel, into New Jersey. Less than ten minutes later, they arrive at the Stadium Club, where the press conference will take place.

The Stadium Club is like most other "public" rooms. Red carpeting, pictures of famous football players on the walls, tables set up throughout the room, with a pad of paper and a glass of water at each seat for the reporters. A long table stands at the front of the room, where she and the other players will sit. The reporters begin to trickle in. Some of the men stop at the bar in the anteroom for a drink. The newspapermen and women riffle through the press kits handed out by Toyota representatives while the television and radio crews set up their gear. Standard procedure. She had seen the process of sports reporting hundreds of times before, yet the end results were still somewhat magical and mystifying. If she beats Martina or Chris in Cincinnati or Kansas City, the event quickly fades into oblivion. But when she wins big in New York, the whole world seems to know about it. That's what she lives for — the wins. The winning is what sustains her through the slumps. And it's a lot easier to salt away the wins when they're accompanied by public recognition.

The room begins to fill up. While Pam and Don chat with Sam McCleery, a Prince representative (the racket Pam endorses), the other players who had qualified for the singles championship arrive: Martina Navratilova, riding the crest of the previous week's win in the Australian Open, which netted her $34,000 and a Toyota Celica, looking more like a movie star than a tennis player with her fur coat and newly bleached blonde hair; Chris Evert Lloyd, who had lost in the finals in Australia, dressed smartly in a wool tweed pant suit: nineteen-year-old Tracy Austin, who had been sidelined with a back injury early in the season and rebounded to win the U.S. Open, appearing to have attained a new maturity in the recuperative process, yet still accompanied by her mother and coach; Hana Mandlikova and Andrea Jaeger, eighteen and sixteen years old respectively, smiling shyly and thumbwrestling in a corner with Hana's coach, Betty Stove; and the two other players, twenty-six-year-old Virginia Ruzici and twenty-five-year-old Mima Jausovec, gazing at the younger players, perhaps wondering when, if ever, they would rise above them.

The young women appear completely at ease with each other. Well they might, for between the thirty-one-tournament Toyota series and the eleven-tournament Avon series, they spend hundreds of hours together each year in hotels, locker rooms, press conferences, parties, airplanes — and, of course, on the court. Above all else, they are competitors. As they mingle with the reporters, they speak of their rankings with the intensity and emotion nonathletes reserve for children or sweethearts.

Martina Navratilova declares that because she has won almost $900,000 in 1981, almost twice as much as Christ Evert Lloyd, she deserves to be number one. Tracy Austin feels that if she wins the Toyota tournament, she should be number one because she would have the best win-loss record against Martina and Chris. And Chris, although she curtailed her tournament schedule drastically in 1981, feels that she deserves the number one ranking, having won seven of the eleven tournaments she played.

By 11:30 all the cameras are set up and Trish Faulkner of the Women's Tennis Association taps the microphone to quiet the crowd, which has grown to about a hundred. The players dutifully take their seats on the dais. The festive atmosphere of the room dies down to anticipation. All eyes are focused on an easel next to the dais, upon which is propped a large cardboard mock-up of the draw, a complex diagram with boxes and arrows in blue and red. First the names of the top four seeded players are fitted into the red and blue boxes: Navratilova and Jaeger are assigned to the red group: Evert Lloyd and Austin to the blue. Then comes the drawing of the opponents, two at a time.

"Mima Jausovec will play Martina Navratilova and Hana Mandlikova will meet Andrea Jaeger. Miss Ruzici and Miss Shriver will go back into the pot," announces Trish Faulkner. She reaches into the box again and proclaims, "Miss Ruzici will play Miss Austin and . . ."

Pam Shriver mischievously simulates a drum roll to herald the foregone conclusion. The nervous tension pent up in the players is released, as they all burst into girlish giggles. Trish Faulkner continues, "and the final and noisiest of the bunch, Miss Shriver, will play Chris Evert Lloyd."

Immediately, players, parents, and coaches start imagining hypothetical match-ups. In one corner of the room, Tracy Austin's mother, Jeanne, and her new coach, Marty Reissen, confer with Hana Mandlikova's coach, Betty Stove. Neither Reissen nor Mrs. Austin understands the confusing process, and Stove tries to explain, without much success. Finally Mrs. Austin and Reissen decide they'll have to wait to get back to their hotel room to figure it all out.

The last minutes of the press conference are devoted to individual player interviews. As the athletes are ushered to their appointed tables, reporters eagerly position microphones under their noses. Most of the television cameras are crowded around Navratilova, Evert Lloyd, and Austin, who are battling for the number one ranking. Six or seven newspaper reporters cluster around Pam Shriver's table. Naturally, she is asked about the unappealing prospect of meeting Chris Evert Lloyd in the first round.

"We've had some close matches — some real close matches," she says brightly. Then her voice drops off. "But actually, I've never even taken a set off her. It will be five games all and then she'll win the most important game. So I've got to play the big games as well as she does or better."

"Are you going to do anything different in this match?" asks one reporter.

"Well, I might strip halfway through," she jokes. "No, seriously, I can't go out there and change a whole lot. Just as she's not going to come out serve-and-volleying. I'm not going to stand around the baseline all night. I'll just have to see how it goes." Pam, like most of the teenagers on the tour, is an intriguing adult-child. A poised and confident nineteen-year-old who can answer reporters' questions with aplomb and whack a tennis serve harder than most men in their prime, she can also be a girl who hasn't quite left the high school locker room.

"She's at a tough stage in her life right now," confirms Don Candy. "When she's away for more than three weeks she gets itchy to return home. But if she's at home for more than three weeks, she wants to get back on the tour. Somewhere sandwiched in there is a tiny slice of adolescence. Pam's drive and ambition are slowly squeezing her childhood away and pushing her toward womanhood. But right now she still comes up with some things that are pure young girl adolescent.

"There's a great emotional involvement in playing professional tennis," continues her coach. "Sometimes people around you can help. In thoroughbred racing you often see a race horse that's been syndicated for $20 million who has a stable dog that's always with him. In tennis, there are coaches like myself who are given $500 a week to help the player along. I know in a year or two I'll be less important to Pam. But right now the tour places a lot of demands on her. She'll get a call from the Women's Tennis Association saying, 'There's a clay court tournament next week. Could you come down?' And as a result, she's playing competitive tennis all year long. That's difficult for anyone, especially a young lady of 19 who is making the transition from adolescence to womanhood."

After the press conference, reporters and players go their separate ways, the reporters to await the start of the tournament the following evening and the players to the practice courts set aside at a tennis club a mile or two from the Meadowlands. In the car, Pam is thinking about her upcoming match with Chris. In one way, drawing Chris had been a real disappointment. But, on the other hand, there is not as much pressure playing Chris. Because Chris is so highly ranked, Pam is not expected to win. She can relax, pull out all the stops.

Pam and Don practice for an hour and a half. She is feeling the ball well the entire time. Although practices can be taken too seriously — things might go differently in a match — she has learned that if she is hitting the ball well in practice, extending to her full height in her serves and volleys and concentrating totally on her ground strokes, she has a good chance of playing the same way in the match. Lately, her game has been coming together. She won the Perth tournament her first week in Australia, won the doubles in Sydney with Martina the next week, and toppled Tracy in the quarterfinals of the Australian Open the last week. Who knows what this week will hold?

That night, she and Don eat dinner at Jim McMullen's. Gene Barakat, a friend of Don's who works for the Ford Modeling Agency, joins them with his friend, Anett Stai, a Norwegian model. Stanley Rumbaugh, Jr., a fashion photographer, arrives with a date. Former tennis champ Fred Stolle and a television producer from Australia complete the party. It is a wonderful evening, the conversation drifting from fashion to tennis to television, and Pam enjoys herself thoroughly. Don and Fred Stolle talk about their days on the Australian Davis Cup team in the fifties, when tennis was strictly amateur. Small and social, a season and an off-season, a sport rather than a business. Things have really changed since professional tennis started in 1967. Now there are 900 male pros; 250 women. Competing on the tour has become like riding a roller coaster. Although some tournaments carry more prestige than others, the results of each are fed into the computer. In the old days there was no computer: if you did well in a few big tournaments, your reputation was made. Now there are forty-two tournaments a year. You only have to play six, but most of the people who can afford the expenses of the tour play at least fifteen or twenty.

At its core, tennis is a sport, but it has also become big business. Because the game has grown so steadily in the seventies, Pam will earn more than $300,000 this year in prize money alone. It seems incredible sometimes, to be paid so well for doing something she loves. To be paid for wearing certain clothes and swinging a certain racket; to be able to afford the coaching and companionship of someone like Don, to be able to buy the tennis club in Maryland where she used to practice. Neither Fred nor Don had been given those opportunities.

But there are trade-offs. There is certainly still camaraderie among the women and often genuine caring. At times Martina Navratilova seems almost like a sister. But above all, there is competitiveness. Each player has to assert her style of play and her belief in herself to emerge victorious. Nothing, not even friendship, can interfere with that.

Having a boyfriend or husband might relieve some of the competitive pressure. At times Pam longs for a male companion other than Don. It would be nice if a tall and twentyish white knight suddenly rode into her life, but looking at things realistically, professional tennis is a consuming occupation. Of the top female pros only Chris Evert Lloyd, Evonne Goolagong Cawley, and Billie Jean King are married, and marriage works for them because their husbands are either tennis players or promoters. They understand their wives' ambitions and are willing to make concessions. And they are older, too. There is still a lot of time left to settle down. If she wants, she can probably slide along at number ten or twelve for the next ten years. But that isn't enough. She wants to be number one — and if that isn't possible, to be in the top four and win some major tournaments. She is only a hairsbreadth below the top. Now is the time to push hard. In a few years, after leaving the tour, she will be able to relax and enjoy a full social life.

Meanwhile, nights like this make a difference. They fight off the demon of loneliness that lurks in the corners of hotel rooms, a demon that can sneak up if you aren't careful. Other people say that being on the tour is an education. Well, she decides, it is. Not in the formal sense of going to museums and seeing things one has studied in school, because sightseeing is simply too exhausting. And only partially in the sense of being exposed to other cultures, because in most cities exposure to strangers is fairly minimal. The real education is internal — organizing oneself. Seeing to it that everything connected with the tournament and practices is taken care of and then filling in the gaps in constructive ways. Sometimes Don comes up with activities, and sometimes the tournament sponsors plan special parties for the players. But the responsibility for using free time well rests with oneself. The tour can be a crushing bore or the opportunity of a lifetime. It is, finally, what each player makes it.

The next day is something of a letdown compared to the fun of the night before. To prepare for the evening match Pam schedules two half-hour practices, one in the late morning, the other ending about an hour before playing time. In between, she rests at the hotel and does her shoulder exercises, lifting the three-pound dumbbells she carries with her when she travels and pulling on a piece of rubber tubing she attaches to a doorknob. Her shoulder is like an old duck; although it isn't lame, it needs proper treatment. When she does her exercises regularly and ices the shoulder before and after each match, it is fine. If she skips the exercises, however, it shows signs of giving out again. After the second practice she does general stretching exercises at the Meadowlands to loosen up, ices her shoulder, and gets some last-minute instructions from Don on match strategy. Then it's time to go. She leaves the locker room, proceeds down the hallway, and enters the brightly lit court.

The Meadowlands arena, despite its pastoral name, is a far cry from the outdoor grass court in Melbourne on which Pam Shriver and Chris Evert Lloyd last competed. A cavernous concrete and steel structure with a capacity for 18,000, tonight about a third of its red seats are occupied. Winter has been sealed out. Below freezing outside, inside the building is comfortably warm. While practicing their shots in the pregame warmup, both players try to get a feel for the court — the speed at which the ball bounces off the thin green "carpet" laid over the cement floor, the glare of the artificial lights, the width of the red carpet that surrounds the court, even the placement of two new steel-gray Toyotas, positioned in opposite corners behind the baseline, one for the winner of the tournament, the other for Martina Navratilova, who has already won the Toyota Bonus Pool.

While the crowd settles into its seats, the players are introduced. Although both wear white-and-red tennis outfits, the similarity ends there. Pam looks like a gentle giant. Of her six feet, about five appear to be legs. Her head is covered with tight tawny curls and her face, with its blue-gray eyes, long lashes, and rosy cheeks, reminds one of nothing so much as a contented cat. Evert Lloyd is less catlike than coltish. A thoroughbred filly, she flicks her ponytail, pats her skirt, and paces the baseline.

As the game begins, Shriver's tabby becomes a tigress. Serving first, she knows there is no margin for error with Chris. She must control the match from the outset. After starting off inauspiciously by losing the first two points, she finds her rhythm — serve and then put away Chris's return with a cool, crisp volley. Four points later, she sighs with relief, walks off the court, and mops her face with a towel. She has won the first game.

In the second game, Chris jumps ahead. She stands one point from clinching the game when Pam recovers. Taking her racket back and carefully measuring her shot, she hits a backhand like a karate chop and ties the game. But three shots later, another backhand volley sinks into the net. "Game Evert Lloyd," the umpire announces. Pam whips the air with her racket in disgust and her face crinkles into the Shriver wince. She can't afford to make unforced errors. Not against Chris.

In the third game, Pam once again finds her groove. She is a study in concentration. Before serving she leans forward, bouncing the ball, glaring at it, almost commanding it to follow a predetermined trajectory. Then she rocks back on her heels, whips her racket back, bites her lip, tosses the ball high, and extending to her full height, sends it zooming across the net. More often now Chris cannot return the ball or returns it poorly. Pam not only has won the next game, but has also gained the intangible but all-important factor never posted on the scoreboard — momentum. Her errors are few, while Chris is missing the mark.

As the players switch courts with Pam ahead five games to

one, the spectators buzz with the prospect of an upset. Suddenly, however, the rallies begin to extend. Chris is hitting with a new authority, as if awakened after a long sleep. She wins the game, and after Pam holds serve, she wins another. The score is now 5–3 with Pam serving. If she holds serve, she'll win the set. If she doesn't, Chris will be in a good position to tie the match.

Pam falls behind 15–30. She mishits the next shot, and as the ballgirl sends the ball back to her, she snatches at it, muttering angrily to herself. One more point and Chris will win the game. She pauses a minute before serving to regain her concentration. Then she unleashes one of her fastest serves, a serve Chris can barely touch. Then another rocket. She has tied the game. But Chris retaliates by zinging a shot that passes Pam's extended racket and nicks the tape. Advantage Evert Lloyd. Pam retaliates with a successful volley. Chris, now back on target, blasts another shot past Pam. Advantage Evert Lloyd. Pam again fights back and wins the next two points. Advantage Shriver. This is it, Pam thinks. I've got to put it away now. She hits a backhand drop shot that trickles over the net and leaves Chris flatfooted by the baseline. "Yeah!" Pam cries, her clenched fist flying into the air in self-affirmation. For the first time ever, she has taken a set from Chris.

When the two take the court for the second set, the spectators sound as if they're at a bullfight. "Wake up Chris!" "Chris, do it!" they scream. In her eleven years of the pro tour, Chris has changed more than her hairstyle and marital status. Her reputation has metamorphosed from that of America's sweetheart to Ice Maiden to Mrs. Tennis. Her amazing composure and consistency, which labeled her an automaton in the middle years of her reign, now command new respect. She is by all accounts — including her own — the toughest competitor on the tour.

So even though she is down a set, the crowd, Chris, and Pam all know that the match is far from over. Indeed, one can almost see her resolve as she serves the first game of the second set.

Whereas in the first set Pam had attacked with her serve and then varied her volleys to keep Chris perpetually off balance, now it is Chris who controls the rhythm of the game. Pam's overpowering first serve falters and Chris is able to pounce on her softer second serve; Pam's groundstrokes become more tentative, while Chris's grow more assured. Chris keeps hammering and chipping away at Pam's game until she has built a commanding 5–1 lead.

But then, as suddenly as Chris's game had jelled, it begins to fall apart. "I didn't know what to do," said Pam after the match. "At 5–1 against Chris you figure that she's going to win the set. I didn't know whether to go for a game, probably lose it, and then start anew in the third set, or try to come all the way back, knowing how tough it is to come back against Chris. And then if I could come back I was thinking, 'Well, what about the third set? Coming back all that way might take too much out of me if I don't make it.' But I kept winning games. And as I kept playing good points, I got right back in it."

Like her distant relative, politician Sargent Shriver, Pam is a polished wordsmith, both on and off the court. In previous years her monologues between points — addressed to the referees, the crowd, herself, and the Lord — have interfered with her concentration. But in her comeback in the second set, she displays a new mental discipline, an air of patient confidence. Miraculously, she withstands nine set points and ties the second set at six games all. The final game of the set will be decided by a nine-point tiebreaker. The first player to win the majority of the nine points will win the set. If it is Pam, she will also win the match.

In the first point of the tiebreaker, Chris entices Pam into playing a backcourt game. Getting into a baseline duel with Chris is like summoning your executioner. She imparts a vicious topspin to her forehand and backhand drives, and at the same time has an almost telekinetic ability to direct the ball within an inch or two of the court's boundaries. Realizing that exchanging shots with Chris is courting disaster, Pam tries a daring backhand drop shot, the same shot that had won her the first set. ("It was a stupid shot to try at that point," Pam said later. "I had just recently started to practice it, although it had worked well in the first set. But this time I wasn't in the right position to execute it well. Then I lost the point on my serve. From there the tiebreaker went downhill. I started off badly and she just steamrolled through, winning the tie-breaker 7–2.")

Pam starts serving in the third set and quickly wins the first two points. But she allows Chris to get back in the game and then win it with a backhand pass down the line. One glance at the two players as they sit on the sidelines between games tells the story. Pam swats the chair with her towel and sits glaring straight ahead before bowing her head in exasperation. Chris, meanwhile, is neatly wiping off her arms and legs with the same motions and lack of expression that had marked her rest periods since the match began.

Ahead 4–3 in games, Chris begins hitting consistent winners, leaving no opportunity for Pam to use her strong volley. Whereas in the first set Chris had made backhand errors while Pam kept her on the run, now the tables have turned. Pam is out of position, looking tired and frustrated. Two hours and ten minutes after the match began, Chris clinches the third set 6–3.

"So near," says a reporter to Pam in the hallway behind the court that serves as a pressroom. "Yet so far," she laughs clutching an ice bag to her shoulder as the television cameras begin to roll. "After the first set I wanted to take that Toyota and just drive out. Then to get back in it in the second set and play a rotten tiebreaker — it's annoying. I wish I could have gotten it close in the tiebreaker, maybe be ahead 5–4 and be serving for the match. Those are the points that show who the heck you are. But I never got there.

"But," she adds, brightening, "I think it was a good match, an exciting match."

A reporter leans forward and speaks earnestly into his microphone, "Do you think you're back?"

"Oh yeah, I'm back," Pam laughs, as if trying to diffuse the intensity of his question. "I feel good," she says, now rolling with self-assurance. "If I keep working hard, and don't expect things too quickly, who knows?"

Who knows, indeed. "She played really well, definitely as well as she ever has," says Chris Evert Lloyd when asked to comment on the match. "Of all the players I could have been paired with, Pam was the one I didn't want to get. Even if I had been playing real well in the first set, it would have been real tough to beat her. She played percentage tennis, getting her first serves in, missing very few volleys, and producing a backhand drop shot that I had never seen from her before.

"Pam knows how to play me and Tracy, or for that matter, anyone who hits from the baseline," Chris adds. "She's very smart that way. After being runner-up in the Open in 1978 she went through a slump and lost her confidence. Now she's beating everyone she's supposed to beat and she's giving all the top players a hard time. That should really build up her confidence. I think she'll need to have more of a weapon with her groundstrokes, because she slices the ball rather than putting topspin on it. And it's hard to hit winners that way. But her serve and volley are definitely there. And she's a great competitor. She keeps hitting and if she misses she doesn't get obsessive about it."

It is to be a grueling week. After a one-day break Pam's next match, against Virginia Ruzici, doesn't finish until 1:52 A.M. thanks to a $3\frac{1}{2}$-hour marathon earlier in the evening between Chris Evert Lloyd and Tracy Austin (Evert Lloyd won). By 3 A.M. a victorious Shriver and Don Candy are taxiing through the deserted streets of New York City, looking for a place to eat dinner. At 5, she is back in her hotel room. She wakes at 11, ready to face another day of tennis. That afternoon, she practices with Candy for an hour in preparation for her two evening matches, the quarterfinal singles match against Andrea Jaeger and a doubles semifinal with her partner Martina.

She wins both, but the doubles match isn't over until midnight. Again, she can salvage only a few hours of sleep. The next evening she plays the singles semifinal, losing to Navratilova. And the evening after that the two take to the court again, this time on the same side of the net, to win the doubles championship.

It is also a rewarding week. Although Tracy Austin takes home the $40,000 winner's check and a new Toyota (which, she realizes with a giggle, is a stick shift, a skill she has not yet mastered), Pam has also fared well. The $19,000 she made by reaching the semifinals of the singles event plus the $14,000 she received for winning the doubles boosts her 1981 prize earnings to $367,000, a sum that is almost doubled by her endorsement income from Prince rackets, Fila clothing, and Nike footwear. At nineteen she has earned more than twice the salary of the president of the United States.

Tennis players and golfers are allowed to enter major tournaments as amateurs, and thus most have at least a taste of the pro life before they commit themselves to the tour. Although they must then become accustomed to a transient life-style, the adjustment can occur over the course of several months. Within the first year, most have either adapted to the pro life or have decided to leave the tour. In team sports, however, the jolt is severe. The introduction to the pro life begins before the player ever faces an opponent, in preseason training camp. "A pro basketball, baseball, and football camp is an emotional jungle," says Dr. Bruce C. Ogilvie, who has traveled extensively with pro teams as a psychological consultant. "You're thrown out there and expected to show your magnificent gifts without any real consideration that this is a very unreal situation with all sorts of things happening, all sorts of confusions. There is tremendous disinterest in you as a human being. You are treated only as a machine. Many youngsters are not ready for that. They've had loving coaches who perhaps may have coddled them unnecessarily, but at least have responded to them emotionally. Now they are thrown in with 120 other gifted young men and told to show the best they've got as a physical machine. But there is no consideration whatsoever as to what is going on inside."

As a result, many college stars never make it out of training camp. Sudden doubts, injuries, or personality conflicts with coaches end their careers. Those who do survive may sign a contract amid great celebration only to find joy soon replaced by other emotions — confusion, boredom, loneliness.

When Bill Bradley was a member of the New York Knicks, he contemplated the pro life: "After so many nights on the road in so many different hotels encountering so many different situations, everything takes on an ephemeral quality; everything ends with the payment at the cashier's desk the next morning. What normally would be out of the question for me becomes acceptable in the self-contained world of Mt. Marriott or Holiday Valley. Normal shyness would prevent me from entering a stranger's hotel room, but on the road there seems to be nothing to lose. Everyone in the hotel sleeps under the same roof for one night and moves on. Loneliness can be overcome only by reaching out for contact: a conversation in the bar, a sharing of dinner, a question in the elevator, a direct invitation, a telephone call to a room, or a helping hand with doors, windows, TV's, locks, or ice machines. The percentages are that if a man spends enough nights in hotels he will meet a woman with whom for that night he will share a bed, giving each a brief escape from boredom and loneliness. Make no mistake: Life in hotels is no continuous orgy. There are months of nights in one's room, alone. And it is rare that an encounter develops beyond the verbal level. It is very unusual when everything feels right and the loneliness of the road oppresses two strangers equally at the same time." The tedium of the pro life causes more divorces than any other profession. It promotes the use of alcohol and drugs. In men, loneliness may result in womanizing; in women it sometimes leads to lesbianism.

The pro life became an artificial one when the sports season stretched from three or four months to seven or more. Training camps began earlier, the number of scheduled games increased dramatically, and play-off series extended ad infinitum. In the 1960s, for example, professional basketball players played 62 games during a three-month season. Now the training camps begin in September, followed by 92 games and then the play-offs, which continue into June, a ten-month season. Pro football now extends from exhibition games in July to the Super Bowl in January, a period of seven months. In actuality, pro football is a full-time occupation. Although the athlete receives a paycheck only during the official season, he is expected to check in and weigh in three times a week during the off-season. In the training camps that precede the exhibition games, athletes must be in shape to do running trials, wind sprints, and weight-resistance training. "Many general managers and coaches would like to have control over their players' lives eleven months a year," says Dr. Bruce Ogilvie. "And in football, with their required weight-training program, it's gotten to be at least a ten-month job. If the players don't do the off-season training, they can't compete. Football is a game of force, and if you don't maintain enough energy to generate the necessary force, your position will be filled next season."

The traveling, the publicity, the fans — all cause a professional athlete to lose perspective. Everywhere twenty-one-year-old hockey star Wayne Gretzky turns, he is analyzed, scrutinized. "Every day I turn on the radio or the TV and I hear 'Wayne Gretzky is two points ahead of his pace last year,' or 'He's two goals behind last year's pace.' So as much as I want to put it out of my mind, I can't. People are always watching to see what I'm going to do."

"The professional athlete lives in a tinsel world of make-believe where the attention is not on the player as a human being, but the athlete as a symbol the fans can identify with and project upon," says Dr. Bruce Ogilvie. "After awhile, if the athlete doesn't realize that this is the game the fan is playing and he expects reality to be this way, he's going to end up in a rather severe depression. He's not going to be able to be fulfilled as a human being. Professional athletes can't have a love affair with the fans. If they do, they are going to be ultimately betrayed. The fans will turn to a competitor or the young man coming up in the next year's draft. If the athlete can say, 'Hey, that's reality, that's competition and professional sports,' the adulation remains in perspective. But when the praise is combined with the root-lessness of the pro lifestyle, some athletes develop neuroses and psychoses. They lose the stable mental base that made them such good athletes in the first place."

How do players escape the grind? Some pursue a particular hobby or business interest. Golfer Ben Crenshaw is an avid bird-watcher, both on and off the tour. Another golf pro, Jim Simmons, is also a registered stockbroker. Yet another golfer, Danny Edwards, is a part-time auto racer. At the beginning of the golf season he studies the tour schedule and the racing schedule and decides for each week whether to don his golf shoes or racing gear. "I don't think my golf has suffered because of my racing," he says. "If anything, racing seems to be good therapy for me. Most of my best tournaments have occurred the week after a race."

The other solution is to take time off. As the number of tennis tournaments and related stresses have risen, more pro players have opted to drop out of competition temporarily. In early 1980 Chris Evert Lloyd's game began to sputter. She suddenly lost four matches in a row to Martina Navratilova and five to Tracy Austin, and her ranking slid to number three. The native Floridian wanted to be outdoors with her new husband, not traveling to one dank, cold arena after another to play on a hard surface ill suited to her baseline game. She had been the number one player in the world for the past five years and had paid her dues. Now all she wanted was time off. The notion of retirement crept into her mind, but aspects of her game needed improvement, and she didn't want to end her career with memories of bad losses to Martina and Tracy. She traveled with her husband, John, to his tournaments and practiced with him an hour a day. She scheduled her return to the circuit in April, in time for the Italian Open.

Chris ended her unprecedented string of ten defeats with a win at the Italian Open. Her comeback was a smashing success. From May until the end of the year she won fifty-nine of sixty-two matches, and for the sixth time was honored with the number one ranking. Her four-month layoff was so beneficial, in fact, that she decided to repeat it every year.

Other players are forced to bow out temporarily because of injury. During the 1980 winter season, after weeks of playing on the unforgiving "carpet," Tracy Austin developed searing pains in her lower back, reaching down into her buttocks. The ailment kept nagging, but she continued tournament play. During the Colgate Series in January 1981, she was whipping her way through the field when, in her semifinal match against Wendy Turnbull, she "felt it go." She played in the finals and soundly beat Andrea Jaeger 6–2, 6–2. But her back problem, diagnosed as sciatica, became so painful that she couldn't play another tournament for five months. During her layoff, Tracy took stock of her tennis career and her life. Everything had always gone so smoothly that she had taken it for granted. Only when she was robbed of the opportunity to play did she realize how much she loved the sport and how it had enhanced her life. Five months after her injury, Tracy returned to the circuit with renewed commitment. A few months later, she won the U.S. Open. She had won the title before, but this time the victory was especially sweet. It symbolized her ability to surmount her first personal struggle.

As more top tennis players realize their need to get away from their sport in order to reassess their careers and allow their bodies to recuperate, it is inevitable that more are going to compete on their own terms, selecting a season and a surface that suits their individual tastes. In fact, this is happening. Andrea Jaeger, suffering a groin injury from too much pounding on the carpet, soon made it clear that she was in no rush to get back to the tour. Despite frantic phone calls from Avon that the series was falling apart because Tracy and Chris had withdrawn (Chris on her winter recoup, Tracy because a waiter in a Los Angeles restaurant had spilled hot tea on her, causing second-degree burns), Andrea defaulted in Dallas and decided that she would also sit out the Avon Championships. Perhaps she was taking a cue from dancer Mikhail Baryshnikov, who said in an interview for the *New York Times Magazine,* "It's funny. I'm very upset about my knee [injured in a dancing accident] but I'm sitting here, relaxed, with a bottle of wine. I seem to take my vacations when I'm injured. That's when I lie on the beach. It's very interesting psychologically — whether I use injuries to relieve the pressure." Or perhaps Andrea was merely following the leads of Chris and Tracy.

Neither tournament sponsors nor fans appreciate it when the top players decide to get off the treadmill for awhile. Sponsors do not like financing a merry-go-round. The cachet and drawing power of their tournaments suffer without the top names, which eventually results in lower profits. Although by scheduling so many tournaments the sponsors have, in effect, made mini-comebacks necessary for survival at the pro level, they are often unsympathetic when players wish to compete in only one of their series tournaments. Such was the case with five-time Wimbledon champion Bjorn Borg, who was barred from the 1982 competition because he hadn't played the prequalifying events on the Volvo Grand Prix circuit.

As Billie Jean King once cynically put it: "The pro tours have created a great opportunity for all of us, to win money and destroy our bodies at the same time."

# 13
# Life after Sports

For the athlete who reaches thirty-five, something in him dies; not a peripheral activity but a fundamental passion. . . . He approaches the end of his playing days the way old people approach death. He puts his finances in order. He reminisces easily. He offers advice to the young. But the athlete differs from an old person in that he must continue living. Behind all the years of practice and all the hours of glory waits that inexorable terror of living without the game.
— Bill Bradley, *Life on the Run*

**F**iction abounds with emotionally dislocated athletes. John Updike's *Rabbit, Run* is a tale of the emotional malaise of a former small-town high school basketball star named Harry "Rabbit" Angstrom. Still living in his adolescent heyday, he cannot form meaningful attachments to women, work, or anything else that drifts into his unstructured life. "That Championship Season," a Pulitzer Prize-winning play by Jason Miller, features four Harry Angstrom types and their coach (who never had another winning season), sitting around reminiscing twenty-five years after they won the state championship. In *Goodbye Columbus,* Ron Patimkin, Brenda's boring brother, sits in his room listening to records of his college basketball glory: 'And here comes Ron Patimkin, dribbling out. Ron, number eleven, from Short Hills, New Jersey. Big Ron's last game and it'll be some time before Buckeye fans forget him.' "

These are all fictional characters, but their withdrawal pains are distressingly real. For as an athlete ascends the competitive ladder and the pressures steadily mount, so does the degree to which self-identity and self-expression become enmeshed with the sport. Moreover, the excitement of the game provides a kind of euphoria that becomes addictive. Senator Bill Bradley wrote about the magic of basketball before he left the game:

The money and championships are reasons I play, but what I'm addicted to are the nights . . . when something special happens on the court. The experience is one of beautiful isolation. . . . It cannot be generally agreed upon, like an empirically verifiable fact, and it is far more than a passing emotion. It is as if a lightning bolt strikes, bringing insight into an uncharted area of human experience. It makes perfect sense at the

United Press International Photo

Bill Bradley goes up to block a shot by Ollie Johnson
of the Kansas City Kings, 1976.

same time it seems new and undiscovered. . . . With my team, before the crowd, against our opponents, no one else can sense the inexorable rightness of the moment. A backdoor play that comes with perfect execution at a critical time charges the crowd, but I sense an immediate transporting enthusiasm and a feeling that everything is in perfect balance.

Rules are made, the stopwatch clicks, the score is tallied, the contestants go home. Like a child's world, the game is simple and finite — in fact, sports keep athletes feeling like children long after their bodies have become adult. To stop competing is to bid farewell to the innocence of childhood, to step out of the familiar black and white world into a gray arena stripped of scoreboards, where the rules are not spelled out in advance and where the game is played with subtleties that lie outside the athlete's realm of experience. The most difficult moment in an athlete's career is usually when it ends.

At thirty-five, Ilie Nastase is in what *World Tennis* Magazine calls his "tragic twilight." Nastase has been deeply — and ferociously — involved in the game for more than twenty years. During his prime he won the U.S. Open and French Open, the Italian Open twice, and the Grand Prix Masters a record four times. But he has failed to win a Grand Prix tournament since 1977. His ranking has slipped a notch or two every year, and he no longer ranks in the top eighty players. "I lost a little speed, maybe a step or two, and I lost some confidence," Nastase says in his broken English. "When you lose your confidence, everything else goes bad. You eat bad, sleep bad, you don't practice. One day I'll wake up and decide I won't play anymore. I don't enjoy losing. But I would miss the tour too much. The tour is something inside me. . . . I suffer when I lose, but I want to be where the show is. I know people say I should retire, but what do I do then? To tell me to retire tomorrow is like saying I must die tomorrow. And I don't want to die."

In a sport like tennis retirement is a decision that the athlete usually comes to by himself. It is possible to gracefully and gradually bow out. In team sports, however, it is usually the coach or owner who decides not to renew the contract. Whatever the method of termination, the psychological process is similar. In fact, the post-retirement period parallels the grieving reaction for other major losses: first shock, then denial, anger, depression, and finally resignation.

The first reaction to retirement is usually a short period of numbness, followed by denial. The athlete may argue with the coach or general manager, continue to report for practice, and insist that a mistake has been made. The intensity of this reaction is related to its unexpectedness. If an athlete has no forewarning the response will undoubtedly be more severe than if the athlete has previously been benched.

But denial cannot be maintained forever. Most athletes next slip into a period of anger and resentment. "The athlete responds to the loss and frustration by projecting anger onto others, including family, coach, the general manager, and peers. Some athletes will generalize their anger and direct it toward God, fate, and life. Still other athletes will direct their rage against themselves. Some manifestations of this internalized aggression include self-destructive behaviors such as overindulgence in drugs and alcohol," says psychologist Bruce Ogilvie.

For the majority of athletes, the bouts of denial and rage are short-lived. What follows is a longer period of depression. "Typically in this stage the athlete withdraws from others, including those significant individuals who could provide much needed support," says Ogilvie. "The athlete may then experience a sense of loneliness and helplessess in this isolation as a result of the withdrawal. At one time consumed by a life-style which provided meaning and purpose, life is now void of significance and direction . . ."

Whereas most athletes retire from the pro ranks in their thirties, forties, and even fifties, Olympic gold medalists usually end their competitive careers in their late teens or early twenties, when they are at (or near) their peak form. Their problem is not postpartum depression but plotting a career path in the face of sudden fame. "The most difficult thing I've done in the last ten years was to make the transition from being an athlete back to being a normal person in the mainstream," Mark Spitz told Ira Berkow of the *New York Times*. "I had never imagined all the attention I would get. It was mind-boggling. My biggest mistake was that I practically became a recluse. I didn't know how to handle it all."

After his victory Spitz tried to make it as a television personality, but on variety shows and as an expert for swimming events, while his demeanor was handsome, his delivery was wooden. His endorsement contract with a swimwear manufacturer wasn't substantial enough to make a career. "After Munich, I never swam competitively again. I felt I had done all I could do in my sport, and now I had to get off the podium," he told Berkow. "At first, it was a real adjustment."

Today, at thirty-two, Spitz is over the emotional trauma. Although he had planned on being a dentist after the Olympics, instead he heads his own real estate development company and endorses swimwear, masks, and snorkels. He has been married for ten years and is the proud father of a one-year-old son Matthew, who has yet to take his first dip in the family pool in Los Angeles. Spitz doesn't do much swimming either. He paddles around the pool about once a week, and when he's in Hawaii checking up on his condominiums he enjoys bodysurfing. His greatest love these days is sailing. Every two years he and a group of five friends and their families compete in a sailing race from Los Angeles to Honolulu. He is proud to have placed third in last year's race, yet winning is no longer his prime objective. "It's nice to look back, but not to go back," he says.

Spitz was a twenty-two-year-old college senior when he won the Olympics and catapulted to stardom. Donna deVarona was only seventeen, and a high school student, when she won two Olympic gold medals in 1964. From her swimming debut at age ten, she had seldom known defeat. By the time she was twelve she was at the top of her age group nationally. Between thirteen and seventeen she set eighteen world records. Swimming was in its publicity heyday and Donna — attractive, extroverted, and crackling with energy — received worldwide attention.

But she had progressed so fast that after her Olympic victories Donna felt lost. She would sit by the pool, watch a workout, and then go home and say to her friends, "I can't make up my mind." One day she'd work out, the next she'd stay away from the pool. "I drove everyone crazy," she laughs in retrospect. "It was just too hard to leave that environment. From the age of 10 I had one goal. I was trained to be myopic, trained so that all my values in life centered around that commitment."

She swam in another competition in Germany and did well, but then she took stock. There weren't any athletic scholarships for women, or any other support that would enable her to continue training until the next Olympics, four years away. Further, she didn't want to quit a loser: she wanted to be remembered as a champion. And so before entering college she retired from competitive swimming. She recalls, "I called up ABC-TV and blurted 'I want you to consider me for a job as an expert on swimming because I can't bear to quit and if you give me the opportunity to stay around it will be much easier on me.' "

There was no mention of money; she just wanted to stay in the sport. Donna got the job. ABC called back and told her that her first assignment would be to cover the men's world championships in 1965. She became the first woman to cover a men's event. In addition to her new part-time job, the seventeen-year-old took on several other responsibilities.

It was a turbulent time, both for myself and the nation. Politics, especially civil rights, meant a lot to me. I had met Wilma Rudolph and Cassius Clay at the 1960 Olympics and I had a great fondness and

Donna deVarona at seventeen after setting a new
world record for the 400 meter individual medley.

respect for them. My boyfriend was drafted to go to Vietnam. I was a college freshman at UCLA, worked for Vice-President Hubert Humphrey's Inner Cities Program, had a contract with Speedo swimsuits, was flying off to cover swim events for ABC, and was hounded by agents who wanted me to do commercials. I found myself leading an almost schizophrenic existence — in Harlem or Newark working with Inner City kids one day and back at UCLA, going to theater classes the next. I was both a political activist and part of the establishment, and that raised a lot of questions in my mind.

One day when I was about twenty I woke up and thought, "I don't want all these responsibilities anymore. I want to go out and be free to drink beer on Friday nights." But that was never going to happen. I loved the television work and, though I knew I had many things to learn, I didn't want to give it up. The challenge then became combining things — my television career, my political interests, and my friendships.

Donna began college as a theater arts major, and one of her greatest thrills was visiting New York to see Broadway plays. Through friends at *Sports Illustrated,* she was introduced to several members of the New York Giants football team. One good-looking Giant, fullback Tucker Frederickson, was especially eager to recruit Donna to New York. "After college, you've really got to come here," he said. "This is the media mecca. If you're really serious about the TV business, come to New York." She did. Her Giants friends helped her find a roommate and took her out on dates. But her financial situation was less rosy. "At ABC we were free-lancers, which means we were only paid for the events we did. And they paid us virtually nothing. I managed to get an apartment on the West Side of Manhattan, which was then a low-rent district. But it was a real struggle to get by."

Professionally, she also felt frustrated. "When I started in TV I was seventeen years old and from California, where people have a very different way of expressing themselves," she says. "I had to devote a lot of time to writing so that I could learn to speak articulately. As a former swimming champion who had

Donna deVarona today, at thirty-five.

also done a lot of research on each competition, I knew I had some good insights to give. Yet how I gave them depended on how confident I was and how much time Jim McKay would let me have. A lot of the announcers who are responsible for covering a meet and have a young person with them aren't so sure that you're going to come through. So a lot of the time I didn't have time to say what I wanted. I developed a fast speaking pattern, which is something I still have to guard against. I also had to worry about my appearance. I had thought, 'Well, just be natural.' At seventeen, I wanted to grow my hair long and wear jeans and be a teenager, free from worry and 6 A.M. workouts. By twenty-two, I realized I had to look good. It was part of my job."

Part of the frustration when she came to New York was the result of unrealistic expectations. "After college, I was ready to take on the world, like I had in swimming. But it was hard to face the reality that I'd have to start all over again, and as a young woman, many of the doors were locked. I began to realize that mastering a profession required a different kind of effort from swimming, where everything had been black and white. It had been me against the clock. If I could swim faster than anyone else, I could reap the rewards. I was suddenly learning that outside the swimming pool one didn't necessarily get places just by working hard. I began to understand that there is a subtlety to real life, especially in the corporate world. Ironically, it was my swimming background, which had created my delusions in the first place, that also saw me through. I refused to give up. I persevered through all the politics. If something didn't work one way, then I'd try another."

Today, at thirty-five, Donna deVarona is a broadcasting veteran. She is eagerly looking forward to hosting the 1984 Olympics for NBC Sports, and now, for the first time, feels truly comfortable in her job. "I really like working with people under pressure," she says. "Live television is like swimming a relay race. The gun goes off and you've got to pull yourself together because you only have one chance. Though I've been at the job ten years, only now am I getting to the point of being very good. I still am not in a position to say 'I want to do this story or that story,' and that's frustrating. But most announcers never have that option. So when I'm assigned an event I just do the best I can."

Donna's political activity is now focused on athletes' rights. In 1976 she took time off from broadcasting to become a special consultant to the U.S. Senate. As a lobbyist, she helped with the passage of the Amateur Sports Act (which gave athletes representation in the United States Olympic Committee and membership on the board of directors in every sports federation) and Title IX (which ensured that equal sports opportunities were provided for men and women in school). Now she hopes to work for legislation that would provide athletes and coaches with federal funds. "A quarter billion dollars is being paid for licensing rights to the Olympics, television networks are making their reputations on how they cover the games, and announcers are making their reputations on how they work the Games," she says. "The only players who don't make money from appearing on prime time in a major entertainment special — which the Olympics has become — are the athletes. . . . The problem is that we are still taking our cue from the national sports arenas. And the two systems — capitalism and socialism — look at money and sports differently. In the socialist countries the athletes are subsidized. You may see Soviet artists defect to the United States but you don't see many athletes defecting. And we have three or four top-level gymnastic coaches in this country who have recently had to close down their gyms because they can't afford to teach. Clearly, we must give our athletes and coaches more support."

Donna's pet program is the Women's Sport Foundation which she, Billie Jean King, and a handful of other prominent female athletes established in 1975. For the past four years she has served as its president and has proudly watched the organization blossom. "Many of us women athletes set a game plan about ten years ago," she explains. "We realized the male establishment would never focus on us. We had to have banquets, dinners, and give awards, like the men do with the Heisman Trophy, to call attention to ourselves as a viable product. In 1979 the Women's Sports Foundation started a Hall of Fame dinner and annual fund raiser in which we honor a top amateur athlete and raise $110,000. As a result, more and more sponsors are being drawn into women's sports. We're helping to get athletes jobs both while they are competing and after they retire."

Donna deVarona is filled with new dreams and schemes. The only area that remains sketchy is her social life. "Marriage is going to be a real problem," she sighs. "I want to be as good a mother as I am a professional. And I haven't figured out a way to balance that yet. I thought it would be possible after 1980. I had been assigned to host the Summer Olympics, and was planning to perhaps end my broadcasting career after that. But with the Olympic boycott my plans, as well as all the athletes' dreams, were thwarted. Now I'm traveling to both coasts as a special consultant to the United States Olympic Committee. I'm going to France tomorrow to cover an event for NBC Sports. I'm spending a lot of time working for the Women's Sports Foundation. And I do a lot of nationwide speaking engagements. I haven't yet decided, 'Enough, slow down, go another direction.' But now the Women's Sport Foundation is functioning well. After the 1984 Olympics things may slow down. I might cut back on the TV work."

In the meantime, swimming provides the antidote to her fast-paced life. "It's harder to fit in my schedule now because of the time demands, and if I don't get bogged down with work during the day. But I love it. It's so freeing and relaxing, like meditation. When I'm on the road, I take my swimsuit everywhere. A few months ago I was going to give a talk in Chicago and when I walked in the gym I saw a beautiful 50-meter pool. It looked too good to pass up. I whispered to my host, 'I've got to swim after my speech.' He couldn't believe that I still love it after all these years. But I do."

As Donna deVarona's story indicates, the retiring athlete faces a convergence of pressures — economic, social, professional, personal. The ability to adapt to retirement ultimately depends on experience and personality. Athletes who have a college diploma, middle- or upper-class parents, internal self-reliance, a strong emotional support system, and a polished image are likely to fare well. Those who are disadvantaged, who have been denied the opportunity to become responsible adults, and who have developed few outside interests are likely to experience a protracted and difficult adjustment period.

Every athlete facing retirement hopes to recapture the particular joy found in his or her sport in another career. Billie Jean King, for example, who has long relished her role as a creative tennis player — running to the net and back to the baseline, darting to the alleys to retrieve impossible shots — hopes that she will be able to find an occupation that incorporates the same flexibility. "Because of this creative drive, when I retire I'll have to find something else that I can get totally involved in," she says. "I don't know what that will be — broadcasting, school, sports, politics? I'm keeping all the doors open. Maybe I'll never find anything I love as much as tennis, but I'm willing to go in search of it."

On the other hand, Chris Evert Lloyd, whose game has been built on steadiness — channeling all her emotional, mental, and physical energies into perfecting her tennis strokes — will be steered by her desire for excellence. "After tennis, I hope I will always have a challenge in my life, something at which I can work hard and feel fulfilled. When I lose my inspiration and incentive I begin to worry." Athletes like Chris Evert Lloyd and Billie Jean King, who have been in the public eye for so long and have built up a polished presence, may well be able to convert their tennis talents into broadcasting or other tennis-related endeavors. And someone like Evert Lloyd, who has earned more than $4 million in prize money alone over the course of her career, does not have to make any immediate career decisions.

But most retiring athletes don't have an economic cushion and must begin another career without delay. Even though there are now greater opportunities for sports-related jobs, with hundreds of athletes retiring each year, the competition for these jobs is intense. Nor are all of them open to everyone. A career as a team trainer, sports psychologist, or sports physician requires years of specialized training. Broadcasting and public relations jobs require an unusual package of attractiveness, poise, and verbal skills. Management of a sports facility requires capital. As a result, only a handful of competitors are able to translate their talents directly into commercial viability.

The economic picture is especially bleak in team sports, in which the average career lasts less than five years, and only those who play longer than this are eligible to receive a pension. Even those who are eligible must wait thirty years or longer to receive their benefits. For the average NFL player, who made only $30,000 or $40,000 a year and incurred hidden costs such as a second home and family travel expenses, the pinch becomes a life-threatening squeeze. To make matters worse, three quarters of professional football players have not graduated from college, a reality that further constricts their career options. They must adjust not only to a salary that often drops from $40,000 to $10,000 a year, but also to the metamorphosis from sports star to business tyro. Many expect their success in sports to translate to success in business. If they fail, they are candidates for severe depression, alcohol and drug abuse, criminal activity, even suicide.

Sports psychologists are now taking an active role in helping athletes to anticipate and plan for retirement. Although the majority of professional football players don't have college degrees, many do have three years of credit toward a degree. Psychologist Dr. Zandy Liebowitz has helped more than two hundred of them investigate nontraditional programs in which they can earn their degrees. She also helps them assess their personal strengths and potential professional skills, and she has set up internship programs to allow athletes to start training for a professional career during the off-season. A key element of her program involves bringing in former athletes to talk to those who are still competing about what they can expect when their careers are over. "We discuss some of the conflicts they may face and reassure them that it's okay to experience the anger and depression. Many guys think they are the only ones who are feeling this extreme loneliness and pain. They won't go near the stadium when their team plays," she says.

Almost no one is exempted from distress. Even children who have not been brought up to believe that winning is everything, who are not raised in the hothouse of big-money sports, who have taken care to become well rounded and well educated, may later pay a price for their talent. A descendant of Benjamin Franklin and an alumnus of Exeter, Princeton, and Yale Graduate School, Franklin Bache Satterthwaite, Jr., was not supposed to become a squash junkie. But the sport captivated him. As a country club tennis player, he was early identified as "good with a racket" (in boys' prep schools the equivalent of a girl's being voted prom queen). At Exeter he excelled in both tennis and squash. The latter, played in a four-walled court with a long, light racket and a small, hard ball, is a faster game, requiring

Frank Satterthwaite in action against
world champion Sharif Khan, 1978.

lightning reflexes and a sharp, strategic mind. The more he played, the more he learned about shot making. With each subtle change in his racket motion he could produce daring and unusual shots. He became obsessed with the game and loved everything associated with it — the smell of the adhesive tape, the showers, the locker room camaraderie, consulting with the coach — and even though he bellyached about the training, he cherished it too, because it put him in touch with his physical self.

But squash, unlike tennis, is a small-time sport. He knew he couldn't make a living from it, nor did he care to. There were other sides of himself that he wanted to develop. He was quick-witted and intellectually curious. And in the schools he attended, although sports skill was admired, it wasn't the prime focus. But what he kept coming back to, day after day, was squash. "It was so much fun and so fascinating that it just sucked me in," he says. "Every weekend I was invited to go to another city and club to go to parties and dances and play in a squash tournament. A loyal squash fan would pick me up at the airport, I'd stay at his house, and we'd talk squash the whole weekend. I became involved in a little world where you can kid yourself into believing that the whole world is a squash court. I was the guest of the world and received as a hell of a guy just for being able to hit a ball with a racket. I had it made both ways — I was a winner and a success: good at the game, and admired for it. And when you're winning, you think you can never lose. It's a fool's paradise."

At every level of the game, at prep school, college, and in the pros, he was consistently near the top of the ranks. Not good enough to be number one, but good enough to beat any of the top players. "When I went on the court I knew I could win. If you get to be number two or number three, there's an incentive to improve your situation. It's like a one-armed bandit. You put money in and every once in awhile you get just enough back to make you keep putting more in."

As he progressed through the ranks, the competition itself continued to fascinate him, but the trimmings started to wear thin. "When I was a young kid, I enjoyed all the trappings — hanging around squash clubs discussing the sport, the parties, the gossip. But eventually I got tired of it all, particularly the institutionalized revelry. And it took up too much time. If you want to perform well, the day of a match you can't be involved in anything else. You have to get psyched up for the event and wind down. And the training, too, was time-consuming and exhausting. I had to do anaerobic wind sprints — both on the court and on a stationary bicycle — to stay in shape. I would pedal so furiously on the bicycle that after thirty seconds my legs were in spasm and I was screaming with pain. Tired of everything but the competition, I developed a fantasy of being parachuted in just for the match and then after the match being able to climb up a ladder through the roof of the court to a helicopter which would then take me away."

Now, at forty, he is about to retire from the pro ranks. "What tells me I'm finished is that I play better in practice than in matches, and it used to be the reverse," he says. "And I've noticed that I can't win when I'm ahead. I'm enough of an old warhorse to get motivated when I'm behind. But when I get a lead it's disastrous. I've lost the sense of the jugular — the ability to put people away. And I'm aware of it because at each tournament I see kids with glazed-over looks in their eyes. They are psyched up, while I'm not all that nervous. In fact, I'm the soul of affability.

"I can do all the things I'm supposed to do," Satterthwaite continues. "I know when to eat, when to dress, when to stretch, when to do warm-ups. And even in the match I can still play good points and put together strategies and games. But once I get an edge on an opponent, I can't put him away."

Now he looks back, thinking about what might have been if squash hadn't monopolized his life — the books that might have

288

been written, the businesses he might have run. "One of the problems was that I could wake up in the morning and know I was one of the top ten squash players in the world. With squash, you are painting on a very small canvas. But if it's the only canvas you know, it looks pretty big. So even though I didn't wake up asking myself how I could improve my game like my fellow pros, I did have the comfort of knowing I was good. It's like an unmarried woman who turns forty and realizes she has in effect chosen not to have children. You wake up one morning and you realize you're at this stage and wonder if you should have done things differently. But you can't just throw a switch and change your life."

At the moment, Satterthwaite is writing a novel, serving as a squash consultant to Dunlop, lending expert commentary to squash matches on cable television, and he has also written and hosted a series of squash clinics for public television. He is doing well, but most of his activities are still squash-related. One wonders whether he might not have achieved success in a wider world had he not devoted so much of his life to squash. He firmly believes, however, that his sports experience is aiding his new careers. "One of the reasons I can tough it out as a writer is the endurance I learned on the squash court. You can dare to lose, for an athlete has necessarily lost. He hates to lose and is afraid to lose, but he has learned how to handle it. And the athlete also knows that winning isn't luck. You have to put in your time to win." At a time when most of his college classmates are feeling bored and stale, he is starting anew.

Most accomplished athletes feel that their sport has given them self-reliance, an appreciation of hard work, and a desire to seek, rather than shrink from, challenge. After what may be a difficult initial adjustment period, most athletes are successfully able to reinvest their motivation and dedication in other activities. Some continue to enjoy their sports as a sideline — either in special "masters" competitions or on a purely recreational basis. Others, especially swimmers who have spent most of their childhoods submerged in a pool, vow they will never swim another lap.

Even after their competitive days are long past, the memories linger. Almost thirty years after receiving her Olympic gold medal in 1956 at Cortina, Italy, figure skater Dr. Tenley Albright recalls, "Winning the gold medal was more than just a feeling of walking up to the podium beside the flame in response to hearing my name, announced late at night, out of doors with the lights shining on the mountains and the bright stars so close overhead.

"The moment itself was one of heightened perception — hundreds of things flashed clearly into my mind at once. Though it was only a matter of seconds, time stood still. I noticed everything around me, recognized the same kind of feeling that I had when I came in first in Eastern Juveniles, and wondered how a sport could seem so very, very important and so connected with *everything* else.

"Everything around me seemed amusing and very serious at the same time," she continues. "Individual faces and colors in the night were, and still are, particularly vivid — and some of the faces I saw so clearly were back home in the United States."

Unfortunately, that moment when body and spirit merge perfectly, that moment John Jerome calls "the sweet spot in time," is all too brief. Eventually, every athlete must strike what former Rhodes scholar Bill Bradley terms a Faustian bargain: In return for the peak moments, "to live all one's days never able to recapture the feeling of those years of intensified youth."

# Acknowledgments

Taking my third skating test was an exercise in terror. But being handed a first book contract and instructed to write 90,000 words was equally mind-boggling. After a few weeks, the initial panic subsided into mere chaos. Thoughts began bouncing around my head like hot-air balloons, and I desperately tried to grab hold of a few strings, lest they fly out of sight (and mind) forever. My editor, Genevieve Young, and literary agent, Wendy Lipkind, often rescued me from this chaos and helped me put my thoughts in order.

Slowly, the book began to organize itself as similarities in the young athletes' lives became apparent. But this point would never have been reached if it were not for the dozens of athletes, parents, siblings, and coaches who graciously allowed me to step into their lives. Many thanks to all — and to the public relations agents who often facilitated the process.

I am also deeply indebted to sports psychologists Bruce Ogilvie, Thomas Tutko, and Rainer Martens, who steered me to relevant psychological research and openly shared their thoughts; and to sport physicians Burton Berson, Lyle Michaeli, and Gabe Mirkin. Deborah Pines of the *New York Times Magazine* also deserves thanks for initially helping me to get a hold on the vast subject. I would also like to thank all the photographers whose pictures enlivened my words and Jill Krementz, David Leonardi, Bob Meade (Sports Fotofile), Joe Luppino (United Press International), and Paula Vogel (Wide World Photos) for their special kindness. And thank you, Peggy Barber, for being the meticulous typist I'm not.

Finally, I wish to offer gratitude to some of the people who kept my spirits high through the months of researching and writing — Robert Karen, Dick Powell, Sally Reigler, Keven and John Bridge, the Semlear family, my sisters Elizabeth and Sally, and my mother, Taube.

# Notes

Most of the material in this book was obtained through personal interviews with athletes, agents, parents, siblings, coaches, and sports physicians and psychologists. This foundation was buttressed with research from newspaper and magazine articles, books, and television documentaries. When possible, references to these sources have been included in the text. What follows is a more complete listing of the sources used in each chapter.

### Introduction

Emily Greenspan, "Little Winners," *New York Times Magazine,* April 26, 1981.

Red Smith, "Sports of the Times," *New York Times,* February 29, 1980.

### Chapter 1: The Rise and Fall of Lisa-Marie Allen

Bob Ottum, "Stumbling to Lake Placid," *Sports Illustrated,* January 28, 1980.

Neil Amdur, "Judging is Clouded for Miss Fratianne," *New York Times,* January 20, 1980.

### Chapter 2: Child's Play

Michael Novak, *The Joy of Sports* (New York: Basic Books, 1976).

*The Perrier Study: Fitness in America* (New York: Louis Harris Associates, 1979).

*Little Winners*

### Chapter 3: Getting Started

Chris Evert Lloyd with Neil Amdur, *Chrissie: My Own Story* (New York: Simon and Schuster, 1982).

*Jack Nicklaus and Jimmy Connors:*
Parton Keese, *The Measure of Greatness* (Englewood Cliffs, N.J.: Prentice-Hall, 1981).

Thomas Tutko and William Bruns, *Winning is Everything and Other American Myths* (New York: Macmillan, 1976).

Dr. Arthur Grayson's observations recorded in *The American Medical Joggers Association Newsletter*, April 1982.

### Chapter 4: Buckling Down

*W. H. Murray, quote:*
James A. Austin, *Chase, Chance and Creativity* (New York, Columbia University Press, 1978).

Sam Moses, "Bobby Unser — I Will Go Fast Until the Day I Die," *Sports Illustrated*, January 11, 1982.

### Chapter 5: The Home Front

Opening quotes from Mrs. Marjorie Healy, interviewed on "Children and Sports," 1980 television documentary with James Michener, Cappy Productions and Emlen House Productions, Inc.; and Mrs. Audrey Leech, "Confessions of a Tennis Mother," *World Tennis*, April 1979.

*Linda Fratianne's reaction to her parents' divorce:*
Linda Kay, "Her Skating Took Its Toll," *Chicago Tribune*, November 30, 1981.

*Sibling rivalry:*
Jeanne Evert and John Austin: Cindy Schmerler, "Is Tennis a Family Affair or Feud?," *World Tennis*, December 1981.

Chris Evert Lloyd with Neil Amdur, *Chrissie: My Own Story* (New York: Simon and Schuster, 1982).

Clare Evert: "Tennis Siblings Try Their Own Shots," *New York Times*, August 8, 1982.

Grant Cassiday: Barry Temkin, "Swimmer Seeks Own Success," *Chicago Tribune*, August 21, 1981.

Beth Heiden: Dave Anderson, "Tears and a Bronze for Beth," *New York Times*, February 21, 1980.

Murray Howe: Steve Marantz, "Enduring the Athletic Name Game," *Boston Globe,* October 13, 1981.

*Information on moral development:*
Erik Erikson, *Identity and the Human Life Cycle,* W. W. Norton, 1980.
Rainer Martens, "Kid Sports: A Den of Iniquity or Land of Promise?," in Richard Magill et al., eds., *Children in Sport: A Contemporary Anthology* (Champaign, Illinois: Human Kinetics Publishers, 1978).
Thomas Tutko and William Bruns, *Winning is Everything and Other American Myths* (New York: Macmillan, 1976).

### Chapter 6: The Coach

*Background on Debbie Meyer:*
Janice Kaplan, *Women in Sports* (New York: Viking Press, 1979).

*Tracy Austin and Robert Landsdorp:*
Bud Collins, "The 200 Percent Solution," *World Tennis,* June 1980.
Jane Gross, "Miss Austin's Coach Takes Some Credit," *New York Times,* March 24, 1980.
Sarah Pileggi, "Rolling Onto a New Track," *Sports Illustrated,* December 21, 1981.

*Psychological impact of the coach:*
Bruce C. Ogilvie and Linda Gustavson McGuire, "How Competition Affects Elite Women Swimmers," *The Physician and Sportsmedicine,* June 1980.
"Development of Talent Project," Dr. Leonard Bloom, University of Chicago, March 1982, as reported by Maya Pines, "Specific Skills Linked to Specific Patterns," *New York Times,* March 30, 1982.

*Carlo Fassi's coaching techniques:*
Carlo Fassi, *Figure Skating with Carlo Fassi* (New York: Charles Scribner's Sons, 1981).

### Chapter 7: The Education of the Superstar

*Lynne Lederer's problems at school:*
Jerry Schnay, "Parents Sacrifice for Gym Star's Dream," *Chicago Tribune,* August 23, 1980.

*Tracy Austin's education:*
Joseph N. Bell, "Tracy's Time," *Seventeen,* June 1980.

*The Stratton Mountain School:*

Holcomb B. Noble, "Schooling for the Olympics," *New York Times Magazine,* February 22, 1981.

*Nick Bollettieri's Tennis Academy:*
  Jim Martz, "Sweatshop with Nets," *World Tennis,* November 1980.
  Barry McDermott, "He'll Make Your Child a Champ," *Sports Illustrated,* June 9, 1980.

### Chapter 8: Sportspolitik

*Background information on the United States Olympic Committee:*
  "The USOC," *The Olympian,* August 1980.

### Chapter 9: Growing Up: Physiology and the Role of Sports Medicine

*Dropout rate:*
*from the twelve-year Medford (Oregon) growth study reported in H. Harrison Clark, "Characteristics of Young Athletes," Kinesiology Review, 1968.*

*Sports injuries:*
Becky Muelhausen's swimming injury discussed on "Donahue," Donahue transcript no. 10261, Youth Sports, Multimedia Program Production, Cincinnati, Ohio.
  Margaret Combs, "Tell Me Where it Hurts: A Rash of Injuries is Plaguing Today's Young Gymnasts," *Women's Sports,* April 1981.
  Neil Amdur, "Women's Tennis Feeling Pain," *New York Times,* March 23, 1982.
  Theodore Clarke, "What Are We Doing to Our Skaters?," *Skating World,* October 1981.

Dr. Vern Seefeldt's quote from "Youth Sports," a segment on "NBC Magazine," aired July 16, 1981.

*Hockey violence:*
*Youth Sports: Is Winning Everything?,* Barton Cox, Jr. Films, San Mateo, California.

*Cardiac capabilities:*
  Donald A. Bailey, "Sport and the Child: Physiological Considerations," in Richard Magill, Michael Ash, and Frank Smoll, eds., *Children in Sport: A Contemporary Anthology* (Champaign, Illinois: Human Kinetics Publishers, 1978).

*Effects of exercise on maturation:*
  Dr. Rose Frisch et al., "Delayed Menarche and Amenorrhea of Col-

lege Athletes in Relation to Age of Onset of Training," *Journal of American Medical Association,* October 2, 1981.

*Other sources on sports medicine:*
Dr. Gabe Mirkin and Marshall Hoffman, *The Sportsmedicine Book* (Boston: Little, Brown, 1978).

Dr. Robert S. Siffert, *How Your Child's Body Grows* (New York: Grosset & Dunlap, 1980).

Dr. John L. Marshall with Heather Barbash, *The Sports Doctor's Fitness Book for Women* (New York: Delacorte Press, 1981).

Lawrence Galton, *Your Child in Sports* (New York: Franklin Watts, 1981).

John Jerome, *The Sweet Spot in Time* (New York: Avon, 1982).

Nathan Smith, "Nutrition in Children's Sports," in Curtis Vouwie, ed., *Sports Injuries in the Child and Adolescent* (Boston: Little, Brown, 1983).

Ken Sprague, *The Athlete's Body* (Los Angeles: J. P. Tarcher, 1981).

Natalie Angier, "How Fast? How High? How Far? Sport Scientists are Probing the Physical Limits of the Human Body," *Discover,* November 1981.

Dr. James A. Nicholas, "Sportsmedicine — Past, Present, and Future," paper presented at the Sixth Annual Meeting of the American Orthopaedic Society for Sports Medicine, New York, July 1980.

*Steroids:*
Dr. Allan J. Ryan, "Anabolic Steroids are Fool's Gold," from the symposium "Drug Abuse in Athletics," presented at the 64th Annual Meeting of the American Societies for Experimental Biology, Anaheim, California, April 1980.

Marjorie Shuer, "Steroids," *Women's Sports,* April 1981.

### Chapter 10: The Sift

*Cus D'Amato quote:*
Robert Riger, *The Athlete* (New York: Simon and Schuster, 1980).

*Psychological factors:*
Bruce Ogilvie and Thomas Tutko, "Sport: If You Want to Build Character, Try Something Else," *Psychology Today,* October 1971.

Bruce Ogilvie, "The Child Athlete: Psychological Implications of Participation in Sport," *Annals of the American Academy of Political and Social Science,* September 1979.

William P. Morgan, "Test of Champions," *Psychology Today,* July 1980.

Richard M. Suinn, ed., *Psychology in Sports: Methods and Applications* (Minneapolis: Burgess, 1980).

Peter Klavora and Juri V. Daniel, eds., *Coach, Athlete and Sport Psychologist* (Champaign, Illinois: Human Kinetics Publishers, 1979).

Thomas Tutko and William Bruns, *Winning is Everything and Other American Myths* (New York: Macmillan, 1976).

Rainer Martens, *Joy and Sadness in Children's Sports* (Champaign, Illinois: Human Kinetics Publishers, 1978).

Dorothy V. Harris, *Involvement in Sport: A Somatopsychic Rationale for Physical Activity* (Philadelphia: Lea and Febiger, 1973).

Richard Magill, Michael Ash, and Frank Smoll, eds., *Children in Sport: A Contemporary Anthology* (Champaign, Illinois: Human Kinetics Publishers, 1978).

William F. Straub, ed., *Sport Psychology: An Analysis of Athlete Behavior* (Ithaca, New York: Mouvement Publications, 1978).

Michael Murphy and Rhea A. White, *The Psychic Side of Sports* (Reading, Mass.: Addison-Wesley, 1978).

Linda Bird Francke, "Riding High," *New York* magazine, December 7, 1981.

*Financial considerations:*
Susanna Schroer, "The 'A' Circuit on a Budget," *The Practical Horseman,* April 1982.

Wally Carew, "Priscilla Hill: Surmounting a Decade of Struggle," *Skating* magazine, June 1981.

**Chapter 11: Turning Pro**

Philip Taubman, "The Exploitation of Dorothy Hamill," *Esquire,* May 1978.

John Radosta, "Roughing It at Golf School," *New York Times,* November 7, 1981.

*Kathy Rinaldi:*
Peter Bodo and Alexander McNab, "Pro Prodigies," *Tennis* magazine, March 1982.

Peggy Gossett, "Latest in Kid Craze: Kathy Rinaldi," *Sporting News,* July 14, 1981.

William Johnson, "The Courting of Kathy Rinaldi," *Florida,* July 14, 1981.

Linda Penz, "Pro Prodigies," *Tennis Week,* March 25, 1982.

*ProServ (agents):*
Pat Sloan, "Dressed to Sell," *Women's Sports,* April 1981.

Tony Scherman, "Money Secrets of the Well-Managed Jock," *Savvy,* January 1981.

Bart Barnes, "Athletes' Lives and Livelihoods are ProServ's Stock and Trade," *Washington Post,* July 19, 1980.

*Isiah Thomas:*
Roy Damer, "The Eyes Have It for Isiah," *Chicago Tribune,* January 19, 1980.

Bill Jauss, "Basketball is Still Only a Game . . . Like Monopoly," *Chicago Tribune,* January 20, 1980.

Roy Damer, "Isiah Undecided on Turning Pro, but Sure of Future as Lawyer," *Chicago Tribune,* March 5, 1981.

Ira Berkow, "At 19, Isiah Makes His Decision to Turn Pro," *New York Times,* April 27, 1981.

*The student-athlete crisis:*
Pete Axthelm, "The Shame of College Sports," *Newsweek,* September 22, 1980.

John Underwood, "The Shame of American Education: The Student-Athlete Hoax," *Sports Illustrated,* May 19, 1980.

### Chapter 12: The Pro Life

Bill Bradley, *Life on the Run* (New York: Quadrangle/New York Times, 1976).

Lawrie Mifflin, "It's Hard for Wayne Gretzky to Keep his Pace," *New York Times,* November 4, 1982.

Billie Jean King with Kim Chapin, *Billie Jean* (New York: Harper & Row, 1974).

### Chapter 13: Life after Sports

Bill Bradley, *Life on the Run* (New York: Quadrangle/New York Times, 1976).

Peter Bodo, "Ilie Nastase: The Tragic Twilight," *Tennis,* May 1981.

*Mark Spitz:*
Ira Berkow, "Mark Spitz, After the Glory," *New York Times,* October 28, 1982.

Neil Amdur and Lawrie Mifflin, "Records are Past," *New York Times,* July 14, 1982.

## Little Winners

*Billie Jean King:*

Robert Riger, *The Athlete* (New York: Simon and Schuster, 1980).

Chris Evert Lloyd with Neil Amdur, *Chrissie: My Own Story* (New York: Simon and Schuster, 1982).

*Tenley Albright:*

Wally Carew, "Gold Medal Memories," *Skating* magazine, July 1979.

# Index

ABC, 241, 276, 278; "20/20," 136

Abdul-Jabbar, Kareem, 234

Academies, sports, 126–127, 144; Nick Bollettieri's Tennis Academy, 63, 64, 68–69, 134–144, 206; Stratton Mountain School, 127–134, 143, 151

Air Force Academy, 156

Albright, Tenley, 173, 187, 290

All-American College Golf Team, 77

All-American Selection Committee, 77

All-American Sport Camp, 135

Allen, Dorothy, 10, 12, 15–16, 21–22, 23

Allen, Lisa-Marie, 162, 173; rise and fall of, 8–23

Amateur Athletic Union (AAU), 43

Amateur Sports Act, 281

Amdur, Neil, 15

American Academy of Pediatrics, 181–182

Amphetamines, 181

Amritraj, Anand, 83

Amritraj, Vijay, 83

Amyx, David, 41, 44, 46

Amyx, Herbert, 41–44, 46–48

Amyx, Jennifer, 41, 42, 44–48

Annacone, Cathy, 64–75, 80

Annacone, Dominic, 64–71, 74, 206

Annacone, Paul, 80–81, 136, 140, 143, 206; tennis career of, 64–75

Annacone, Steve, 64–75, 80–81

Anthony, Earl, 221

Arias, Jimmy, 135, 136, 141, 142, 143, 144

Ariel, Gideon, 184–185

Armagh, Nina, 133

Ashe, Arthur, 142

Ashe, Neil, 198

Ashford, Evelyn, 179

Aspen Cup, 148, 149

Aspen Highlands Company, 149

Aspen Ski Club, 148–149, 162, 163

Aspen Ski Corporation, 146, 148, 149

Austin, Doug, 98

Austin, George, 98

Austin, Jeanne, 98–99, 100, 101, 102, 252–253

Austin, Jeff, 98, 100

Austin, John, 83, 88–90, 98

Austin, Pam, 98

Austin, Tracy, 25, 83, 137, 225, 248; bond between coach and, 98–103, 118; competition between brother John and, 88–90; conflict between school and sports for, 125–126; earnings of, 228; Evert Lloyd's losses to, 267; financial status of, 232; injuries of, 171, 267–268; and Pam Shriver, 249; and Toyota Series championship, 250, 252, 253,

Austin, Tracy *(cont.)*
262, 263; her winning of U.S. Open, 25, 100–101, 125, 126, 251, 268
Australian Davis Cup, 255
Australian Open, 249, 251
Avon Championships, 268
Avon Indoor circuit, 248, 251
Avon International Women's Marathon, 46–48
Axthelm, Pete, 241

Babashoff, Shirly, 126, 232
Babilonia, Tai, 19, 21, 172, 232
Bailey, Donald, 176
Baryshnikov, Mikhail, 268
Baseball, 223; salaries in, 222
Basketball, 222, 223, 265; players, black, 234–242
Bassett, Carling, 135, 136, 138–139
Bassett, John, 135
Bassler, Tom, 203–204
Baxter, Tori, 229
Bell, Ivan, 27–33
Berkow, Ira, 275
Berson, Burton, 177, 180
Bloom, Benjamin S., 103
Bodo, Peter, 99
Bollettieri, Nick, 70, 71, 72; his Tennis Academy (Bradenton, FL), 63, 64, 68–69, 134–144, 206
Bolt, Tommy, 26
Borg, Bjorn, 229, 269
*Boston Globe*, 87
Bowling, professional, 221, 223
Boxing, 221–222
Braden, Vic, 98, 99, 101
Bradley, Bill, 264–265, 272, 290; *Life on the Run*, 243, 270, 271–273
Brandi, Andy, 233
Brill, Frank, 217
Broadmoor Ice Arena (Colorado Springs), 18, 20, 22, 23, 116
Brown, Billy Ray, 77
Brown, Charlie, 77
Budge, Don, 40
Bunge, Bettina, 225
Burge, Wendy, 18
Button, Dick, 20

Candy, Don, and Pam Shriver, 249–251, 253–256, 257, 262–263
Casale, Pam, 136
Cassiday, Grant, 87–88
Cassiday, Stacy, 88
Cassiday, Sue, 87–88
Castellucci, Lisa, 204–205
Cawley, Evonne Goolagong, 248, 256
CBS, 241; "Sports Spectacular," 96
Chaffee, Suzy, 223, 231
Chapa, Rudy, 203
Chapman, Jeanne, 18
Chavoor, Sherm, 95, 97, 98
*Chicago Tribune*, 79, 87
Children's Hospital (Boston), 177
Clarke, H. Harrison, 167
Clay, Cassius, 276–278
Coaches, 94–95; attrition rate of first-level, 108; bond between athletes and, 95–103, 120; in gymnastics, 108–116; in skating, 104–108, 116–120
Cohen, Tiffany, 168–170
Colgate Women's Games, 26, 192–195, 267
Collins, Bud, 101–102
Comaneci, Nadia, 52
Connors, Gloria, 36
Connors, Jimmy, 36, 220
Cordero, Angel, 57–58
Corrigan, Jim, 172
Cosell, Howard, 221
Cousins, Robin, 116
Cox, Barton, 174–175
Crenshaw, Ben, 266
Curry, John, 116, 117

D'Amato, Cus, 188
Davis, Scott, 72
DeBus, Chuck, 184
Decathlon, 155, 159–160
Deford, Frank, 84
Delinger, Bill, 203
Dell, Craighill, Fentress and Benton, 228
Dell, Donald, 71, 228
Delsing, Jay, 77
Delsing, Jim, 77

Dempsey, Jack, 222
DePalmer, Mike, 71
de Picciotto, Phil, and Kathy Rinaldi, 228–234
deVarona, Donna, 223, 275–276, 282–283; retirement of, from swimming, 276; and Women's Sport Foundation, 281–282; her work in television, 276–281
Diamond, Jerry, 171–172
DiMauro, Steve, 55, 56
Diving, 27
Dominguez, Richard, 171
Donahue, Phil, 171
Douglass, Dana, 210
Dropping out of sports, 203–206, 212–213
Drug abuse, 181, 183–186
Duran, Roberto, 221
Durbin, Brahm, 84

Eclipse Award, 56
Edwards, Danny, 266
Edwards, Harry, 237
Eid, Mark, 162–165
Emerson, Roy, 100–101
Emotional stability, of athletes, 191
Endorsements, 229–231, 232, 263
Erving, Julius "Dr. J," 234
Esposito, Phil, 83
Esposito, Tony, 83
*Esquire* magazine, 216, 218, 219
Europa Cup, 150–151
Evert, Chris, see Lloyd, Chris Evert
Evert, Clare, 84–85, 86
Evert, Drew, 84
Evert, Jeanne, 39, 83, 84–85
Evert, Jimmy, 39–41
Evert, John, 84

Fassi, Carlo, 16–17, 18; Lisa-Marie Allen's training with, 19, 20; skating coached by, 116–120
Faulkner, Trish, 252
Federation of International Gymnastics, 172
Fleming, Mrs. (Peggy's mother), 119

Fleming, Peggy, 8, 116, 223, 231
Flexibility, 178–179
Football, 175, 223, 265, 284–285; Monday night, 220–221
Fortune 500 companies, 160
Francke, Linda Bird, 204
Fratianne, Linda, 8, 13, 15, 16–17, 18, 205; million-dollar contract of, 21, 79; her parents' troubled marriage, 79–80
Fratianne, Robert, 79–80
Fratianne, Virginia, 79–80
Frazier, Walt, 4
Frederickson, Tucker, 278
French Open, 226, 273
Furtado, Juli, 133

Gardner, Randy, 19, 21, 172
Gargel, Doug, 146, 149, 150, 163
Gargel, Lee, 146, 148, 150, 159, 162, 163; his fall in downhill race, 198; goals of, 165
Garrison, Kelli, 111
George, Bill, 53–55
Gerulaitis, Vitas, 4, 135
Gettling, Tom, 51–52
Giammalva, Sammy, 83
Giammalva, Tony, 83
Gifford, Frank, 221
Golf, 26, 36, 77–78, 224
Gonzalez, Pancho, 141
*Goodbye, Columbus,* 271
Goodell, Brian, 126
Goolagong, Evonne, see Cawley, Evonne Goolagong
Gottfried, Brian, 144
Grand Prix circuit, 72, 88, 273
Grant, Gayna, 104–108, 120
Grayson, Arthur, 43n
Gretzky, Wayne, 87, 265–266
Grossfeld, Muriel, 110
Guidolin, Bep, 93
Gullikson, Tim, 83, 224
Gullikson, Tom, 83
Gustavson, Linda, 103
Gymnastics, 27, 52, 200–203; coaching of, 108–116; dropout rate in, 203; injuries in, 172

Gymnastics Team, U.S. National, 123

Hamill, Dorothy, 3, 17, 116, 190, 205; charisma of, 13; exploitation of, 216–219; million-dollar contract of, with Ice Capades, 21, 215–216, 217–218; Olympic win of, 16, 215, 217
Hamilton, Scott, 51, 118
Hampton, Jackie, 51–52
Harkins, Bob, 153–154
Harmon, Rodney, 143
Harris, Stan, 217
Heiden, Beth, 85
Heiden, Eric, 5, 85, 157, 158–159
Heiss, Carol, 19
Hellman, Frances, 128
Hellman, Tricia, 128
Hellman, Warren, 127, 128
Hill, Priscilla, 205
Hill, Ralph, 205
Hnatov, Michael, 28
Hockey, 85–87, 175, 223
Hockey Team, U.S. Olympic, 5
Hoffman, Barbara von, 14
Holden, Mike, 153
Holiday on Ice, 104
Honda Civic Classic, 248
Hooper, Chip, 142–143, 144, 220
Horvath, Kathy, 135
Howe, Gordie, 85–87
Howe, Mark, 83, 87
Howe, Marty, 83, 87
Howe, Murray, 85–87
Hunterdon Academy (Pittstown, NJ), 127

Ice Capades, 19, 20, 23, 104; Dorothy Hamill's contract with, 215–216, 217–218
Indianapolis 500, 52
Injuries, sports-related, 167–175; fear of pain and, 197–200
International Olympic Committee, 155
International Paper Corporation, 128
*Intrepid*, U.S.S., 151
Italian Open, 267, 273

Jaeger, Andrea, 25, 83, 126, 225, 248; and Colgate Series, 267; earnings of, 137; injuries of, 171, 268; and Toyota Series championship, 250, 251, 252, 263
Jaeger, Richard, 134
Jaeger, Suzy, 83
Jausovec, Mima, 222, 251, 252
Jenner, Bruce, 231
Jerome, John, 290
Jockeys, 53–61
Johnson, Earvin "Magic," 222
Johnson, Ollie, 272
Johnson, Robert, 230
Joslin, Charles, 66, 67

Kaplan, Janice, *Women and Sports,* 96
Karate, 51–52
Kathy Corrigan's School of Gymnastics, 172
Kay, Linda, 79, 80
Kees, Timmy, 210
Khan, Hashim, 83, 84
Khan, Mohibullah, 83, 84
Khan, Roshan, 84
Khan, Sharif, 83–84, 286
King, Billie Jean, 179, 222, 248, 256, 269; retirement of, 283, 284; and Women's Sport Foundation, 281–282
Knee surgery, arthroscopic, 186
Knopp, Kate, 131–132
Konihowski, Diane, 185
Koopman, Amy, 111–112, 115
Korita, Eric, 72
Kovak, Janet, 198
Kramer Club, 98, 99
Krementz, Jill, *A Very Young Gymnast,* 202

Landsdorp, Robert, bond between Tracy Austin and, 99, 100–103, 118
Laver, Rod, 141, 220
Lawliss, William, 230–231
Le Coq Sportif sportswear, 230
Lederer, Gloria, 122–123
Lederer, Lynne, 111–112, 113, 122–123

# Index

Lendl, Ivan, 144
Lenox Hill Hospital (New York City), 186
Leonard, Sugar Ray, 221–222
Leone, Armand, 83
Leone, Mark, 83
Leone, Peter, 83
Lewis, Carl, 179
Lieberman, Nancy, 223
Liebowitz, Zandy, 285
Little League, 103, 174, 178
Lloyd, Chris Evert, 25, 83, 86, 179, 223, 248; Tracy Austin's loss to, at Wimbledon, 100; *Chrissie: My Own Story,* 35, 84; defeats of, 267; earnings of, 284; injuries of, 171; low-key attitude of, 39, 40; marriage of, 256; retirement of, 283–284; sibling rivalry in family of, 84–85; and Toyota Series championship, 250, 251, 252, 253, 254, 257, 258–262
Lloyd, John, 267
Lopez, Nancy, 223, 229–230
Lotto tennis shoes, 230
Louganis, Greg, 126
Louis, Joe, 222
Ludington, Ron, 18

McCleery, Sam, 251
McEnroe, John, 135, 142, 220, 224
McKay, Jim, 280
McKinney, Tamara, 153
Maclay Championship, 26, 197–198, 204, 206, 210–211
McNamara, Julianne, 127
Madsen, Beth, 174
Mahre, Phil, 83, 153, 173–174
Mahre, Steve, 83
Mandlikova, Hana, 25, 248, 251, 252
Maple, Eddie, 57–58
Marantz, Steve, 87
Marshall, John L., 247–248; *The Sports Doctor's Fitness Book for Women,* 179–180
Martens, Rainer, *Joy and Sadness in Children's Sports,* 199–200
Martin, Dean-Paul, 219
Martin Downs (tennis resort), 231

Mascarin, Susan, 225
Mathias, Bob, 155–156, 158–161
Mayer, Gene, 83, 220
Mayer, Sandy, 83
Menstrual cycles, 177
Meredith, "Dandy" Don, 221
Methany, Linda, 127
Meyer, Debbie, 95–98, 204
Michaeli, Lyle, 177, 180
Michigan State University, Youth Sports Institute at, 174
Mid-America Twisters, 110
Migliore, Richard, 53–61
Miller, F. Don, 155
Miller, Jason, 271
Miller Brewing Company, 159n
Mirkin, Gabe, 180–181, 185; *The Sportsmedicine Book,* 168
Mission Viejo, CA, relocation of Natadores swim team in, 126–127, 168–170
Monahan, Katie, 222
Mondale, Walter, 151
Morolt, Bill, 148
Moros, Julio, 137, 139, 141–142
Morris, George, 127, 209
Mt. Sinai Hospital (New York), 177
Muelhausen, Becky, 170–171
Muelhausen, Walter, 171
Mulvihill, Dick, 127
Murray, W. H., 49
Muscle fibers, fast-twitch and slow-twitch, 179
Mutch, Ronnie, 210

Namath, Joe, 4
Nastase, Ilie, 273
Natadores swim team, 126, 168–170
National Basketball Association (NBA), 234, 235, 236, 237, 240, 242
National Federation of State High School Associations, 237
National Figure Skating Championships, 8, 19, 22, 27, 123
National Football League (NFL), 196, 223, 284
National Governing Bodies (NGB), 156

National Gymnastics Academy (Eugene, OR), 127
National Hockey League (NHL), 87
National Institute of Health, 41
National Sports Building, 156
National Sports Festival, 154–155
Naturite Track Club (Northridge, CA), 184
Navratilova, Martina, 101, 144, 229, 248, 249; Evert Lloyd's losses to, 267; and Toyota Series championship, 250, 251, 252, 253, 255, 257, 263
NBC Sports, 280, 282
NCAA championship, 72, 240, 241
Newman, Clea, 127
*Newsweek,* 241
*New York* magazine, 204
New York Ski Ball, 151
*New York Times,* 5, 15, 133, 275
*New York Times Magazine,* 268
Nicholas, James, A., 186–187
Nicklaus, Charlie, 36
Nicklaus, Jack, 36
Nicks, John, 18
Noble, Holcomb, 133, 134
North American Open, 83–84
North American Trophy Series (Nor-Ams), 150, 151
Novak, Michael, *The Joy of Sports,* 24
Nutritional faddism, 181–183
Nyad, Diana, 171

Ogilvie, Bruce C., 61, 75–76, 103, 173, 191; on neck injuries, 175; on pro life, 263–264, 265, 266; on reactions to retirement, 274; on stress in athletes, 192, 195–197; his studies of Olympic gold medalists, 213
Ogilvie, Terrie, 76
Olympics, 5, 159; (1956), 173, 187; (1960), 183; (1968), 95; (1972), 27; (1976), 52; (1980), 5, 8, 16, 19, 80, 85, 147, 172–173; (1984), 47, 158, 159n, 162, 280; (1988), 47

Olympic Training Center (Colorado Springs), 154, 155–161, 162, 195–196
Olympic Trials, 154

Palmer, Arnold, 220
Pan-American Games, 159
Perry, Chris, 77–78
Perry, Gaylord, 77–78
Perry, Jim, 77–78
PGA, 26
Pikes Peak Fourth of July climb, 52
Pingatore, Gene, 239
Poetzsch, Anett, 16
Politics, sports and, 4–5
Port Washington Tennis Academy, 135
Powers, Barrett, 143–144
Pressures, on athletes, 190–192, 195–197
Preuss, Heidi, 130
Prince rackets, 228, 229, 230, 231, 251
Professional Bowler's Tour, 221
ProServ, 71, 228, 232–233
Psychologists, sports, 196–197, 199–200, 285
*Psychology Today,* 191

Racing: car, 52; horse, 53–61
Rainey, Carol, 194
Rainey, Ellen, 192–194
Rainey, Meredith, 192–195, 198–199, 212
Rainey, Schuyler, 192–194
Reece, Kevin, W., 28
Reggi, Raffaela, 135, 142
Rehe, Stephanie, 102
Reissen, Marty, 102, 252–253
Retirement: decision about, 273–274; reactions to, 274–275, 283–285, 289–290
Reyes, Douglas, 98
Riding, 26, 197–198, 204, 206, 210–211
Rigby, Cathy, 223
Rinaldi, Bill, 233

Rinaldi, Dennis, 228, 231, 232, 233–234

Rinaldi, Denny, 233

Rinaldi, Kathy, 25, 126, 225, 227; endorsements of, 229, 230–231, 232; financial status of, 231–233, 234; image of, 230; turning pro by, 226–230, 233–234

Rinaldi, Lindi, 228

Rinaldi, Tina, 233

Road Runner's Club, 43, 44

Robert Landsdorp Tennis Academy (Vista, CA), 102–103

Robinson, Sugar Ray, 222

Roche Cup, 148

Rockefeller family, 135

*Rocky*, 197

Rodgers, Bill, 48, 179

Rolles, Barbara, 18–19

Rudolph, Wilma, 276–278

*Runner's World* magazine, 203

Running, marathon, 38–39, 41–48, 168

Ruzici, Virginia, 251, 252, 262

St. John, Peter, 144; and Stratton Mountain School, 127–134 *passim*

Sands, Bill, 120, 203; gymnastics coached by, 108–116

Santee, David, 196–197

Satterthwaite, Franklin B., Jr., 285–289

Scarborough Fayre, 207, 208–212

Scatena, Kathy, 184

Schroer, Susanna, riding career of, 206–212

Seefeldt, Vern, 174

Shea, Joe, 56, 59

Shelton, Bill, 71

Shriver, Pam, 25, 244–247; comeback of, 249; endorsements of, 263; shoulder injury of, 247–249; and Toyota Series championship, 249–263 *passim*

Shubert, Mark, 126

Sibling rivalry, 80–83, 84–90

Simmons, Jim, 266

"Skate Canada," 161–162, 170

Skating, figure, 3–4, 27; coaches in, 104–108; injuries in, 172–173; rise and fall of Lisa-Marie Allen in, 8–23

Skiing, 146–154, 162–165; injuries in, 173–174

Sloan, Jim, 63

Sloan, Pat, 63–64

Sloan, Susan, 63–64, 139–140

Smith, Anne, 229

Smith, Barbie, 18, 23

Smith, Red, 5

Smith, Robyn, 223

Spitz, Mark, 27, 50, 77, 275

Spitz, Matthew, 275

*Sports Illustrated*, 38, 84, 235, 278

Sports medicine: and drug abuse, 181, 183–186; future of, 185–187; and nutritional faddism, 181–183; role of, 175–181

Squash, 83–84, 285–289

Steroids, anabolic, 181, 183–185

Stolle, Fred, 255

Stove, Betty, 251, 252–253

Stratton Corporation, 128

Stratton Mountain School (Stratton, VT), 127–134, 143, 151

Super Bowl, 33, 265

"Superskates," 170

Swimming, 27, 50, 88, 95–98, 126, 168–170; and cardiovascular fitness, 176 and n; injuries associated with, 170–171

Talavera, Tracee, 127

Talos Digitizer, 158

Tanvier, Catherine, 126

Tarinelli, Deborah, 127

Tarinelli, Donald, 127, 128

Tarinelli, Donald, Jr., 127–128

Taubman, Philip, 216, 217, 218

Teacher, Brian, 102

Television, hours of programming devoted to sports on, 4, 52

Teltscher, Eliot, 99, 102

Tennis, 25, 36, 39–41, 63–75; bond between athlete and coach in, 98–103; professional, 223–224; retirement from, 273–274; sibling teams

Tennis *(cont.)*
in pro, 83; Toyota Series championship in, 249–263 *passim*
Tennis Academy, Nick Bollettieri's (Bradenton, FL), 63, 64, 68–69, 134–144, 206
*Tennis* magazine, 99
Testosterone, 181, 183, 184, 185
Thatcher, Mark, 232
Thomas, Isiah, 237–242
Thomas, Mary, 237, 239
Thomas, Ruby, 240–241
Thompson, Fred, 194–195
Tickner, Charlie, 23
*Time*, 85
Tinling, Ted, 230
Title IX, 281
Toddler Movement Education Program (New York City), 27–33
Touring Professional's Association (TPA), 224
Toyota Corporation, 154, 161
Toyota Series championship, 249–263 *passim*
Track and field, 26, 27
Tracy Austin Enterprises, 102
Turnbull, Wendy, 248, 267
Tutko, Thomas, 33–34, 38, 90–92, 191, 199, 205; *Winning is Everything and Other American Myths*, 33

Unser, Bobby, 52
Unser, Robby, 52
Updike, John, *Rabbit, Run*, 271
U.S. Figure Skating Association (USFSA), 11–12, 16–17, 161–162, 173; competitive categories established by, 106
U.S. Olympic Committee (USOC), 151, 154–156, 281, 282; branches of, 155; job opportunities program of, 160; junior development project of, 161
U.S. Olympic Fund, 170
U.S. Open, 40, 72, 78, 84, 102; Tracy Austin's winning of, 25, 100–101, 125, 126, 251, 268; Ilie Nastase's winning of, 273; and Pam Shriver, 245, 246, 247, 248

U.S. Ski Association (USSA), 151, 154, 155
U.S. Ski Educational Foundation (USSEF), 128, 132, 151
U.S. Ski Team, 148, 150, 151–154, 164, 174
U.S. Tobacco Company, 153
U.S. Volleyball Association, 156

Valley Professional School (Garden Grove, CA), 11
Van Aarsdale, Dick, 83
Van Aarsdale, Tom, 83
Vassalho, Jesse, 126
Vitamins, 182–183

Waitz, Grete, 48
*Washington Post*, 38
Weintraub, Jerry, 216–217, 218–219
Welch, Kelly, 105
White, Anne, 135
White, Wendy, 229
Williams, Gus, 83
Williams, Ray, 83
Wimbledon, 88–90, 100, 102, 226, 247
Winfield, Dave, 222
Women's Sport Foundation, 281–282
*Women's Sports* magazine, 184
Women's Tennis Association, 171, 222, 252, 254
Wood, Stan, 77
Woodworth, Richie, 130
World Championships, 111, 125, 170, 204
World Cup, 150, 151, 153, 163, 165
World Series, 77
World Swimming Championships, 183–184
World Tennis Association, 247
*World Tennis* magazine, 25, 88, 101–102, 273

YM–YWHA, 27–29
York, Clifton, 201
York, Janet, 200, 202–203

# Index

York, Torrance, 202–203, 212
Young, Faye, 83
Young, Kaye, 83

Zausner, Hy, 135
Zayak, Cindy, 81
Zayak, Elaine, 17, 27, 124–125, 173,
205; cost of her career, 81, 206; education of, 123–124; injury to, 50–51; sibling rivalry in family of, 81–83; travel of, 161–162, 170
Zayak, Jeri, 81–83, 123–124, 161–162
Zayak, Richard, 81, 206
Zayak, Ricky, 81